LEOPOLD STOKOWSKI

A PROFILE

Also by Abram Chasins

Speaking of Pianists
The Van Cliburn Legend
The Appreciation of Music
Music at the Crossroads

LEOPOLD STOKOWSKI

A PROFILE

ABRAM CHASINS

HAWTHORN BOOKS
A division of Elsevier-Dutton
New York

To the people of National Public Radio and the
Corporation for Public Broadcasting for perpetuating
Leopold Stokowski's lifelong purpose—to bring the joy
of music to the widest audience

Acknowledgments

FOR NUMEROUS COURTESIES and for invaluable assistance in assembling the materials for this book, I am indebted to many people.

I want especially to thank Evangeline Merrill, formerly Mrs. Leopold Stokowski, for her hospitality, memorabilia, and graciousness in sharing so many recollections. Other members of the family to whom I am indebted are Sonya Stokowski Thorbecke and her mother, the late Olga Samaroff Stokowski, in loving memory.

I am also grateful to Thomas Lask, Virgil Thomson, Henry Pleasants, Dr. Louis R. Thomas, Nicolas Slonimsky, and Daniel Webster for being immensely helpful.

My appreciation is extended to many cooperative and kind people in the following organizations: Anne B. Shepherd (Cincinnati Historical Society); Helen Reed (McKelvin Library at the University of Maryland), who made available the fruitful James Felton Collection; Fred Keller (*The New York Times*); Jean Mann (*The New York Times*, London Bureau); David R. Smith and Wendall Mohler (Walt Disney Archives); Philippa Thomson (The Royal College of Music); and the Reverend Bruce W. Forbes (St. Bartholomew's Church, New York).

I am grateful for the wellspring of information gleaned from the writings of Hubert Roussel, Dr. Louis R. Thomas, and James Felton. I also owe especial thanks to Sophia Yarnell Jacobs, Sylvan Levin, Stewart Warkow, Philip Kahgan, and Joseph Sharfsin, who gave Stokowski so much of themselves. It would be remiss of me not to thank Freda Pastor Berkowitz, Gustave Janossy, and Elisabeth Waldo for supplying copious and useful information.

Special gratitude is owed Jane Courtland Welton and Elizabeth McCormack Law for their meticulous and constructive perusal of my unkempt manuscript.

Everyone quoted within this book is identified, naturally, but it would be neglectful of me not to make special mention here of Ernest Fleischmann, Paul Myers, and David Raksin, who spared more than the few hours they have to talk with me at length.

In terms of gratitude, my deepest thanks belong to Judith Sachs, for her warm-hearted and cool-headed editorial guidance and encouragement. I also want to offer hearty thanks to my colleague Leland Lowther for his historical precision and musical enthusiasm.

To many others—friends, correspondents, kindred spirits who generously sent pictures, letters, descriptions of personal encounters with Stokowski—I extend cordial thanks which are no less sincere because the limitation of space prevents the publication of their contributions or names.

Prologue

"I ALWAYS WANT TO BE FIRST. I'm what's known as egocentric. It's a disease, a mental disease. I'm egocentric."

This understatement opened Leopold Stokowski's last public appearance in a telecast shortly before his death on September 13, 1977, at his home in Nether Wallop, England. He was in the midst of fulfilling an astounding six-year recording contract, signed on his ninety-fourth birthday, a formidable project that would have taken him up to his centenary.

Stokowski never stopped astounding the world. The man was a human dynamo with unlimited power to excite other musicians to achievements far beyond their normal capacities, to mesmerize audiences, and to provoke critics and colleagues to unprintable condemnation, even as they extolled his unique conductorial genius. Over the years I myself have alternated in the roles of critic and colleague, as well as what we may loosely call "friend," for although he never told me a deliberate lie, I never knew a man who told me less of the truth about himself.

For almost three-quarters of a century, the unfathomable Stokowski was as much a legend to his vast public as were any of the Olympian gods. To women especially, he was an object of inscrutable mystery and fascination—and each year he seemed to radiate more glamour and to pique more curiosity.

What were his true origins? Was his name really Leopold Boleslawowicz Stanislaw Antoni Stokowski, as some biographies state? Or was it simply Leo Stokes, as some skeptics insist? Was his great-grandfather the Polish-born General Stokowski who marched with Napoleon's army? Or was this London-born musician the son of an Irish mother and an English father, without any ancestral ties to Poland? Yet how could that be, considering Stokowski's indeterminant Slavic accent? Did he derive it naturally from immigrant parents— or was it merely the acquisition of a keen showman who learned early that an accent, especially for an artist, has charms to seduce and soothe the Anglo-Saxon breast?

Various encyclopedias cite conflicting birthdates, and Stokowski himself variously recorded three different dates and birthplaces, but long before he died, everyone knew his correct age. Fifty years earlier, I asked Stokowski's first wife, Olga Samaroff, how old he was.

"How should I know?" she answered with a shrug. "Don't ever forget—my husband is a professional beauty!"

"Stoki," as he was affectionately known, intrigued the world not only because his physical elegance and artistic power seemed to escape time but also because he was an irresistible combination of Saint Francis of Assisi, Maharishi Mahesh Yogi, Beau Brummell, Don Juan, and a Trilby to his own Svengali. He was a Leo despite his April birthdate; above all, he was the last in a long line of podium lions who revolutionized the symphonic world, and it was he who established the incontestable supremacy of the Philadelphia Orchestra.

Stokowski conducted hundreds of broadcasts and world premieres; thousands of recordings; the first transcontinental orchestral tour; and the revolutionary film *Fantasia*, which introduced stereophonic sound, brought symphonic music to mass audiences, and established his orchestra and himself as popular institutions.

A perennial pioneer, Stokowski dispensed with the baton as well as the score, taught his audiences concert etiquette, inaugurated self-managed youth concerts, became expert in acoustical science, and made the first electrical recording of a full-length symphony, Dvořák's *New World,* for RCA in 1927. Two years before he had recorded Saint-Saëns's *Danse Macabre* in the first electrical recording of a symphony orchestra. He was the foremost propagator of this century's most significant music as well as the bold experimenter, instigator, and utilizer of every technological device and resource related to its transmission.

Stokowski was always the driven perfectionist pursuing a golden sound that he alone heard within himself and produced on his "instrument," the orchestra. An unpredictable tyrant, streaking on and off stages, he was a bully, ruthlessly stepping on anyone who stood in the way of reaching his momentary goal. His orchestras loved and loathed him, and at the very same moment. Audiences fought for admission to his concerts and walked out on his revolutionary, modern programs. Musicians attacked him for the outrageous liberties that he took with scores. He was the perfect caricature of our ambivalent century.

I met Stokowski in Philadelphia in the spring of 1926 when I walked into the spacious, walnut-paneled lobby of the Curtis Institute of Music, whose faculty I was joining in the fall. Mary Louise Curtis Bok, the school's founder, was descending the stairway with a tall, courtly, handsome, blond gentleman whose perpetually photographed face was internationally familiar. Mrs. Bok introduced us and then excused herself.

Stokowski greeted me casually but cordially, putting me instantly at my ease. He seemed so much warmer and friendlier than I had imagined, having heard from so many musicians of his remote and challenging manner. That day, he was all smiles and offered me a cigarette. We sat down on a comfortable sofa, and without preliminaries, he launched into what sounded like a conscientiously prepared speech in his obscure accent. What "a *mahvelous wooman*" Mrs. Bok was, how much pride she took in bringing the school's students such superb musical "*no-ledge*" and how much joy it gave her to take so "*ahkteef*" a part in their personal welfare. "She has collected the finest teachers in the world," he said. "She is giving us an endowment of $12 million, the largest single private fund ever devoted to the advancement of '*mu-seec*.' This will become the most important musical institution of our country, perhaps of the world. Forgive me for saying 'our' country, but I became a citizen in 1915 and you will hear me boast of it very often." He looked at me intently, and from my smiling face he could tell that I was fascinated and flattered. Seeing that he had captivated me evidently pleased him, and we parted warmly. Such camaraderie, I thought. How gracious.

Our Philadelphia meeting marked the beginning of a relationship that brought Stokowski and me together professionally and socially several times each week during my pedagogical decade in Philadelphia. We were also artistically united when I was his soloist in the world premiere of my Piano Concerto no. 2 in 1933 and again when we were teamed together for a few months on acoustical research at the University of Pennsylvania. Our association continued on and off, hot and cold, intimately and formally for some fifty years.

The last time I saw him was in his New York apartment on upper Fifth Avenue around his ninetieth birthday in connection with an article I was writing called "Stoki, the Ageless Apollo." He seemed to like the title, and I had chosen it because to me he remained glamorous to the end. But not to a former Philadelphia Orchestra musician who, upon seeing the title, wrote me, "Baloney. Stoki began looking like a witch twenty years ago. You should've called it 'Stoki, the Tarnished Apollo.'" And that is just one of the many—often diametrically opposite—opinions of our subject which makes him so utterly intriguing, a perfect subject for a biography.

The pursuit of objective and accurate accounts from interviews and communications is the biographer's cross. Always there are the sycophants who use an illustrious name to aggrandize their own, and always there are the fanatical derogators with a chronic mote in the eye. Neither, naturally, is capable of doing the subject justice. The biographer attempts, as I have done here, to achieve a balanced evaluation.

The old question as to whether history makes the man or the man makes history does not apply to Stokowski. He was a nineteenth-century man and a twentieth-century musician with a twenty-first-century outlook. Stokowski was born at the perfect moment—the budding of the orchestral age—for obviously his mission was to contribute uniquely to its fullest flowering. Given his fear of air travel, the sheer number of performances he conducted on every continent during his long life is remarkable. The mere thought of getting on a plane was terrifying to him ever since he had experienced a narrow escape on a harrowing flight. Thereafter he took ships and rationalized by saying, "Flying makes no sense. Everyone admits that it takes three days to recover and function normally. I use those days having a wonderful time studying and relaxing on board." Stokowski's rejection of air travel was typical of the incongruity of this ultramodern man, whose research and astounding experiments in recording technology enabled music to be reproduced with unprecedented sonic and technical perfection.

Yet in spite of—perhaps even because of—Stokowski's perversities and eccentricities, the man and artist were always in absolute control. He had final approval over every aspect of his recordings, as he had over his concert performances, from their production to their promotion. He spared nothing and no one to get exactly what he wanted, and from his beginnings the world gave him total sanction.

What I see as central to the understanding of Stokowski is the nature and extent of his musical influence, the things he thought about, the questions he asked, and the answers he offered. And by answers, I do not mean to imply that the Maestro ever sat on only one side of the fence. There is no getting around it. Even the most factual and objective description of Stokowskiana almost inevitably emerges vague or inconclusive or contradictory. For example, one reads of him as the staunch "defender of human rights, civil rights, minority rights." All true. And so are the conflicting accounts from numerous and venerable members of his orchestras who had worshipped their leader but had suffered indignities imposed by the man's "cold-hearted inhumanity." Any confraternity, any semblance of warmth, was bestowed but momentarily, with a lordly air of one who mingles democratically with the below-stairs help. Stokowski eschewed professional intimacy. Musicians do a lot of backstage fighting and what one does and does not know quickly becomes evident. Obviously, Stokowski did not want to risk involvement. He also relished the role of the Brahmin in the caste system of "Orchestralia."

"Stokowski has no class consciousness," I once read. For the record, he was not only class-conscious, but he was extremely self-conscious about class, as reflected in his constant reluctance to discuss his childhood environment, in his manufactured and mercurial accent, and in his propitious marriages. He courted society women as though they were chambermaids, and vice versa. They all loved it, for a while.

Again we meet ambivalence in Stokowski's convictions that "music is a universal language" belonging to everyone, everywhere, while acting at the same time as though it were his royal domain, with himself as czar, surrounded by favorites of the court required to keep him on the throne. Unfortunately he needed an orchestra to play upon and an orchestral board and a manager to do the dirty work, to combat, and to manipulate. And most of all, he needed an audience, preferably music-lovers who could understand, appreciate, and remember the sounds they heard. The rest of the world was no-man's-land to Stokowski, except for the patrons and professionals of the other arts who associate with musicians for mutual cooperation and benefit.

Stokowski always had his eye on the music-lover, because to him "the customer is always right." He knew that throughout history it was the approval or disapproval of that listener in the balcony which spelled the life or death of music and its interpreters. Individually, musical laymen made mistakes; collectively, they had an unerring ear for quality. The layman grew tense when he heard new music he could not quite follow. But not for long if it was good music. He rarely missed. Musical laymen are sensitive and valuable people who have to be handled firmly. No one did that so well as Stokowski, who understood that in a way they were like children. While often inattentive, they themselves craved attention. Stokowski lavished it on them in massive doses, scolding them for arriving late and leaving early, for coughing and knitting, for gossiping while the music was going on. In the next breath he would praise them for reacting, even for hissing, but he included them in all things, year in and year out.

Mainly, he spanked them for their a priori condemnation of the modern music he served up in such huge portions. Audiences loved Stokowski the preacher even when he punished their hostile reaction by a complete repeat of a novelty. Meanwhile, he hit the headlines, packed the halls, and shaped a group of instrumentalists into an incredible unity of sound.

Stokowski's harshest judges have not disclaimed his genius. Nor have his most formidable rivals denied the many debts owed him and the paramount place that the orchestra occupies in our daily lives because of him. But more than that, he paved the way for others: for composers, conductors, and performers who would have had a much harder time in the artistically unfledged environment that was pre-Stokowski America.

George Szell, on hearing him conduct the NBC Symphony in 1942, said, "When Stokowski stops acting the Apollo Belvedere and concentrates on the music, one realizes what a great musician he might have been. A born conductor he always was."

"Beyond any question, Stokowski's conducting is sheer genius," said Sergei Rachmaninoff, and no less than Stravinsky, Sibelius, Shostakovich, Vaughan Williams, and Ravel expressed the opinion that in Philadelphia he had created the greatest orchestra in history.

My memories of Stokowski conducting the Philadelphia Orchestra date from the 1920 season of their celebrated Tuesday evening concerts at Carnegie Hall. The programs were richly varied and artfully calculated to display the full opulence, grandeur, and virtuosity of the orchestra that Stokowski had brought from mediocrity to unexcelled prestige within eight short years.

Famous critics with astonishing unanimity termed the instrumental performances "glorious," "flawless," "miraculous," while taking the conductor to task for "tasteless interpretative liberties." Stokowski was judged to be "uncomfortable in the classic style" of the great symphonic literature, taking refuge in altering its texts and instrumentation, distorting its tempi and rhythms, melodramatizing its noble lyricism, and thereby "damaging when not actually destroying" its stately proportions. These reactions applied principally to his Bach orchestral arrangements, to the overtures and symphonies of Beethoven, and to the tone poems and symphonies of Tchaikovsky. But there were few occasions when Stokowski was not under fire on some controversial ground.

That is precisely how he wanted it, and it was in great part his defiance and independence that led all musically inclined youngsters to become his rabid fans. Not only could we admire his fabulous music-making but also we could esteem and signalize the man himself for his indomitable courage on every level of his life and work. From start to finish, Stokowski never hesitated to lay his professional life on the line.

It was a common experience during the forties and fifties to walk into a living room reverberating with a fight over Stokowski. The battleground was inevitable. "Is Stokowski a charlatan or a genius?" For that I had my stock answer: "First of all, genius and charlatanism are not mutually exclusive. Stoki did quite enough to validate both contentions, but if you'll stop arguing with each other long enough to put on his recordings of Mahler's Second Symphony or of Rimsky-Korsakov's *Scheherazade,* you'd realize that your argument is irrelevant. You'll be reconciled to all his absurd furbelows and foibles if you'll just listen to those incomparable sounds."

Apropos, Irving Kolodin wrote, "One cannot mark him down as either a charlatan or a poseur, for his accomplishments are too considerable, his attainments beyond belittling, whatever one may think of this manifestation or that." But then, Kolodin elucidates, "Quite bluntly, I cannot understand how, after so long a period of absorption in so demanding an art, he still remains outside its fundamental sense of order, its demand for mental discipline, its logical, arithmetical organization."

Although this is a fair expectation, there is no inconsistency in maintaining that in art, nothing is of ultimate value which does not explain itself through the evidence of that art alone without the aid of technical erudition. Stokowski did not have erudition and did not claim it. Dealing with music as music was quite enough for him and more than enough for most musicians.

LEOPOLD STOKOWSKI

A PROFILE

1

STOKOWSKI HIMSELF GAVE HIS BIRTHPLACE AND DATE in his own handwriting to the *Hugo Riemann Musiklexicon* around 1950. The listing reads: "Krakow, Poland, 1887." That musical polymath and editor of *Baker's Biographical Dictionary of Musicians,* Nicolas Slonimsky, received a letter from the editor of a Finnish encyclopedia "correcting" the Stokowski data, saying, "The Maestro himself told me that he was born in Pomerania, Germany, in 1889."

The Maestro himself once "explained" the discrepancies as follows: "When I got to London on my way to America in 1914, I was afraid that my Pomeranian birth certificate would make me eligible for the draft. I therefore asked a powerful friend of mine to remove this birth certificate from Somerset House and substitute one which said I was born in London, England, and to change the date so that I would be too old to be drafted for the British army." Getting into Somerset House and altering one of their certificates would be comparable to breaking into Fort Knox and walking out with a gold ingot in each hand.

The birth certificate of Leopold Anthony Stokowski, as signed by J. Claxton, registrar at the General Office, Somerset House, London, in the All Souls County of Middlesex, attests to his birth on April 18, 1882, in 13 Upper Marylebone Street, in the St. John's section of London. His Polish

1

father was Kopernik Joseph Boleslaw Stokowski, a cabinet-maker. His mother was Annie Marion Moore, of Irish parentage.

The household, when Leopold joined it, consisted of his parents and, according to Stokowski, his paternal grand-father. In 1884, his mother gave birth to a daughter, Lydia-Jessie, and six years later to another son, Percy James, known as Jim and eventually as Uncle Jim to his brother's children. Few people knew, and I never knew, of the existence of either a Stokowski sister or brother.

In 1975 I met a British violinist in Los Angleles who said that he had just recorded a Wagner album in London with Stokowski and added with a smile, "I got a pleasant surprise when a friend introduced me to a jovial old man named Percy Stock, who turned out to be Stoki's younger brother! He changed his name to Stock long ago. Do you know him? Delightful man."

"Stoki's brother?" I asked in astonishment. "Not once has he mentioned him. Are you sure?"

"Well, it's curious but understandable because I was told that they'd been estranged for over fifty years and that they were reunited only recently through Sonya, Stoki's daughter. He runs an auto business—rents cars to tourists, sells cars, something like that."

Suddenly it dawned on me. Possibly this was the origin of the absurd legend that Stokowski's real name was Leo Stokes and that he had adopted the name Leopold Stokowski for professional advantages.

Subsequently, I went to England, found the Stocks, and in a revealing talk with Mrs. Stock learned that Percy, who died in 1978, never liked his first name, so he used his middle name and thought that Stock would be an easier name than Stokowski for clients to handle. In the last years of Leopold's life, his daughter Sonya came to England to visit him, and got in touch with her uncle. "It was so nice," Mrs. Stock told me, "and eventually we met all of Leopold's children and two of his grandchildren, a son and daughter of Sonya's."

When I asked whether she had ever inquired about the reason for the estrangement of the brothers, she shrugged. "Well, perhaps their being in such different fields, of different citizenry, and living in such different and distant countries could possibly account for it, but I really don't know."

No one I questioned had any recollection of the Stokowski family. Evidently they all got along so well that they were rather unremarkable. I gathered that the Stokowskis were not overinvolved in intellectual pursuits. Leopold never went beyond grade school for his academic education. Stokowski, years earlier, told me that his family always lived in some *"leedle coddage,"* was never impoverished, and enjoyed a simple, comfortable home life.

According to Stokowski, his first contact with music came at age seven when "my grandpa took me to a club where the members spoke only Polish, Russian, and German. They sang their native songs, lusty ones which shook the rafters and sad ones which made them cry into their beards. It was here that I first saw and heard a violin. 'What's that wonderful instrument?' I asked my grandfather. 'I want one.' So grandfather got me a quarter-sized violin and an instructor."

Although Stokowski related this tale frequently and it found its way into many authoritative texts, it is utterly impossible that he could have had these experiences with his Polish grandfather. Leopold Stokowski, after whom his grandson was named, died in the county of Surrey, at the age of forty-nine, on January 13, 1879, three years before Stokowski's birth. Stokowski's other grandfather, of course, was Irish, and it would have been highly unlikely that Polish songs were sung at his club! Stokowski continued, by the way, to call the violin his favorite instrument despite the fact that his school records do not indicate that he studied violin at all.

Ever since his first exposure to instruments and voices in

church, Leopold had demonstrated an obvious talent for music and a resolute perseverance in obtaining instruction. The family moved to 10 Nottingham Street West, and their modest budget was stretched to include a piano and piano lessons. Leopold managed to find his way to a pipe organ on his own. One of his playmates was the son of a sexton, and Leopold coaxed the boy into getting permission for him to practice on the church organ.

As a beginner on the organ his legs were so short he could use only the instrument's four manuals. As his legs grew, he was able to reach the middle pedals and then, as the months and years passed, the next and the next. When he could at last reach the low C and the high F of the pedals, he said that he had played his way through "all the organ music of Bach —my favorite composer always."

Another childhood incident he frequently described was the exciting opportunity to conduct at age twelve when he was the pianist of a children's orchestra. The regular conductor had suddenly fallen ill, and Leopold was allowed to be his substitute. "That did it," he often said. "It was the discovery of my real identity. That night I didn't sleep a wink. I had but one thought—to become a conductor!"

A member of the congregation who had witnessed the boy's struggles at the organ and his ever-growing mastery sponsored his entry to the Royal College of Music (R.C.M.) in London on January 6, 1896, when he was thirteen. Sparse information is available regarding Stokowski's scholastic achievements in his major or minor subjects. In the choir boys' quarterly report of September 29, 1897, Stokowski is listed under "Altos Cantores" thus: "Conduct, excellent. Voice, excellent. Is of great service to the precenter." It is further noted that he was elected to membership of the Royal College of Organists on June 25, 1898. He won additional diplomas in 1899 and 1900, entitling him to add *Choirmaster* to his name.

The R.C.M., an extraordinary school of music, was started the year Stokowski was born and had been reorganized from the National Training School, founded a half-century before. It had a remarkable staff of superior teachers and administrators. All were first-rate in their subjects and guided their students with unusual interest and warmth of heart. Leopold spent nearly four years there, until December 16, 1899. Although the organ has always been considered his main instrument, the R.C.M. records state that on his entering, piano was his principal subject and organ was secondary. Two years later, organ took precedence, and composition and analysis were added. He continued in all of these subjects until he left the college.

Stokowski had the good luck to be first taught piano and organ by the organist Stevenson Hoyte and later by the organist, composer, and conductor, Henry Walford Davies. His professor of composition was the eminent composer Sir Charles Villiers Stanford, who also conducted the orchestra and the opera class. Although Sir Charles Hubert Parry is invariably listed as Stokowski's composition teacher, this also appears implausible, for the distinguished composer had succeeded Sir George Grove as director of the R.C.M. in 1894, two years before Stokowski entered, and did not teach thereafter.

There is no further official record available of Stokowski's musical studies or activities from the time he left the R.C.M. until 1902. The intervening two years seem to have been spent in self-study and travel to Paris and Berlin. In 1902 he entered Queen's College at Oxford for two semesters. The college secretary, Susan P. William, stated in a letter to Edward Johnson, editor of *Stokowski—Essays in Analysis of His Art* (1968), that "Stokowski was not a full member of the college but was attached to it as a student studying for the bachelor of music degree, which he took in 1903. It seems he was only at Queen's for that one year and that his main place of study was the Royal College of Music." Stokowski re-entered the Royal College on November 16, 1903, where he completed his courses on July 27, 1904.

Is it not puzzling that a young musician possessed of such a burning ambition to be a conductor never utilized the chance to study conducting or his "favorite instrument," the violin, under the most opportune circumstances either at the R.C.M. or Queen's College? It remains one more of the many mysteries surrounding Stokowski.

It is set down in several publications—and more than a few people have quoted Stokowski confirming it—that in his student days he had studied conducting with the great Artur Nikisch and had also played under his direction in the first violin section of the Berlin Philharmonic, that he had studied composition with Sir Edward Elgar, and that he had also studied at the Paris Conservatoire. The records also disclose that among Stokowski's associates at the R.C.M. were indeed such future celebrities as Gustav Holst and Ralph Vaughan Williams, frequently mentioned by Stokowski.

In lieu of grades and marks and a correct roster of colleagues and teachers during this period, one is fortunate to have a few letters, as delightful as they are revealing, from H. C. Colles's comments and book on Stokowski's teacher, *Dr. Henry Walford Davies* (1942):

Stokowski was, as he would himself confess, and indeed his letters prove it, the least ruly of Doctor's pupils. They disagreed about everything and most about God, and "Sto" rebelled truculently against Walford's attempts to subdue him to his own unorthodox orthodoxy. The written evidence of their tussles need not be reproduced here, but a note written when Stokowski had obtained his first substantial appointment at St. James' Church, Piccadilly, attests the gratitude and affection in which, despite all their differences, he continued to hold the Doctor:

> 10 Nottingham Street
> London W
> 10 March 1902

DEAR DOCTOR,

I am sure you will be glad to hear that I was appointed to St. James's Church this morning. I can never, of course, repay in any way your kindnesses to me. I can only hope to have an opportunity of passing them on to another.

> Your affectionate pupil,
> LEOPOLD STOKOWSKI

The author then quotes a letter written six years later from New York, signed, "Always with affection and gratitude, your ugly duckling, Sto." Colles then adds,

> Stokowski's brilliant career has carried him far from the traditions of the Temple Church, but it was the offer of an important church organistship in New York which first took him to America; and when I heard him some twenty years later conducting the famous Philadelphia Orchestra in Bach and Beethoven, it was easy to perceive that he was still passing on, not to another, but to many thousands of others, some of the lessons which he had learnt in the old practice room.

A postscript from Edward Johnson:

> Stokowski's whole approach to music-making is spontaneous, improvisatory, and abhorrent of the metronome. When he entered the Royal College of Music as a boy of thirteen he must have memorized the college motto on his very first day: "The letter killeth, but the Spirit giveth Life." It has been his credo ever since.

At a Curtis Institute faculty meeting in 1927, Stokowski himself recalled:

> I was very lucky with teachers, even before I got to such masters as Parry and Stanford. They never held back my enthusiasm. None of them ever told me I must learn to walk before running. I wanted to run. Walking bored me and so would exercises. I wanted to get to the heart of music, and I refused to learn things that would only develop my technique. My teachers understood that I was in love with music and that I wouldn't go in for anything that made me hate it. They let me play Bach before I knew the key signatures or could name the chords.

That was the first clue I had to one of Stokowski's frailties. He had not been obligated to acquire a basic technique in anything but keyboard playing. He was never made to assume all the disciplines of a systematic education. The disadvantages were obvious, and he spent much of his life making up for the fact that he had taken the shortest route. Most of us would have done the same. What youngster does not hate drudgery? But most successful musicians have had teachers who persuaded them that many long hours of drudgery are indispensable, that discipline is the only road to freedom. But Stokowski took every shortcut. He was a law unto himself, and a self-protective instinct enabled him to build a wall around his limitations.

In his musical language, I think Stokowski supplemented his haphazard study of the techniques of music by a supreme intuition for sonic phenomena. For him, music was not merely a history of stylistic practices and traditions. Apropos, the noted American conductor of the Atlanta Symphony Orchestra, Robert Shaw, told me, "Stokowski's interest and his genius were not directed toward musical structure or style, but toward color and sonority. We are accustomed in our time to accord structure and style an intellectual superiority, and I think that is fair. They do call for more information and keener intellectual apprehension and judgment. But it's also possible to examine or exhibit wearisomely the arid nether regions of musicology and analysis. And I recall (abruptly at this very instant) that the first symphony orchestra I ever heard (at a woefully late age) was the Philadelphia in 1936 with Stoki on tour in Los Angeles at the Shrine Auditorium playing the Franck D-minor Symphony—and life never has been the same."

Every account of Stokowski's professional career starts off with his appointment as organist to St. James's Church in Piccadilly around 1900. The following letter from A. H. Surridge, one of Stokowski's choirboys in 1900, will correct this assumption:

> 15 Fongmead Rd.
> Tooting, London
> SW 17
> 1 October 1973

To LEOPOLD STOKOWSKI, ESQ.

DEAR SIR,

Seeing you on television yesterday and reading of you in the *Daily Mirror* today, I felt that I must write, as one of your old choir boys. You came to St. Mary's Church, Charing Cross Rd. in 1900–1901, when the church was rebuilt, (I think from St. Marylebone Church) and formed the choir at St. Mary's, of which I was an alto; after approximately 12 months, you went to St. James's Church. I have a photograph of the choir, with yourself, the Rev. G. C. Milton, and the brother Steads (tenors) which I greatly cherish; you must then have been around 18 years of age. One thing I always remember is a man with a fruit barrow, always appearing on Friday nights (full practice night) when you used to purchase a hand of bananas, giving us lads one each, saying that they were good for the throat. In conclusion, I trust that God will give you many more years of life, with good health.

Yours very affectionately,
ATT. SURRIDGE (now 83 yrs)

When Stokowski accepted the appointment at St. James's, he followed a distinguished line of musicians associated with an equally distinguished edifice. The building was designed by Sir Christopher Wren and was consecrated in 1684. Three of its rectors later became Archbishop of Canterbury, and the church has been famous for its fashionable and eminent congregations as well as for its musical programs.

The organ, built for James II and intended for his Roman Catholic chapel at Whitehall, was given to St. James's by Queen Mary, his daughter, in 1694. Bumpus, in his *London Churches,* says, "This favorite old instrument, originally built by the celebrated Renatus Harris in 1678, was entirely rebuilt by Bishop in 1852 on a much more comprehensive scale, but retaining the old pipes—for these, the mellowing of time had rendered of more than ordinary value."

John Blow and Henry Purcell are known to have tested the original instrument, according to the annals of St. James's, and it is likely, although unrecorded, that George Frederick Handel would have had access to the organ when resident in the parish from 1712 to 1720.

The years that Stokowski spent at St. James's were extremely fruitful. His musical objectives were becoming ever more clearly defined, and with philosophical patience he marked time by utilizing his position as organist and choirmaster to play a vast and varied literature. He organized and conducted vocal soloists, choruses, and instrumentalists to perform a magnificent choral, symphonic, and operatic repertory, from Palestrina's motets through Bach concertos, to scenes from Beethoven's *Fidelio* and *Missa Solemnis,* all of which provided some firm foundations for his symphonic repertory.

In short order, this tall, radiant, and adventurous young organist attracted unusual attention and, at twenty-two, was invited by a producer to expand his musical activities from the church to the theater. On the nights of November 16 and 17, 1904, Stokowski made his formal debut conducting a pit orchestra, performing an overture and intermission music for Jerome K. Jerome's three-act play *Woodbury Farm.* The program included Nicolai's Overture to *The Merry Wives of Windsor,* the "Valse Lente" from the ballet *Coppelia* by Delibes, and Elgar's "Salut d'Amour."

At St. James's Stokowski's imaginative programming made a deep impression on a musical visitor, Dr. Leighton Parks, the distinguished rector of St. Bartholomew's, an impressive church in New York City. Stokowski told Rollin Smith (for London's *AGO-RCCO* magazine) of his conversation in 1905 with Dr. Parks:

> "Our organist has left and I have come to England looking for an organist," he said. He had been speaking to many famous people, evidently, and had all kinds of big names. "We want a good organist, but one who is not too British, and everybody said, 'Take Stokowski.'" I suppose that was because I was always criticizing things which went too slowly.
>
> And so he asked that I come to be their choirmaster and organist. Saint Bartholomew's is, of course, a Protestant church and my Catholic origin made it at times a little difficult for me.

Flattering as the invitation was, Stokowski hesitated, weighing its chances of furthering his major ambition. He was becoming uncomfortably aware of his unwillingness to accept the doubtful fortunes and anonymity of a church organist. Yet no other door was open to him. He had to weigh the alternatives: England or America?

"Das Lande ohne Musik" had long been a popular phrase in Germany to assert its artistic supremacy over that of its economic rival, Great Britain. The disdainful appellation had its sole source in the almost insurmountable obstacles placed before aspiring young British musicians, especially those who would play upon that most expensive of all instruments, the orchestra.

England was certainly not a land without music. Indeed, there was a good deal of great music and a good deal of money being paid to hear it; but it was totally under the domination of foreign artists, who played the great music of the eighteenth and nineteenth centuries, written by composers whose native language was their language—German.

The American environment showed many similarities to the English, including the sparsity of native composers and performers, especially conductors. But by 1905, Theodore Thomas's prodigious developmental work and conductorial influence had launched America full sail in the dramatic development of its musical life. More and more American orchestras of excellent quality were arising, their indigenous personnel was constantly increasing in numbers and skill, the leading European conductors were being engaged to bring them to ever-higher standards of performance in ever-larger repertories, and the greatest virtuosi were among their soloists.

Further, classical music was rapidly becoming an important part of the fiber of American daily life. Children were studying not only piano and voice but also orchestral instruments, concert-going was becoming a family activity, and chamber music was being played and heard in many homes. Stokowski was made aware of all this. He had more than a hunch about the musical potentials of America. He also had the good sense to realize that in America he would have the advantage of being a foreigner, and a foreigner who could speak English! It seemed like a good tree to be under when the apples started falling.

Almost all that I know of Stokowski's three years at St.

Bartholomew's stems principally from two close friends: Dr. Thomas Tertius Noble, organist of St. Thomas's Church on Fifth Avenue from 1912 to 1947, two of whose assistants were choirboys at St. Bartholomew's under Stokowski's "reign," as they put it; and the conductor's first wife, pianist Olga Samaroff Stokowski, as she still called herself when we first met in 1925, two years after their divorce.

Tertius Noble was born in Bath, England, in 1867. He too had trained at the R.C.M. and became an assistant to Charles Villiers Stanford at Trinity College. While Stokowski was at St. James's, Noble was the highly esteemed organist at York Minster. He had visited London and had seen and heard Stokowski quite frequently. "Stokowski's playing was so individual and colorful," he said, "that afterward I would spontaneously go forward to express my appreciation. He always accepted it smilingly as his due, but I wince at the remembrance of his blank stares and hollow disinterest when some others came up to thank him. I often wondered whether he was not utterly indifferent to public approval."

Not at all. Stokowski eagerly sought public approval, but it was part of his duality to appear above it. He played this role to the hilt at the church. It worked with the snobs, and there were many. The church also wanted to hold on to Stokowski, for this was an era of great organs and great organ playing, and major churches of all denominations were in spirited competition to hire the best they could find. For Stokowski, whose ambitions transcended his instrument, this prestigious post provided a firm foothold in the musical community.

Stokowski said that he had not been in America more than an hour when he knew that this was to be his country. It was love at first sight, a love not fully reciprocated for some time. Stokowski had to flap his wings quite a bit, because a church organist does not get much chance for exposure. He transcribed baroque choral works into full-blown productions of operatic scope. Noble's assistants reported that Stokowski would conclude an electrifying performance of some great work, after which he would remain motionless and stare

heavenward without moving a muscle to display the Prince
Charming profile. The men of the congregation distrusted
him. But of course. The women adored him.

To Caroline Willis-White, Leighton Parks's great-grand-
daughter, must go my appreciation for several delightful
letters she wrote to me:

When Stokowski came to New York, my great-grandfather
had recently been widowed. It was Leopold who was responsible for nicknaming the rector's three daughters the
World (Alexandra), the Flesh (Ellen), and the Devil
(Georgette, who was my grandmother).

Aunt Ellen died in 1973. She was very dear to me and
often told me stories of her experiences with grandpapa.
She never married, and while she never directly said so, I
suspect that there was a strong romance between her and
Leopold. She was a marvelous cook—and Leopold loved
to eat. There are relationships built on less. However,
there was an impediment. Grandpapa did not "approve"
of Leopold. He was not beyond using his talent to draw
crowds to church, but he surely did not want one of his
daughters involved with such a man.

My Grandmother Georgette died when my own mother
was thirteen. She was active in the early Feminist Movement and once outran a policeman on horseback making
her way back to St. Bartholomew's and actually rode her
horse into the church, where the policeman gave up the
pursuit. Apparently she and Leopold were somewhat both
of a wild and fiery temperament.

This account recalls the time when Stokowski was expected
to put in an appearance at the Church Choral Society's performance of Handel's *Messiah* at another church. He showed
up an hour late and in full riding habit walked the length of
the church to take his place in the front pew.

Evidently, it took very little time for Stokowski to feel very comfortable anywhere, even at stylish St. Bartholomew's. The Episcopal Church is a member of the worldwide Anglican communion, which has always had a commitment to education and art. St. Bartholomew's had its own distinctions and venerability dating from 1835, when it was an aristocratic little façade below the Bowery on Lafayette Street. When Stokowski joined it in 1905, it had moved to larger and handsomer quarters on Madison Avenue and Forty-fourth Street.

The American pianist Olga Samaroff came into Stokowski's life through Marie Dehon, a parishioner of St. Bartholomew's, a prominent society woman, and a patron of the arts. Marie was a close friend of the operatic idol Geraldine Farrar, who asked her to entertain Olga. When Olga visited Marie's handsome home on lower Fifth Avenue one fateful day in 1906, she invited Olga to St. Bartholomew's the following Sunday morning to hear "our marvelous organist, Stokowski, who looks like a poetic Viking."

Olga went, saw, and was duly conquered even before she and Stokowski met for the first time that afternoon.

Marie had asked many people for tea after the services, and her spacious living room quickly filled with a colorful mixture of personalities. But for Olga there was only one person. "The moment he arrived," she said, "we got into a corner. I could hardly wait to tell him that my real name was Lucie Hickenlooper and that I was born in San Antonio, Texas. He roared with laughter. It turned out that we were both twenty-three and had the same musical ideas and ideals. After an hour the only thing we didn't know about each other was that we'd be married within five years. I remember thinking what a flair Leopold had for the fair sex and what a difficult man he'd be to deny." Stokowski and Olga were as alike as fire and water. He was poetic and quiet; she forceful, even aggressive. He was thin; she robust. He was blond and fair; she brunette and swarthy.

But Olga too had lived the professional musical life since childhood, when it became obvious that she had a genuine pianistic talent and a capacity for hard work and concentration. In those days, there was only one possibility for an American musician who sought a career—European tutelage and acceptance. For the Hickenloopers, this required great sacrifices, for although the family had been among the earliest and most prosperous southern settlers, the Civil War had crippled their financial resources. But Lucie's mother and grandmother were women of unusual vision and determination. They had many personal and social connections, many powerful and wealthy friends.

Olga's maternal grandmother, Lucie Palmer, was a frustrated concert pianist. When the family became penniless, she was forced to turn to teaching. She was Olga's first teacher and therefore doubly determined to overcome every handicap that might stand in the way of the fulfillment of her granddaughter's talent. At the very least, Olga should develop musically to a point where she could make a living at it "if she had to." Otherwise, if some male came around who was warm and willing, she would have no choice. She had been brought up in the old southern tradition, after all, which accounts for Olga temporarily giving up her career at the beginning of her unsuccessful marriages.

With Grandma as chaperone, Olga became the first American pianist to win a scholarship at the Paris Conservatoire de Musique. When she walked into her first lesson with the "eccentric M. Delaborde," his first words were, "Why do you try to play the piano? Americans are not meant to be musicians!" The remark wounded her, but eventually, Olga became his favorite pupil.

After a rigorous year, in which the eighteen-year-old Olga kept a staggering schedule, she left with Grandma to study in Berlin. Her family meanwhile pondered ways and means of launching her with a Berlin piano debut, as she had now developed into a pianist of professional caliber. At this point, a young Russian civil engineer, Boris Loutzky, entered her life. In line with her social background and in view of the precariousness of a career, she chose marriage and promptly abandoned the idea of becoming a concert artist. She did not exactly settle for a "domestic life," however. Her husband was attached to the Russian Embassy in Berlin and the couple spent three and a half years in a chic diplomatic atmosphere, partly in Berlin and partly in St. Petersburg. For Olga this was not enough, not nearly enough. Following an annulment of the early marriage by the pope and a legal divorce, Olga headed back to New York with few prospects and fewer dollars. But now she was free to pursue her real love, the piano.

Another fortunate meeting, this time with the brilliant concert manager Henry Wolfsohn in 1904 changed her life —and her name—and opened the door to a concert career. Almost the first thing that Wolfsohn told her was, "Look. It's hard enough to make a pianistic career when you're a woman, especially an American woman, but with a name like yours, even if you played like Liszt, it would be impossible."

That is when Lucie Hickenlooper climbed the family tree and plucked the name of a remote Russian relative—Olga Samaroff. And so she joined the Foreign Legion.

She made an auspicious debut on January 18, 1905, with the New York Symphony Orchestra under Walter Damrosch in a program of two concertos—the Schumann and the Liszt E-flat—and a group of Chopin solos. It was evidently successful enough for a skillful manager like Wolfsohn to capitalize on. Within an incredibly short time he had booked Olga in Europe and throughout the United States in recital and as soloist with leading orchestras under Nikisch, Muck, Mahler, and Gericke. She also toured in joint recital with Geraldine Farrar. Olga was in a good spot to be of enormous assistance to Stokowski's early conductorial career, and she used every resource at her disposal.

From the moment Olga met Stokowski at Marie Dehon's, she started to utilize the artistic respect she was gaining and her considerable connections to pry open every door for the handsome young organist. The church job was just a stopover: He had never strayed from the vision of himself as a conductor. He confided his dreams to Olga, and they became her dreams too.

Olga pulled strings, wrote letters, got people to do things and to get other people to do them. In New York, she saw to it that Stokowski was invited to all the right places on an equal social and artistic footing with the elite, not only of New York but of London, Paris, and Munich, where they spent several vacations at the great music festivals.

No one knew better than Olga that performers have always been subdivided into three main classifications: the "run-of-the-mill performers," who come and go; the "superstars," who inspire worship, become public idols, and bring glory not only to themselves but to all who pay them homage; and the "artists," who command wide respect and choice engagements and who invariably deliver high-caliber performances without the drawing power to attract capacity audiences. Although the artistic qualities of the last group may sometimes equal or even surpass those of some superstars, these performers are seldom able to establish a public of vast proportions.

When Olga and Stokowski first met that afternoon in Marie Dehon's home, Olga was well on her way toward being included in the third category as an established pianist. He was not even in the first. Indeed, he was not yet even a conductor but an organist and merely one among many. But Olga knew instinctively that within this man was the fire and the ecstasy that mesmerize audiences long before they hear a note. She herself never claimed to have it. "As a pianist," she told me, "I was beginning to play splendid dates at good fees, getting good notices and coming along nicely. But as a personality, as a woman, I felt like a grim-faced brunette compared to this blond beauty. From the moment I heard him and then met him, I knew he had that unique thing given to the few and that his career was headed toward heaven."

After three months Stokowski was widely known as the aristocrat, as well as the autocrat, of church organists. With an eye on his inevitable conductorial future he worked and searched with feverish exhilaration, discovering not only the great organ repertory but also a vast symphonic and choral literature, which he transcribed and performed week after week, adding surprise and excitement to the musical scene. He even managed to endow the organ with rhythmic articulation comparable to Landowska's matchless effects of accentuation on the harpsichord. Stokowski was being constantly invited to appear as guest organist at every institution that housed a great organ, including Wanamaker's famous department store in downtown New York. And it was evident now that if he wished to make his musical mark in a capacity greater than church organist, he was in the right place at precisely the right time.

In the first decade of this century, New York was rapidly becoming a world center of music. The demand for the best and the money to buy it provided a huge harvest for the many brilliant, creative, and interpretative personalities heard day and night at Carnegie Hall and the Metropolitan Opera. What an opportunity for the ambitious Stokowski! Not only were there two New York symphony orchestras— the Philharmonic and the Symphony—but also the orchestras of Boston, Chicago, Pittsburgh, St. Louis, and the Metropolitan Opera, all under virtuoso conductors.

In those days the matinee idols were primarily singers, such vocal stars of the Metropolitan Opera as Enrico Caruso, Lillian Nordica, and Louise Homer. Next in the ability to compete for public acclaim were the famous foreign instrumentalists: Ignace Paderewski, Eugène Ysaÿe, Fritz Kreisler, and Moritz Rosenthal. Hero worship caused music fans to behave like barbarians in battles for tickets. Mob mania prevailed at the recitals of such child prodigies as violinist Bronislaw Huberman and pianist Josef Hofmann. The musical life of New York when Stokowski arrived proved to be even richer than that of Paris, Berlin, Leipzig, or Munich in their heyday. His exposure to this musical community was tantamount to having a working vacation with pay. It was as though they were waiting for him.

2

THROUGHOUT THE HISTORY OF MUSIC, there have been periods when the time, the place, and the personalities, creative and interpretative, were fortunately fused to make a golden age or era of some specialty. Sometimes one overlapped another. Early in the nineteenth century, a revolutionary era of violinism was initiated by Paganini's first appearance in Paris. A golden age of pianism followed when Liszt caused a mad frenzy by not only emulating but surpassing Paganini's devilish powers. The latter part of the nineteenth century precipitated an operatic golden age, personified by Patti, Melba, Battistini, and the de Reszke brothers, all of whom possessed the basic ingredients of emotional and technical wizardry and mesmerizing personalities.

A golden age of conducting began in the second decade of the twentieth century in the United States, exemplified by Stokowski, Koussevitzky, and Toscanini. Their eminent predecessors in the twilight of the nineteenth century were Hans von Bülow, Artur Nikisch, Gustav Mahler, Hans Richter, Richard Strauss, Anton Seidl, Vassily Safonov, and Theodore Thomas. Charles Russell, in his distinguished book *The American Orchestra and Theodore Thomas,* says,

> But when all other influences together have been recounted and reviewed, . . . there is one man whose contri-

bution went incontestably beyond all the rest. Forty-three years he devoted himself to this work and traveled up and down the land to originate and prosper it. . . . Wherever Theodore Thomas went in his restless wandering he left his mark. To a great and always expanding constituency he gave the first real conception of musical elation and gave it in ways that made it permanent. . . . Assuredly, before him, in his time, and after him, were great men . . . other conductors who gave beautiful concerts, produced excellent music, interpreted great thought to entranced audiences. This man alone had his mind fixed upon a sequence of public instruction that extended over the span of his life and beyond it. . . . Other conductors played for today and often played magnificently; he alone played for tomorrow and all the tomorrows that are to be.

How fateful it seems that the year of Stokowski's arrival in New York was the very year of Theodore Thomas's death in Chicago, the city whose great orchestra was his own god-child. It was as though the torch, the task of bringing America to symphonic maturity, had been transferred from one to the other. And it was miraculous that one with so slight a background as Stokowski would soon make the flame blaze on a scale of unimagined magnitude.

In music, just as the eighteenth century had witnessed the development of the dramatic style, so did the nineteenth century reach the peak of romanticism. The years of Stokowski's youth bridged the gap between a fading lyricism and a metallic twentieth century, which precipitated an era of bold experimentation and a symphonic golden age. Stokowski's pioneering spirit symbolized them more than any conductor of this century.

He had the vision not only to follow but also to further the speedy transition that had occurred within three decades from classicism (in 1882 Brahms was yet to complete the third of his four symphonies) through impressionism (Debussy's *Afternoon of a Faun,* 1894), to Schoenberg's destruction of tonality (Three Piano Pieces, 1909) and Stravinsky's atomic treatment of primitivism (*The Rite of Spring,* 1913).

Stokowski often referred to the period 1905–08 as among the happiest and most fruitful of his life. Ever since his late teens, he had managed to spend his summers on the Continent, especially in Germany, the ideal place for an aspiring young conductor. He had heard Nikisch, Mahler, Strauss, Richter, Karl Muck, Wilhelm Furtwängler, and Felix Weingartner in unforgettable symphonic and operatic performances, at which his own conductorial style was being formed. At various times, Stokowski would name various conductors "the greatest one I ever heard" and express his gratitude for what he had learned. He limited himself to three: Nikisch, Richter, and Furtwängler—one at a time.

In 1931 I had a chance to inquire about Stokowski's visits to Germany from Felix Weingartner and Bruno Walter. I was making my debut with the Vienna Philharmonic as soloist in my own Piano Concerto no. 1 under the baton of Carmen Suder, a gifted protégée of Weingartner's. I saw Weingartner almost every day for weeks at rehearsals and at social gatherings frequently attended by Bruno Walter.

From both I learned that Nikisch taught very little and had few pupils, all of whom were well known and had been heard in Berlin, Leipzig, Munich, and Vienna. Nikisch gave them chances to fill in during rehearsals with the symphony and opera orchestras of those cities and to conduct at least one or two complete concerts under Nikisch's "merciless guidance." Weingartner and Walter spoke at length of those who were most in evidence: Adrian Boult, Albert Coates, Muck, Mengelberg. And at my insistence they also spoke of their own work with Nikisch. They did mention Serge Koussevitzky's constant presence in Berlin, not as a member of Nikisch's conducting class but as Nikisch's soloist on the double bass, of which he was the leading virtuoso at the time.

Neither of them could recall seeing Stokowski during those memorable days, though both were certain from his manner of conducting that he had carefully observed and emulated Nikisch. Both admired Stokowski tremendously,

Walter for his "passionate involvement" and Weingartner for his "magnetic effect on the orchestra and the audience." Both agreed that Stokowski never had the time or opportunity required to master the violin sufficiently to play in any orchestra under Nikisch, himself a first violinist under Wagner at Bayreuth. Both were equally firm that Stokowski never actually studied conducting with Nikisch.

So what? It is part of Stokowski's duality that he could, on the one hand, insist that "one can learn the technical fundamentals of conducting in a half-hour lesson—the rest must come from within," and then, on the other hand, still claim Nikisch as his teacher. Obviously he was driven to cover himself: He believed it necessary to assuage the suspicion that he was inadequately prepared to meet his objective, and therefore, he needed Nikisch. My inclination is to ascribe this partially to modesty, partially to wanting Nikisch's approval; possibly he wanted to convey the thought that he was very capable in demonstrating that imitation is the sincerest form of adulation. Nikisch was an inspiration which helped to support his own confidence in himself.

I myself never heard Stokowski claim any direct connection with Nikisch except to express sheer worship of his art and gratitude "for what he taught me, taught us all." Koussevitzky, however, told me in great detail about his own ardent hopes and persistent and unsuccessful efforts to study with Nikisch. This was puzzling because Nikisch had heard Koussevitzky play the double bass in Russia, had come backstage bubbling with enthusiasm, and had spontaneously invited him to appear under his direction at the Leipzig Gewandhaus. But the engagement was not officially endorsed by the orchestra board. Later, when Koussevitzky reminded Nikisch of his invitation, Nikisch explained in great embarrassment that the board did not consider the double bass a classical instrument. Characteristically, Koussevitzky did not let this stop him and immediately announced two solo recitals in Leipzig. The board of directors was invited to the first and witnessed a sold-out house of the city's elite give Koussevitzky an ovation. The next day a hand-delivered official letter arrived, inviting Koussevitzky to appear as soloist with Nikisch's orchestra.

Nevertheless, Nikisch would not and did not accept Koussevitzky as a pupil. Perhaps he had learned that Koussevitzky had conductorial gifts and ambitions. Perhaps he felt that with great tutelage, Koussevitzky's artistic reputation, persuasive personality, and ability to subsidize any orchestra single-handedly would produce a competitive force quite impossible for Nikisch's pupils and protégés to overcome.

In those days, competition raged furiously at the schools of orchestra conducting. Everyone wanted to study with the world's paramount maestros: Hans von Bülow, Nikisch, and Mahler. Their classes abounded with a brilliant array of young students who soon took the world's great cities by storm and became stars of the first magnitude, among them Muck, Furtwängler, Boult, Thomas Beecham, Otto Klemperer, Mengelberg, and Walter.

Obviously, Koussevitzky and Stokowski had never studied with any great conductors. Both of them had worked independently. Both had studied conducting by watching and hearing the concerts of the supreme masters of the baton.

"Koussy," as he was affectionately called, and Stoki both told me that their method was to study thoroughly every score of these concerts and to take the scores along to the performances to make meticulous markings regarding every detail of the art of these virtuosi of the baton. From them, they evolved their own techniques, their own methods.

Koussevitzky devised a further method of his own, which served him throughout the rest of his life: Once having memorized a score he would engage a pianist to play a piano version while he stood in front of a mirror and conducted. This process was repeated time and again until he had acquired a thorough familiarity with the music and mastery of the gestures necessary to convey his interpretation of it to the orchestra. When he had formed his own artistic convictions about the composition and had no doubt of his ability to remember the score, he faced a student orchestra.

Stokowski told me much less about his own learning devices, emphasizing the *"eenspeeration"* he got from every aspect of the performance of his conductorial idols. Obviously, both Koussevitzky and Stokowski came to their enormous successes despite imperfect early training in theory, score reading, and historic styles. Yet, as Virgil Thomson wrote in *The Art of Musical Criticism,* "They contributed more of value to the glory of their art than most of the first-prize-in-harmony boys ever have." This does not diminish the superbly cultivated art of a Reiner, Rodzinski, Szell, or Karajan. Their mastery is unquestioned. As for Stokowski, Munch, Koussevitzky, Toscanini, and Beecham, "great artists all," Thomson concludes, "They bought, muscled, or impressed their way in, and they settled down to learn their jobs. They succeeded gloriously."

No complete appreciation of Stokowski's fantasies is possible without an understanding of the bitter struggles one encounters in order to survive, to obtain an education, and finally to make any sort of career in an artistic milieu. Who can find policies and practices more dictatorial, more filled with jealousies and intrigue than those within musical institutions? When nationalism compounds the problem and is added on top of professional hostilities, the struggle can unhinge the soundest mind. In Berlin at the turn of the century, Teutonic musical supremacy was unarguable. The names Stokowski and Koussevitzky inevitably carried slavonic elements with them, and therefore neither man could gain entry to the privileged conclave.

The three years in New York, where the impatient Stokowski had been experiencing everything and everybody, sealed his decision to escape from the prison of his organ loft. The cul-de-sac of a cathedral post was no longer for this musician, whose imagination was generations ahead of his time. Moreover, "the king of instruments" had become too small for him. Human beings would become his instrument, the fusion of a hundred instrumentalists with variegated means of musical expression.

Before leaving for Europe in the spring of 1908 for a holiday with Olga, Stokowski tendered his resignation at St. Bartholomew's. His dedication to the idea of conducting was so irrevocable that it was easy to give up the assured indigence of a church organist's life.

After the summer, he returned to London hoping to find an orchestra, a chorus, anything that needed a conductor. Evidently, nothing arose of enough significance for him. Then he tried his luck on the Continent, making a living by coaching and playing piano accompaniments for singers and instrumentalists. Early in October of 1908, Stokowski opened a studio in Paris, hoping to organize some concerts. "It was a difficult period," he once said in a surprisingly candid mood. "There were few jobs, very few pupils, and a lot of discouragement." This stuck in my memory because Stokowski so rarely deigned to describe anything about his professional past that was not *"seemply wahnnaful."* But, of course, Stoki had an ace in the hole.

"Just when things looked darkest," he said dramatically, "I received a letter saying that the *Ceenceenahti Orchéstra* was *eentrested* in my becoming its conductor." Who wrote the letter he did not say. But fifty years later, Olga's closest friend, Ruth (Mrs. Theodore) Steinway, told me the details. It seems that Olga had written Stokowski from New York in feverish excitement, telling him that she had just accidentally run into Mrs. Christian R. Holmes, the president of the Cincinnati Orchestra Association, who was busily engaged in the re-establishment of the Queen City's orchestra. Born Bettie Fleischmann, she was a member of the family that ruled the yeast dominion, a great patron of the arts, and "passionately devoted to music." She and Olga had taken to each other immediately, and Bettie had confided that the Cincinnati Orchestra Association was looking for an exciting new conductor. That is where Stokowski came in.

In an uncharacteristic burst of openness, Stokowski once told me that at the age of six, his mother had asked him what he wanted for Christmas. Without a moment's hesitation, he said, "A magic wand." Few musicians have been so accurately cast at so early an age.

For a long time now, the world has known that Stokowski was a born conductor. But in 1909, the Cincinnati Symphony board displayed either a remarkable clairvoyance or a fantastic naïveté in considering this golden lad, for he had so little to offer in the way of conducting credentials. The apparently crystal vision that caused the Cincinnati Symphony Association finally to select Stokowski can be more easily understood if one knows the story of that city's orchestra. I was never able to extract more than a few cryptic and quite uninformative words from Stokowski about Cincinnati or his experiences there. The little I do know was learned from Olga Samaroff; another close friend, Leonard Liebling, whose interest in Stokowski began when he covered the Cincinnati debut for *Musical Courier*; and from Dr. Louis R. Thomas's excellent dissertation on the history of the Cincinnati Symphony from 1895 to 1931.

The Queen City, according to Dr. Thomas, had provided lukewarm support to a local orchestra conducted from 1895 to 1907 by the efficient, but unexciting, Texas-born Frank van der Stucken. Previously, Cincinnati had been host to a number of notable visiting orchestras and conductors, most notably Theodore Thomas and his Chicago Symphony.

In 1907 the board of directors announced that no effort would be made to maintain the orchestra, because of lack of public interest and support. The excessive cost of maintenance, especially in a depression year, did not justify the orchestra's consistent inability to bring artistic prestige and renown to the community. Consequently the board decided it would be a better plan to sponsor a series of five pairs of concerts by visiting major orchestras and celebrated soloists for the 1908–09 season.

To be featured were the Theodore Thomas (formerly and latterly, Chicago Symphony) Orchestra under Frederick Stock, the Russian Symphony Orchestra under Modest Altschuler, the New York Symphony under Walter Damrosch, the Pittsburgh Symphony under Emil Paur, and the preeminent Boston Symphony Orchestra under Dr. Karl Muck, who engaged no soloist and charged $5,000! Soloists included baritone Emilio de Gogorza, violinist Fritz Kreisler, and two pianists, Ernest Hutcheson and Josef Hofmann.

At the termination of the 1907–08 symphonic season the board reconvened for an evaluation of the year. "Although the orchestra reduced its ticket prices for the symphony season, only sixteen hundred season tickets were sold," reports Dr. Thomas, "25 percent fewer than the previous season." The deficit of $6,500 was assumed by the advisory board, which included Charles Taft (brother of the president of the United States) and Julius Fleischmann. Mrs. Holmes, who headed the board, stated that "the financial situation of the country was possibly largely responsible" for the unexpected deficit, but equally relevant was "the lack of interest in an undertaking which aroused no feeling of local pride and enthusiasm." She further stated that the exposure to five "major" orchestras had been enough to convince the Cincinnati Orchestra Association that "our orchestra was not as far behind them as we thought." In fact, the defunct home orchestra was "more than the equal of most" of the visiting orchestras, according to Mrs. Holmes.

It was then recommended that the board forgo the sponsorship of a symphonic series during the 1908–09 season in order to achieve three goals: first and foremost, the establishment of a five-year guaranty fund of $50,000 per annum for the reestablishment of the Cincinnati Symphony Orchestra in 1909. Second, selection of a suitable conductor who would merit the respect of musicians and audience alike; and finally, the choice or construction of a smaller concert hall, better suited to the needs of the orchestra association.

In 1873, the indefatigable Theodore Thomas had extended his activities as guest conductor of the Cincinnati Symphony to organize the May Festival, an annual series of symphonic concerts with guest orchestras, conductors, and soloists. The first few featured Thomas conducting his famous Chicago Symphony Orchestra. Later, with other guest orchestras and conductors, it became the inspiration for other cultural events staged at numerous annual festivals whose significant impact has been felt throughout America. The venerable Music Hall, a 3,600-seat barn and the only available concert hall, was appropriate for the festival and for large town meetings, but it was far too large for the regular symphony series by a seventy-two piece orchestra and its audience. The Friday afternoon audiences of less than 1,000 and the Saturday evening audiences of nearly 2,000 were swallowed up in the enormous reaches of the hall.

Fortunately, Mrs. Mary Emery, widow of a distinguished Cincinnati capitalist, donated to the Ohio Mechanics Institute the sum of $500,000 in October 1908, as a fitting tribute to the memory of her deceased husband. The funds were to be used for the construction of a new building to include an ideally proportioned auditorium. The building was slated for completion in 1912, and the auditorium was offered to the orchestra.

The next problem to be tackled was financial, and the board ran into some frustrating delays. The primary stumbling block in garnering support for American orchestras, unlike their European counterparts, is the near-total dependence on private, nongovernmental support and patronage. Of the prodigious costs of maintaining a symphony orchestra, less than one-half is produced by ticket sales. Mrs. Holmes, who was in charge of raising the first $50,000, set an

April 1 deadline. The goal had not been reached by April 20 in spite of private and public appeals for contributions. She had to find more direct measures. Mrs. Holmes and the ladies of the board marched determinedly into the offices and clubs of Cincinnati's businessmen and convinced them that the orchestra was a benefit to the city and a sizable asset commercially as well as artistically. Their persuasive pitch paid off, and they reached their goal within two weeks. One muses ruefully that today $50,000 would have to be augmented by at least $2.5 million to open the first year of a major symphonic series.

The least difficult, but most crucial, problem was all that remained—engaging the right conductor.

What Cincinnati needed was another Theodore Thomas, the godfather of all American symphonic projects. His inestimable effect on musical taste in America is nowhere better exemplified than in the "historical cycle" of programs from Giovanni Gabrielli to the latest symphonies of Tchaikovsky, first presented with his Chicago Symphony during the 1901–02 season and to SRO halls in Boston, New York, and Cincinnati. He had performed Beethoven's *Missa Solemnis* and Ninth Symphony at the Cincinnati May Festival of 1904. Previously, he had presented a performance of Bach's B-minor Mass to which he had devoted two years of preliminary study so as to achieve stylistic accuracy. He devoted no less time and effort to attaining variety in his programs by presenting Berlioz's *Requiem* with an augmented orchestra, a brass band in each of the four corners of the auditorium, sixteen kettledrums, ten pairs of cymbals, a huge chorus, and the organ, unleashing the thunders of the universe.

In short, Cincinnati was no artistic hinterland, and Olga carefully coached Stokowski to appreciate the cultural aptitude of the city. Actually, he was being given an opportunity to effect a renaissance, for as early as 1873 and again in 1875 and 1888, the redoubtable Theodore Thomas had staged musical festivals that had placed Cincinnati in an aesthetic position "hardly second to Boston itself."

This background and potential were perhaps the most powerful incentives for the fierce and unyielding campaign that Olga and Stokowski waged for the job. Cincinnati provided not only a fabulous chance but also a fantastic challenge. Stokowski loved nothing better.

Olga had done all she could to sing his praises to Bettie Holmes; now it was up to Stokowski. He must write immediately to Bettie. This woman of such energetic and determined character who exercised so enormous an influence over Cincinnati's orchestral life and was so stimulated at the idea of recommending Stokowski, had to be the one, Olga felt, to make Stokowski's ship come in.

He therefore had to devise a striking dossier that would hit the mark, and Olga counseled him to send it as soon as possible. She also asked him not to mention her name if things developed to a point of negotiation so that she could act most effectively behind the scenes. She urged him to cooperate to the fullest and, if things proceeded as she hoped, to "accept whatever proposals and conditions are made to you without any objections."

This sounded like the real thing. From that moment, all of Stokowski's hopes and actions were predicated on this eventuality. It was a long haul. Through an incredible chain of circumstances it worked at long last, the first miracle of many that studded this man's fantastic career for almost seventy more years.

On October 19, 1908, Mrs. Holmes reported to the orchestra board that among the first applications received for the post of conductor was one from Leopold *Stokovski*. Stokowski was evidently so fed up with mispronunciations of his name that he changed the *w* to a *v*. He never should have changed back. He is still called *Sto-cow-ski* by a shocking number of people. Milton Marcus of Omaha, Nebraska, recalls that many years ago, as a young musician in New York City, he attended a panel discussion in Town Hall. The moderator introduced Stokowski with a glowing account of his many accomplishments, mispronouncing his name repeatedly. At the conclusion of her lengthy preliminary, the Maestro slowly rose and said, "Thank you, my dear young lady," and then added, "I want you all to know that there is no *cow* in my name. It is pronounced *Sto-kov-ski*." With that he sat down and did not say another word.

Stokowski's dossier was obviously effective enough to be pitted against those of many eminent and prodigiously experienced competitors for the position. However, the most adroit evasions could not conceal the fact that Stokowski had virtually no experience in conducting and none whatsoever in directing an actual symphony orchestra.

While lengthy negotiations took place with a large number of impressive candidates, letters of high recommendation arrived on Stokowski's behalf from the prestigious Welsh tenor Daniel Beddoe and the celebrated soprano Marcella Sembrich. Olga had also enlisted the support of powerful New York colleagues and of her Cincinnati family, headed by the retired Yankee general Andrew Hickenlooper. Olga made weekly calls to Bettie Holmes, who strongly advised her to urge Stokowski to make every effort to prove his conductorial ability by getting an orchestral appearance and newspaper reviews, even by hiring an orchestra if necessary. Bettie had long since made up her mind that Stokowski was "it," and this conviction was strengthened by another visit to Olga in New York, where Wolfsohn; Leonard Liebling, now editor of *Musical Courier;* and Vassily Safonov, the New York Philharmonic's principal conductor, were present and had strongly approved of Stokowski. Stokowski, meanwhile, had initiated his own postal campaign from Paris, hinting at "invitations to conduct" and "pending engagements."

Finally, it was Stokowski's sagacity that tilted the scales. On April 19, 1909, Mrs. Holmes announced at an orchestra board meeting that "Mr. Stokovski is on his way to Cincinnati to have a personal interview with the ladies in about a week or ten days." Stokowski arrived on April 22, and the next day was granted an audience by thirteen members of the board, which had especially convened for that purpose.

The conductorial candidate was evidently his most irresistible self. Bettie, meeting him for the first time, noted, "Everyone felt that he apparently possesses many of the qualities
which we deem essential to the man who is to become the
conductor of the new orchestra." She confessed on many
occasions that personally, she had instantly become what Stokowski's daughter Sonya described to me as "one of those
innumerable female satellites who orbited around Daddy
throughout his life."

But the facts were indisputable. Stokowski's conducting
experience was nil. Try as he would, he could not hide these
inadequacies from the orchestra board. Buying an orchestral
appearance was financially out of the question. Some other
way had to be found.

Olga found it. She was scheduled to play an all-Russian
concert in Paris on May 12 with the Colonne Orchestra. Suddenly, the conductor fell ill and canceled. As soon as Olga
heard the news, she cabled her mother, "Take Stoki instantly
to orchestra manager Gutman. Say famous Slavic conductor
delighted to substitute. If his fee can't be met, will contribute
services. I honored to play under him." The recommendation was impressive, the price was right, and Stokowski's personality and accent did the rest. He was engaged on the spot.

Promptly and proudly, Bettie announced to the Cincinnati
board that her candidate had just been invited to conduct
"the world-renowned Colonne Orchestra" in Paris, with Olga
Samaroff as soloist. And, as fate would have it, Lucien Wulsin, founder of the Baldwin Piano Company in Cincinnati
and a prominent member of the orchestra's advisory board,
was in Paris at that moment and would stay on to attend the
concert. He was to be joined by J. Herman Thuman, music
critic of the *Cincinnati Enquirer*. Together they were to attend the concert and report it in fullest detail to the Cincinnati board.

Three weeks after Stokowski's visit, the Cincinnati board
made its decision and cabled Wulsin, "Stokovski selected unless your report decidedly unfavorable." In the meantime,

Wulsin had interviewed Stokowski in Paris and had received a "pleasant impression." After attending the crucial concert, he cabled Bettie Holmes on May 13, throwing the ball back to her: "Stokovski all right. Conducted very well. I think your decision good."

Bettie cabled Stokowski the official invitation the same day.

Meanwhile, another apple had dropped into Stokowski's lap. The violinist Francis MacMillan, hoping to make a conspicuous appearance in London, had engaged an orchestra called the New Symphony to accompany him in Saint-Saëns's B-minor Concerto and in Lalo's *Symphonie Espagnol* and was seeking a conductor. Stokowski was suggested and found available and decidedly willing.

In cabling his acceptance to Cincinnati, Stokowski added that his manager had arranged a London appearance on May 18, which he would fulfill before returning. The Mac-Millan concert opened with Beethoven's *Coriolanus* Overture, and after intermission Stokowski performed Ippolitov-Ivanov's *Caucasian Sketches*. There is no greater testimony to Stokowski's personal magnetism than the way MacMillan's concert was reviewed in the London *Times* and the *Musical Times*. The critics wrote as though they were covering an orchestral debut. Clearly, Stokowski was the star. Especially remarkable was his ability to win such serious praise and unusual attention within the comparatively slight opportunities which that program offered a conductor to display his true qualities. But it worked.

The timing was perfect. Stokowski was in orbit.

From the board's point of view, Stokowski was the least expensive and the most persistent and desirable contender for the position. He had peppered the Cincinnati Symphony Association with monthly inquires and bulletins from Europe and was the one suitable candidate willing to sign a single-year contract and accept the $4,000 salary. With Olga's work behind the scenes and the impressive reviews he was getting for his Paris and London concerts, Stokowski landed the job.

If his relative inexperience was of minor concern to the management, it was quickly apparent to the members of the orchestra. Indeed, their new conductor floundered so badly at the initial rehearsal that the concertmaster felt constrained to whisper a few suggestions pointedly in his ear. Stokowski, probably for the first and last time in his life, took the advice and came on strong. But he was always a quick study.

What he learned in Cincinnati in three years set the pattern for his entire meteoric career. Diligently, he laid out a course of self-instruction in how to tyrannize a board of directors, then, how to win the respect and support of an orchestra, and next, and perhaps of most importance, how to hypnotize an audience. He wooed them and cajoled them, flattered them and gently reproved them. When they grew fidgety, he shamed them into attentiveness and concentration. "Please don't do that," he once admonished an audience of program shufflers. "We work hard all week to give you this music. Now you must do your part. I'm here to give you my best. If you don't want it, then I'll give you nothing."

This was one of his many set speeches, memorized and repeated almost verbatim, time and again before new audiences that displayed anything less than worshipful attention. Later, when his programming grew more adventuresome and the audience grew liberated enough to hiss, Stokowski was cunning and hedged, saying, "That's all right! If you feel strongly enough and need to express your feelings, that's good! What is bad is to sit and feel nothing!"

So at twenty-seven this musical unsophisticate headed an orchestra. Not a great orchestra, but an orchestra with a great tradition in a great American city. Cincinnati was a metropolis of 364,000 souls, only 100,000 fewer than today. When he arrived, he began exploring. Walking through the business district, observing the theatrical and shopping areas, Stokowski saw many fine buildings of brick, blue limestone, and a grayish-buff freestone. Of particular interest to him was the dumpy, disproportionately large Music Hall and the exquisite Church of Saint Francis de Sales, built in 1888 and possessing a famous bell he had heard about as far away as Europe. Cast in Cincinnati and weighing fifteen tons, it was said to be the largest swinging bell in the world. The most arresting and elegant statuary in the city was an impressive bronze fountain, displaying fifteen magnificent figures, one a female reaching forty-five feet above the ground.

The city also boasted a wire suspension bridge across the Ohio River, designed in 1867 by John A. Roebling, the engineer who built the Brooklyn Bridge in New York two years later. Cincinnati had also been an important station on the Underground Railroad; one site had been the home of Harriet Beecher Stowe.

Fifteen thousand blacks lived in Cincinnati, and the largest group among the whites by birth or ancestry was German. The residential districts—formerly suburban villages—were connected to downtown by electric railway cars. Cincinnati had slaughterhouses and meat-packing plants, and its industrialists manufactured clothing, boots, and shoes, brewed beer, and built carriages. Now, young Stokowski was going to shake the rafters of the bloated old Music Hall and make the entire city pay attention.

Cincinnati was known as the Paris of America, its Champs-Elysées was Vine Street, and it was not an easy town to dazzle. It had its full share of saloons, burlesque houses, concert halls, restaurants, theaters, celebrities, and festivals. The Cincinnati Baseball Club became America's first professional team in 1869, and the the smart set had tennis and golf at the racquet clubs.

World-famous sports figures such as John L. Sullivan, Jim Corbett, Tom Sharkey, Kid McCoy, Jack Dempsey, and Jim Jeffries decorated the bars on Vine. The famed stickup artist, Frank James, gambled and lost there. The Peoples' Theater featured Buffalo Bill, Sarah Bernhardt, and Lillian Russell.

In 1901, according to the annals of the Cincinnati Historical Society, the town had been honored with a visit from Carrie Nation. At the Atlantic Garden, haunt of the whores and gamblers, the little lady with the hatchet who had smashed the windows and glassware of so many barrooms tried to guide a female lush down the path of temperance. Soaking the crusader's bosom with crocodile tears, the big blonde promised she would become a good girl. Carrie was touched in more ways than one; the weepy penitent lifted her earrings.

Yes, Cincinnati was a swinging town. Stokowski had his work cut out for him. All the top-drawer hot spots featured fine food, drinks, panoramic views, and music. But what music! Wilert's Garden flaunted a forty-piece band, and the Lookout House presented the visiting Theodore Thomas's symphonic orchestra nightly.

In April, the new conductor and the orchestra's manager, Bernard Sturm, auditioned musicians who had come from Chicago, Minneapolis, and St. Louis. At the end of a tough week, only partially promising, Stokowski left for New York, and Sturm headed for Chicago, both to find more and better players. First consideration had been given to local musicians, and in the end approximately one-third of the orchestra came from Cincinnati. Stokowski had promised the musicians' union, whose rules were designed to improve the climate for American musicians, that he would attempt, if possible, to hire Americans. A foreigner was required to show naturalization papers or at least evidence that he had taken the first steps toward naturalization. Characteristically, Stokowski himself would not be pushed. Taking his own sweet time, he applied for his first papers in 1914 and became a citizen the next year.

Public favor ran counter to union rules in the musical world: A musician at that time was unlikely to be highly regarded unless he was imported. Stokowski was in every way the perfect combination: born a foreigner, educated on the right side of the Atlantic, with some (at least a little) European musical experience, and the only conductor of a major American symphony whose native tongue was English. Considering the capriciousness of his accent, let me posit that his mother tongue was broken English.

For all of Stokowski's ingratiating and forceful qualities, he was a gamble for Cincinnati, for the orchestra board, and particularly for Mrs. Holmes. Obviously, they were aware of it, and yet he had given the orchestra board a great deal of "information" that led them to believe that "his credentials were quite impressive."

Immediately after the appointment was announced, Stokowski was widely interviewed and favorably portrayed. Mrs. Holmes was able to breathe freely again. Thomas notes that reporters were always impressed with Stokowski's gracious, unaffected manner, his clean-cut, young executive appearance, the absence of musical eccentricities or temperament, and the catholicity of his interests. However, noted a reporter, "He adroitly sidestepped those questions which probed too deeply beneath the surface or which sought to explore his previous conducting experience."

J. Herman Thuman's review of the Paris concert with the Colonne Orchestra that Olga had maneuvered appeared on May 29, just as Stokowski arrived in Cincinnati. A "most pronounced success," Thuman proclaimed, saying that "Stokovski was accorded an ovation at the conclusion of the concert such as is seldom bestowed upon a conductor in this city." Not only Mrs. Holmes, but Cincinnati, could relax. Paris was selective, hard to please, and *très* sophisticated. And Cincinnati was going to have the man Paris applauded.

Stokowski took a bachelor apartment in Mount Auburn, one of the more handsome residential sections of Cincinnati. There was much music to learn after auditioning the orchestra. At his June meeting with the board, he had insisted that all the programs for the season be decided on promptly and published well in advance. He dedicated himself primarily to the meticulous scrutiny of the many compositions with which he had little or no experience but which he planned to conduct during the 1909–10 season. He innately possessed courage and magnetism but had yet to garner the judgment, technical skill, and authority to develop the personnel and the working conditions that produce a great orchestra.

As Dr. Thomas notes, "Stokovski was fully aware that, whereas many of the principal players enjoyed the security of a five-year contract, he, their leader, had been engaged for one year only. Stokovski, not the orchestra, was on trial; and he was expendable. It was exceedingly important that Stokovski earn the respect of the orchestra musicians from the outset, and this he succeeded admirably in doing."

I learned from Leonard Liebling that within two weeks of the first rehearsal Stokowski was in full command, conducting with complete confidence. A warm rapport had been established between conductor and orchestra. The men were especially appreciative of the courtesy and respect that Stokowski accorded them. Concertmaster Hugo Heermann reported that "all the men admire and respect him extremely, both for his deep musical knowledge and his kindly, courteous treatment of them."

Olga told me of eyewitness reports of this unknown young man when he arrived in Cincinnati. These convey the efficacy of Stokowski's radiant personality, his youthful freshness, his rapid changes of mood—one moment irresistibly charming, the next wildly satanic. It took two years for him to gain the security to unleash the dictatorial approach and to implement his innate conviction that one cannot run anything right without having full control of all its elements. This commanding drive would have to be concealed for a while until he had the authority to express it. He was a born ruler with a goal that he would have to bide his time to attain. Ultimately, he would have to exercise absolute authority, alternately frightening and flattering his associates to overcome all opposition.

3

LONG BEFORE THE CINCINNATI PUBLIC had heard one note from its new conductor, Leopold Stokovski—with a *v*—was a household name. The glamorous corona about his head, his romantic pallor and aquiline profile, every idealistic word of his that the press had quoted, all had established the Stokowskian charisma.

His long-awaited debut in the Music Hall on Friday afternoon, November 25, 1909, attracted a huge and semihypnotized audience, excited and prepared for an occasion that promised to be not only a musical event but also a metaphysical experience. Stokowski had never had to study the art of being a public idol. Genius was a birthmark upon him.

Unpredictable man that Stokowski was, he opened his American premiere program with Wolfgang Amadeus Mozart! This may induce a mite less condemnation of Stokowski's seemingly unaccountable neglect of all but a handful of masterpieces by the musician's musician. I have no intentions nor means of explaining or defining this baffling blind spot of Stokowski's, for every question I ever posed him on the subject was met by stubborn subterfuge. But the opening work heard by that expectant audience was the Overture to *The Magic Flute,* Mozart's masonic fairyland in which the spirit of universal brotherhood is brilliantly reflected.

Before the new conductor came onstage, the lights were dimmed and a hush fell over the hall. Then the audience gasped as it got its first glimpse of this tall, lithe, haughtily handsome blond youth with icy blue eyes and a small, thin, sensuous mouth. Suddenly, he straightened up to his full height, with the stance and dignity of a Roman senator. The orchestra tendered him the traditional "tusch," a triply repeated token of welcome accompanied by the flourish of brasses and winds, drum rolls, and the tapping of string-players' bows on music stands, while the crowd hailed him with deafening applause. Abruptly, Stokowski leaped upon the podium and stabbed the air with his baton. "The music started, the audience came alive, and the air was filled with electric sparks such as I had experienced only once," said Liebling. "It happened the year before, at Toscanini's debut at the Met. This was the same kind of overwhelming atmosphere."

At the conclusion of the Mozart overture, the audience was moved "to one of the sincerest outbursts of applause ever heard in the Music Hall," as the *Cincinnati Post* reported. After the pandemonium had subsided, came the big work of the evening, that most battle-scarred of symphonic pieces, Beethoven's Fifth Symphony. Stokowski had announced in advance that his debut concert was to be an all-orchestral program of familiar masterpieces "to give the audience a full opportunity to measure me by compositions they know and which they have heard before. It is by comparison that judgments are made possible."

All the reviewers raved. Thuman wrote in the *Enquirer*, "Stokovski presented a unique interpretation of this orchestral war-horse, including an overly fast fate theme and slower first and third movements than tradition had established. But before the program was half over, there was not one in the audience but was not captivated by his personality, delighted with the graceful manner of his conducting, and immensely pleased with the musical acumen he fervently demonstrated. The ice had been broken. Stokovski had come and conquered."

Liebling wrote that "Stokovski's interpretation of the Beethoven Fifth was both original and reminiscent of the best efforts of Nikisch, Mahler, and Weingartner." He knew what he was talking about, for they had been his heros during his student days at the Berlin Hochschule. He also came to worship Stokowski uncritically as the friendship developed. Whereas Thuman's enthusiasm gradually turned into disillusionment, Liebling's loyalty never faltered. He recognized Stokowski's genius and refused to limit his judgment to "narrow, orthodox insistence on adherence to traditions. Even Toscanini defined traditions as the ingrained mistakes of musical performances." When the purists began to attack Stokowski for his "distortions" of the Bach style, Liebling wrote, "He plays Bach as though he enjoys him and wishes his hearers to enjoy him too."

Stokowski was also learning how to manage a management. He knew there must be only one head, himself, and in order to lead, he made everyone believe that they were merely followers. He put up his demands, and he had his way. Eventually he settled for nothing but the best. For the moment he demanded better musicians, better instruments, better rehearsal conditions, better tour arrangements, better salaries (including his own). The Cincinnati management knuckled under quickly, for they did not want to lose this young dynamo, who was putting the Queen City on the musical map. They gave him everything he wanted—adequate money to enlarge the personnel of the orchestra and to import anywhere in the world the most expert instrumentalists available.

They soon approved an extensive western tour for the orchestra. Stokowski's fame began to expand, and the young conductor began to attract nationwide attention. The board accepted Stokowski's suggestion that the orchestra not appear in New York. "The orchestra is not quite ready," he said in 1911. Little did they know that he was casting eyes eastward for one that was ready or shortly would be.

Cincinnati was overjoyed with their spellbinding maestro and with his critical acclaim. On February 8, 1910, they offered him four more years on top of his one-year contract, and the board made inquiry about other major orchestra conductors' salaries. They found that Frederick Stock in Chicago earned $10,000; Max Fiedler in Boston, $18,000; and Gustav Mahler in New York, $25,000. On February 24 they offered Stokowski—beyond the $4,000 he was under contract for in the 1909–10 season—the next season at $6,000, the next at $7,000, the following year at $8,000, and the last year, the 1913–14 season and his fifth year with Cincinnati, $10,000, the "same stature as other conductors." Stokowski accepted: "I am very happy in my work at Cincinnati. [The] musical environment of the Queen City is unusually artistic. . . . I have been encouraged by the real love of music that prevails."

Bettie Holmes felt justifiably proud: "Your Board of Directors," she told the orchestra stockholders, "feels that it is greatly to be congratulated upon the wisdom of its choice. We feel confident that the Cincinnati Symphony Orchestra will soon rank with the foremost orchestras of today."

The programs that Stokowski presented had been immediately notable for the ingenious variety they offered and for the novelty of their organization. His originality was again demonstrated, for example, in an all-British program of the 1911–12 season, with contemporary masters such as Sir Arthur Sullivan, Sir Edward Elgar, and Sir Charles Stanford, an obeisance to his master at the R.C.M. They shared the program with such ancient masters as Byrd, Farnaby, and Purcell. Stokowski's regime initiated an exceptionally fertile repertory, including compositions from every school and period.

When constructing a program, Stokowski explained, the

first number "should be solid and the last number should be impressive and effective." Despite tradition, he did not want a soloist on the opening pair of concerts, because "a ragged orchestra is more in evidence accompanying than in straight work." Stokowski also suggested that no program should exceed two hours in length and that there be an intermission on each one for the benefit of the orchestra players, "as they work better" with a rest. Once or twice during Van der Stucken's tenure there had been an intermission during the all-Wagner request programs. But the practice of having an intermission at each and every Cincinnati Symphony Orchestra concert was inaugurated by Stokowski during the 1909–10 season. He also elevated the last two rows of the orchestra with risers for improved audibility.

During that first season, Stokowski and the new orchestra were quickly introduced to the rest of Ohio. In addition to the ten pairs of subscription concerts given in Cincinnati, the orchestra performed twenty-one concerts on the road. It was on these tours that the orchestra evoked the greatest enthusiasm. As early as December 1, 1909, after Stokowski and his men had performed together but four times, the *Piqua* (Ohio) *Leader* proclaimed that "the new Cincinnati Symphony Orchestra is greater than the old."

Profuse praise flowed from reviews in Columbus and Dayton, but it was sophisticated Cleveland that tendered the most lavish tributes. The orchestra had appeared there many times before under Van der Stucken, but Stokowski's appeal undoubtedly accounted for the audience of 2,500. In order to insure an artistic and financial success, the celebrated operatic soprano Marcella Sembrich had been engaged as soloist. But that night the popular Sembrich played a secondary role. Stokowski and his orchestra completely captivated the audience and the critics. The *Cleveland News* described Stokowski as "fresh, forceful, magnetic and ambitious. . . . The consensus of opinion judged the Cincinnati Orchestra as good stuff—youthful, strong, and promising of splendid development with its young Jupiter of a leader." Wilson G. Smith, of the *Cleveland Press,* declared the occasion to be "the most notable concert ever given locally by the Cincinnati Orchestra," and as for Stokowski, "He has the spark of interpretative genius that knows no age." The Cleveland *Town Topics* reviewer was particularly impressed by Stokowski's interpretation of Tchaikovsky's Sixth Symphony: "Cleveland has heard this symphony interpreted many times, but never has it produced such a wonderful effect. Stokovski is a genius, and before he has reached the age of forty he will have become the most wonderful conductor in America."

The first rip in this neat seam came with the unexpected resignation of Stokowski's concertmaster, Hugo Heermann, in early March 1910. Heermann seemed not to have been at odds with Stokowski but rather with the city itself. "Cincinnati is barbaric in its musical taste," he said. Cincinnati women were appreciative of good music, but the men were not—"They don't care about music at all"—and it was impossible too, he added, for a musician in Cincinnati to support a family. Heermann was going back to Germany, and right away.

Stokowski spoke up for the audiences of Cincinnati and of America: "This is a young country," he said, "and the men are too busy building it up, building railroads and cities to take time for the enjoyment of art and music."

The men of the orchestra were members of the Cincinnati musicians' union, and the recent relations between the union and the management had been stormy. Nevertheless, when the 1909 season began, harmony reigned. There had been no Cincinnati Symphony the season before, but now there was a new conductor and very different conditions of employment. The orchestra members were now to be on salary for the full twenty-week season, the same rules were going to apply to all members, and the musicians were no longer permitted to be farmed out for other jobs. Furthermore, the musicians were allowed to serve on faculties and to play outside dates so long as their service and their dates did not interfere with their Symphony work.

A rent occurred in the otherwise peaceful first season when the May Festival took the spotlight away from Stokowski. Frank van der Stucken, Stokowski's immediate predecessor, conducted the Theodore Thomas Orchestra of Chicago at the opening-night performance of Handel's *Judas Maccabaeus,* with President and Mrs. Taft in the audience. Stokowski exhibited Machiavellian diplomacy and restraint by ignoring the obvious snub to Cincinnati's own orchestra and conductor.

Following the May Festival, the Cincinnati Orchestra was reconvened to perform for the national convention of the General Federation of Women's Clubs. In what Dr. Thomas calls "the most ironical anticlimax in orchestral history," Stokowski was thrown a bone: The orchestra concluded its extracurricular activities as the primary attraction of the Connersville, Indiana (population 7,738), May Festival. Stokowski was so hurt by this situation that he never mentioned it to the board. Instead, he waited until it would provide the moral justification to walk out on his contract.

Stokowski was at the height of his artistic success in Cincinnati during the second season, 1910–11. He and the orchestra were recognized as the city's leading cultural export. The number and scope of the out-of-town concerts increased to thirty-two and widened to include Indianapolis, Buffalo, Omaha, and Wichita. The orchestra was enlarged by the addition of nine string players, a "Popular Concert" series was presented on Sunday afternoons, and Stokowski's request to extend the 1911–12 season to twenty-three weeks was approved by the board.

Nevertheless, there was trouble in the second season—not musical and not of Stokowski's making, but real trouble for which he had to take some responsibility. The orchestra had played in Buffalo on March 9, 1911. On the trip back to

Ohio, the Jewish musicians—there were fifteen of them—
were segregated from the others and located in the rear car
of the train. Segregation was followed by insult: Some members of the orchestra walked through the car singing offensive songs. The Jewish players signed a letter informing Stokowski of the anti-Semitic incident and threatened to resign
immediately if this behavior went unchallenged. Stokowski
"promised an early investigation into the charges and the
dismissal from the orchestra of anyone found guilty of such
discrimination," Thomas reports.

This was a sad contrast to the rapport Stokowski and the
musicians enjoyed during the first season's tour, when the
Maestro had purchased baseball bats, divided the musicians
into teams, and indulged in daily games while the nonplayers
formed a brass band and cheered. During the second season,
on a trip to Kansas, the orchestra took twelve hundred bottles of Cincinnati beer along "because they had heard that
Wichita was dry." Shortly after, as reported in the *Wichita
Beacon,* Bettie Holmes noted that "several breweries have
solicited [the] patronage of the orchestra."

Nothing more was heard of the anti-Semitic incident.
Three weeks after it, the season ended. Stokowski gave the
orchestra a luncheon. The orchestra gave Stokowski a set of
diamond cuff links.

Stokowski and Olga were quietly married on April 24,
1911, in St. Louis, her family's home. For their honeymoon,
they returned to Munich, Germany, the scene of several romantic summer vacations they had taken in previous years.
Munich was the home of summer music festivals where the
operas of Mozart and Wagner were performed in an atmosphere of indescribable charm. Writers, painters, and dancers, as well as musicians, flocked there, not only because of
the superb performances but also because of the proximity
of the Alps. They provided opportunities for delightful day-

time excursions to contrast with the evening performances, invariably followed by a *gemütlich* supper at the *Keller* in the Vierjahreszeiten Hotel.

The summers were calm, pleasant—typical of Stokowski's life. Mendelssohn is probably the only other musician who enjoyed such constant fruition and good fortune. Both had intrinsically sensitive and subjective natures. From the beginning, Stokowski's entire existence was guided by personal feelings, by likes and dislikes, by pleasant and unpleasant memories. The only reliable recollections of Cincinnati that I ever extracted from him related to his remembrance of being appreciated. He said that he had felt "very fortunately placed, for the time being." Perhaps he meant, but did not say, not overexposed. He remembered feeling "very optimistic" about his future. He had every reason to be.

When Stokowski and Olga returned from Munich to Cincinnati in October, his third season with the orchestra promised to be even more successful than the last. Through generous contributions the orchestra was again enlarged. The new auditorium was nearly completed; and the road trips, while fewer, would take the orchestra to larger musical centers, Chicago and St. Louis. Stokowski was confident enough to correct the continual misspelling of his name as "Stokovski." He announced that "he would henceforth use the correct form of his correct name, 'Stokowski,'" in the erroneous belief that the public had learned to pronounce it correctly.

The first concerts of the season were acclaimed by all the Cincinnati critics except J. Herman Thuman of the *Enquirer*. His solitary invectives, with the exception of his very first, complimentary review, had hounded Stokowski since the first season. He had since become a local manager of imported events.

When the orchestra returned from still another equally triumphant and critically successful tour of Akron, Cleveland, Pittsburgh, and Columbus, the entire membership signed a statement addressed to the editor of the *Enquirer* in protest to the unduly severe musical criticisms and prejudice of Thuman.

How, the *Musical Courier* earlier asked, can the *Enquirer*'s music critic be allowed "to be a musical manager of artists, manager of the May Festival, and manager of imported opera companies? How can he remain unbiased?" It also pointedly suggested that Thuman's unsuccessful bid to be appointed manager of the symphony might also have colored his opinions.

Editor Leonard Liebling, Stokowski's champion, supported the musicians' protest and added, "The crux of the problem is that Mr. Thuman is a professional music critic and a musical businessman at the same time, and the two activities do not mix ethically." Thuman's criticisms became less severe immediately following the publication of the protests, and for the balance of the season he was often quite complimentary.

In the midst of this controversy, the orchestra traveled to St. Louis for the first time. On the December 13 concert, Olga was the soloist in Tchaikovsky's First Piano Concerto. The audience was rapturous and the critics raved.

Back home, the concert of January 6, 1912, which inaugurated Emery Auditorium, impressed even Thuman, who went so far as to acknowledge, "Stokowski grasped the meaning of the Franck D-minor Symphony far better than any of the several ones [symphonies] he has yet given here."

The February tour to Chicago, again featuring Olga, elicited such critical enthusiasm that the *Tribune* remarked, "The Cincinnati Symphony Orchestra was better than the New York Symphony Orchestra when it appeared in Chicago under Felix Weingartner."

The orchestra Stokowski had trained had brought greatly advantageous results to Cincinnati's reputation and prestige.

Stokowski's tangible value to Cincinnati was becoming ever more apparent, especially in this time of intense economic expansion and cultural rivalry. The sine qua non of a great metropolis was a preeminent symphony orchestra, and without the slightest doubt, Stokowski had made Cincinnati the "Midwestern musical capital."

While the orchestra was out gathering laurels for the city, a rivalry had arisen between the president of the board, Bettie Holmes, and Anna Taft, the principal financial supporter of the orchestra. When the board denied Stokowski's request in early January for a New York tour as financially unfeasible, Stokowski surreptitiously asked Mrs. Taft to subsidize the trip. Mrs. Holmes was offended that Stokowski would attempt to circumvent the authority of the board, and her relationship with him and Mrs. Taft cooled considerably.

An outright catfight developed between the two women in a dispute over the administrative control of the organization. Dr. Thomas's examination of the board minutes disclosed that on January 30 Mrs. Holmes suggested a reorganization of the management of the orchestra so that a single manager, not the entire board, could handle the orchestra both in town and out on the road. Mrs. Taft, among the original founders of the Orchestra Association Company in 1894, offered to "take the responsibility and direction of all out-of-town engagements of the orchestra," replacing the current manager.

Stokowski had received an invitation from London to conduct a concert in the spring and had informed the board that he was planning to accept. The board had refused to allow him to leave Cincinnati before the season's end. Further, it had complained of the "heavy nature of the music" at the last two Popular Concerts.

Since Mrs. Taft was away, Stokowski took the matter up with Mrs. Holmes, who ruffled the young conductor's feathers in such a manner and to such a degree that on that very evening he submitted his resignation in a letter addressed to the advisory board, delivered to Lucien Wulsin:

March 23, 1912

DEAR SIR:

During an interview which I had this afternoon with Mrs. Holmes, she made the statement that I had "insulted her more than she had ever been insulted in her life" by approving of Mrs. Taft's offer to finance the outside engagements of the Cincinnati Symphony Orchestra.

This unjustifiable view of the matter is doubtless caused by the unfortunate friction which has existed between us for some time owing to our inability to agree regarding the affairs of the orchestra.

When I assumed the directorship of the Cincinnati Symphony Orchestra I had hopes of building up a really great institution which would take its rank as a national feature of American music.

The conditions prevailing in this city and the policies of those controlling the orchestra, convince me that this is impossible, and therefore feeling that this disappointment makes it impossible for me to continue my work here with the same enthusiasm which has inspired me during the past three years, I am writing to beg you to grant my release from my existing contract with you.

It was his intention, Stokowski said, "to return to Europe and devote myself in the immediate future to guest conducting."

Olga said years later that Stokowski "always found something to complain about—the hall, the inefficient management, an ever-less-happy alliance with the board. He was growing disillusioned." However, she said, she was just as surprised and startled as everyone else when he actually resigned.

This I have reason to doubt. So did Leonard Liebling, who assumed that he enjoyed Stokowski's full confidence during the time preceding the abdication. He told me, "There was never any justification for Stoki to break his contract. There was nothing on God's green earth that Cincinnati wouldn't have given him. I can't ever accept his reasons for leaving. Something was going on behind the scenes that I wasn't in on until later."

The advisory board made no public acknowledgment of the receipt of the Maestro's letter. But Stokowski immediately notified the newspapers that he had asked for his release, although he declined to reveal what his grievances were and refused to mention any names.

The board assembled on March 25 and announced that Stokowski would probably remain to fulfill his contract and that the differences between the conductor and the members of the board could easily be resolved. Yet on March 26, after spending two hours with a special committee from the advisory board, Stokowski told the afternoon papers that he had not changed his mind about resigning. In this statement he aired one grudge that he had evidently been harboring for three years: "There is no other city that has a musical festival and has at the same time an orchestra that is capable of performing at that festival, but would have its own orchestra for that occasion," he said bitterly. "Instead, a Chicago orchestra comes down here for the festival."

Pleas from the entire city poured in, begging him to remain in Cincinnati and expressing appreciation for his talents. But Stokowski was as determined to resign as he had been determined to acquire the post in 1909. On March 27 he issued to the *Cincinnati Post* a public statement that enumerated the causes of his discontent. It was fundamentally a matter of lost enthusiasm, a disaffection stemming from a number of reasons: "The slight of my orchestra concerning the May Festival . . . has deeply hurt me personally and has done me professional harm in the musical world outside. . . . From one of the leading critics of the city [Thuman] I endured persistent persecution, manifestly of a personal nature, . . . and it was owing to the indignant protest of my orchestra that this condition was ameliorated. . . . I have been much discouraged by the coldness of our Symphony audiences as compared with the cordial receptions tendered the same work by the same orchestra everywhere else." Stokowski refused to divulge his difficulties with the board of directors, because "they were of a nature which could be adjusted" and the board had expressed its willingness to adjust them. "What cannot be adjusted is the loss of my enthusiasm."

Lucien Wulsin, incensed at Stokowski's self-righteous statement, wrote a disdainful letter to Henry E. Krehbiel, the eminent music critic of the *New York Tribune:*

March 29, 1912

MY DEAR KREHBIEL:

It may interest you to get the enclosed cuttings, which give some idea of the present condition of Stokowski, who, I may add, is a nervous, hysterical young fellow with a good deal of native ability and charm, but who has not in him either physically or from the standpoint of the technically skilled conductor the power to do what he has undertaken to do. The most unfortunate thing is that certain personal quality which he has, has carried away a lot of people in Cincinnati, . . . that this young man has been praised to an extent far beyond his deserts and takes all this thing for gospel.

What does one do in such a case as this where a party comes here and after a year's trial deliberately makes a contract for four years more and then proceeds as is now going on?

Krehbiel promptly replied on March 31, 1912:

I cannot say that I am at all surprised at your letter concerning Stokowski. If the Tafts are grieved by the turn affairs have taken, they have only themselves to blame, for it was they who persisted in believing that the young nincompoop was a great man, . . . a second Nikisch. Well, watch and see.

The famous music critic was way off target that time.

On April 5 Stokowski received the official decision of the special committee of the advisory board: "After full consideration in all its phases, we have unanimously concluded not to grant your request. The contract has still two years to run, and we expect you to complete it."

"Stokowski's immediate retaliation is so insulting and offensive," Dr. Thomas notes, "that it undoubtedly alienated forever the majority of the men and women who had theretofore been his staunchest friends and admirers":

In sending you my letter of resignation I most certainly never supposed that men and women of honor would ignore the moral responsibility devolving from the agreement I have with the President of your Association. . . .

I shall most certainly sever all personal relations with everyone who countenances such an outrageous breach of faith or such a personal insult to me.

In all my dealings with the present situation I have, as a gentleman, refrained from mentioning my difficulties or disagreements with women. However, a woman, if vested with official authority, ought to be just as responsible for her actions as a man. I therefore demand of Mrs. C. R. Holmes, President of the Orchestra Association, a recognition and fulfillment of the compact under which I signed my existing legal contract with the Cincinnati Symphony Orchestra and that she, as President of the Orchestra Association, should grant me the full and unqualified release from my legal contract, which, in justice, it is my right to demand.

I also state that Mrs. C. R. Holmes affirmed to me that she was fully authorized by the Board of Directors in all her business dealings with me, and in all other matters her power to act has been recognized by the Association. I therefore hold you bound with her.

If you ignore any longer my just claims for release from my contract, I shall make the whole matter public both in Cincinnati and elsewhere.

Again Stokowski notified the press before the advisory board could officially act upon his letter. In a letter to the editor of the *Enquirer* he restated his contention that a verbal agreement existed between Mrs. Holmes and him which allowed either party to dissolve the contract at the end of any given season.

Though Stokowski was always capable of being "undeniable," as Olga put it, he was also capable of being his own worst enemy. The board finally capitulated on April 13 and officially accepted Stokowski's resignation:

Your letter of April 5, answering that of this committee of same date, having been considered by the Board of Directors of the Cincinnati Symphony Orchestra Association and their Advisory Board, the undersigned special committee, duly authorized, hereby notify you that your recent behavior and repeated aspersions upon members of the Board of Directors of the Association, and your unfounded reflections upon the musical public of Cincinnati, have destroyed your usefulness to the Cincinnati Symphony Orchestra Association Company, and we now notify you that you are released from your contract and the same is hereby cancelled.

This letter included a check for $875, the final installment of Stokowski's $7,000 salary.

By obtaining his release in such a callous and shocking manner, Stokowski was the subject of a great deal of verbal and reportorial abuse. The *Musical Leader* on April 18 reported:

> Words are lacking to describe the disgust that exists among true loyal music loving Cincinnatians at the manner in which this young climber has treated this city.

And from the *Cleveland Leader* on April 28:

> Thus ends for Cincinnati, at least, the drum and cymbal career of Leopold Stokowski—né Stokovski—who brilliantly and quickly rose from an inconsequential position in the East to the leadership of one of America's greatest orchestras; who made Beethoven dance on his ears; who made Brahms a puling, sickly sentimentalist; who calcined Strauss in more clashing and fighting colors than Strauss ever knew; and who Stokowski-ized each composer whom he took into his directorial hands; who clenched his shaking fists, threshed the air with his arms and distorted his body to secure innocuous and unconvincing effects; and who in violation of all professional ethics caused his pictures to be published far and wide above columns of fulsome matter which had Stokowski for its subject.

Stokowski's response to the press came on the morning of April 15, 1912, the day he departed from Cincinnati, "headed for Europe," he said. Stokowski wrote: "I was mistaken in my belief that the Cincinnati public did not appreciate my work. I want to acknowledge very cheerfully that I was wrong in my criticism of the attitude of Cincinnati audiences. Especially since my resignation they have shown by every move possible how friendly they are toward me and how warmly they appreciate the work of the orchestra. I feel now that the public is with me, and it is with very great regret I leave Cincinnati." From the *Times-Star:* "One must admit he kept up appearances." (Either that, or he had an extraordinary ego—which he did!)

En route to New York, Stokowski and Olga stopped in Philadelphia to meet with the board of directors of that city's orchestra, which was still under the baton of Karl Pohlig. Undercover negotiations with Stokowski ensued and were concluded in New York on April 29, the day before they left for Europe. Andrew Wheeler, a backer of the orchestra and the secretary of the Philadelphia Orchestra Association, offered Stokowski a secret contract, which he signed, to conduct the Philadelphia Orchestra as of the 1913–14 season.

Pohlig, who was in Europe at the time, got wind of this, rushed back to Philadelphia, and was all set to sue for breach of contract, as his had still one year to run. This gave the Philadelphia board the chance it was seeking. The *Musical America* of June 15 gave the facts: "The Philadelphia Orchestra Association, rather than have Mr. Pohlig bring suit in an attempt to prove a conspiracy to oust him, paid him $12,000 for the unexpired year of his original contract, and accepted his resignation, effective June 10, 1912." Stokowski was notified in Munich, where he and Olga were vacationing, and he agreed to begin his Philadelphia conductorship in the fall of 1912.

Rumors immediately flew out that Stokowski had already been signed sub rosa to conduct the Philadelphia Orchestra for the season 1912–13 as early as January 1912 and that this was the actual reason he abandoned Cincinnati.

Further evidence surfaced in 1925, which revealed that Stokowski had been interested in the Philadelphia position even before he was hired by the Cincinnati orchestra. The *Philadelphia Inquirer,* covering the twenty-fifth anniversary banquet of the Philadelphia Orchestra Association, reported that Andrew Wheeler recalled that Stokowski had first ap-

plied for the conductor's post of the Philadelphia Orchestra
in 1908. Stokowski had been refused consideration because
of his youth and inexperience.

Forever after, Stokowski denied that the Philadelphia offer
had anything to do with his resignation from Cincinnati.
Olga denied it, and the Philadelphia board denied it. But
years later it was verified for me beyond doubt by Arthur
Judson, manager of the Philadelphia Orchestra; by Ruth
O'Neill, vice-president of Columbia Artists Management and
secretary to Stokowski in his early Philadelphia days; by
Mary Louise Curtis Bok; and by Alexander Van Rensselaer,
president of the Philadelphia Orchestra Association.

Nothing could have been more natural than for Stokowski
to fall into the job in Philadelphia, what with Olga spending
so much time there, playing, socializing, and proselytizing.
Every major figure in the Philadelphia orchestral hierarchy
was her very good friend and sincere admirer. It was equally
natural for Stokowski's reputation to have captured the
imagination of ambitious Philadelphia itself, a city in dire
need of the cultural prestige enjoyed by New York, Boston,
and Chicago.

No one can blame Stokowski for coveting the conductorial
post in so eminent and ascendant a place as Philadelphia. Yet
it was undeniable that since the Queen City had placed faith
in him despite his inexperience and since he had delivered so
magnificently and had brought so much civic pride to Cincinnati, another way of severing the connection should have
been found. As objective as one tries to be, one can only
regret that what began as a beautiful romance should have
turned into a humiliating, backbiting brawl.

On April 30, Stokowski sailed for England, where he was
engaged to conduct two London concerts. One, with the New
Symphony Orchestra, featured the reappearance of the
famed American soprano Lillian Nordica. The critical reactions were gratifying. Said the *Times* of June 15, 1912:

In this remarkable performance Mme. Nordica had an admirable colleague in Mr. Leopold Stokowski, who conducted the New Symphony Orchestra both with her and in some Wagner selections for orchestra alone. He showed great power in dealing with the *Götterdämmerung* scene, and particularly in carrying out the fine conception of the music which Mme. Nordica had placed before us up to an overwhelming climax in the orchestral ending of the opera.

The other concert, with the London Symphony Orchestra and the budding Russian violinist Efrem Zimbalist as soloist, had great historical significance, for it initiated the longest-lasting association of Stokowski's numerous orchestral alliances. The reviews were glowing. From the *Manchester Guardian* of May 25, 1912:

> Mr. Leopold Stokowski . . . has a quiet but authoritative manner, his gestures are restrained, and there is much healthy and judicious moderation in his style. . . . His reading of Brahm's First Symphony was broad and strong, and its thoughtfulness was not made an excuse for dullness. There was picturesque refinement without affectation in his reading of Debussy's *Prélude à l'Après-midi d'un faune*. Mr. Zimbalist played Glazounov's Violin Concerto remarkably well, and was admirably accompanied. Mr. Stokowski certainly impressed one as a conductor likely to achieve a reputation.

And from the *Daily Mail* of May 25, 1912:

> The London Symphony Orchestra, playing yesterday at Queen's Hall under M. Leopold Stokowski, as on Monday they did under Herr Nikisch, gave displays of orchestral playing as fine as it has ever been one's lot to hear. The band's American tour appears to have sharpened the edge of their virtuosity.
> M. Stokowski is a young musician of brilliant ability, holding his men in a firm grip and revelling in the amassing of mighty crescendos.

At the very least, here was a young conductor to keep an ear and eye on, and he had entered the arena at a moment of intense ferment in orchestral interest and popularity.

After a period of elder statesmen and heavily mustachioed Germans who had dominated the entire symphonic scene, the public was ready to lionize a handsome, youthful hero.

In Cincinnati, the selection of Stokowski had been as fortunate as it was unorthodox. In Philadelphia, his appointment was inevitable. The man was ascending true to form, the career right on schedule. There was no conductor on the horizon with his personal distinction, individual force, and fire. From the instant he arrived in the City of Brotherly Love, he lit the flame and kept it crackling for over a quarter of a century. Immediately, he emerged not only as a musician of immense vitality but also as an extraordinary organizer and motivater.

In his unique and unrivaled way, Stokowski stood majestically alone.

4

When Stokowski was about to take orchestral command in Philadelphia, there were some twenty American cities that could boast of viable professional orchestras. New York and Boston each took pride in two impressive symphonic organizations.

Although the Philadelphia Orchestra had had an auspicious first seven years under the direction of Fritz Scheel, it had plummeted downward after his tragic death in 1907 and failed to recover until Stokowski came to the rescue in 1912.

At this point in the glorious history of the American symphony, the maintenance of a major orchestra was already a formidable financial operation. It had to pay off in prestige and publicity or go under. Its reputation directly reflected not only a community's cultural status but also its economic development.

For centuries in Europe, the unavoidable gap between costs and receipts from ticket sales had been fully met by state subsidies. In the United States, during the early, formative years (1842–82), orchestras were primarily sustained by the orchestra musicians themselves. The nation's oldest permanent orchestra, the New York Philharmonic Society, had been founded in 1842 as a cooperative endeavor. Its members paid dues, drew modest fees, and shared the profits. At the end of the first season the players' dividends yielded $25 per man. Such sacrificial service became fairly common in quite a few communities, which hoped in this manner eventually to create vital and lasting local institutions. This plan succeeded splendidly but usually only after long, lean stretches: In New York it took more than fifty years.

Gradually, the orchestral musicians' responsibilities were lightened by increasing public attendance, voluntary contributions, and the work of industrious women's committees. As civic pride swelled and as costs mounted, deficits were increasingly assumed by wealthy patrons. It was not until the middle of the twentieth century that assistance in sharing the costs of artistic institutions emerged from governmental, foundational, and industrial sources.

At the time of Stokowski's entrance into the major symphonic league, it was still up to private donors to subsidize local music. Only the enthusiastic support of a broad public would win donor support. And this necessity in turn required the presence of a conductor with the artistic skill and personal magnetism to attract a large and loyal following and a laudatory press.

For the second time, Stokowski proved to be the right man in the right place at the right time. Philadelphia and its orchestra needed him desperately. Despite Scheel's many gifts and splendid achievements, the orchestra could not brag about such conductorial talent as its rivals in New York, Boston, and Chicago.

Olga's delicate hints to the "powers that be" of Stokowski's growing discontent in Cincinnati activated the Philadelphia fathers to approach Stokowski quietly and diplomatically, through Olga, early in 1912. Edward Bok, editor, publisher, husband of Mary Louise Curtis Bok, and a powerful member of the Philadelphia Orchestra board of directors confirmed this often-disputed fact, as did Mrs. Alexander Biddle, Mrs. Samuel Fels, and Mrs. Gertrude Gimbel Dannenbaum, all among the most stimulating and active music-lovers in Philadelphia's cultural set. Undeniably, it was Olga's coup that provided her husband the means, in an incredibly few years, to create perhaps the greatest orchestra ever known.

In Boston, she had become friendly with Col. Henry Lee Higginson, a musically talented man who, upon returning to his hometown from a European education, had become Boston's leading financier. He contributed huge philanthropies to Harvard; to the Boston Symphony, which he subsidized single-handedly; and to the building of one of the greatest auditoriums in existence—Symphony Hall, which stands today as a model and a monument.

From Higginson, Olga gained a lot of firsthand knowledge of symphonic operations, from public relations to deficit financing. She also made it her business to make firm friends of the cultivated philanthropists in other cities, to whom music soon owed what it owed the colonel in Boston. Harry Harkness Flagler, Felix and Paul Warburg, and Otto Kahn in New York, John Severance in Cleveland, Marshall Field and Charles Norman Fay in Chicago, the Charles Tafts in Cincinnati, and Alexander Van Rensselaer in Philadelphia, all warmly praised Olga's persuasive musical convictions. She and her flamboyant conductor-husband shared the belief that the beauty and refinements of great music could be made available to all the people.

Olga and Stokowski arrived in Philadelphia during the early, balmy fall of 1912. Stokowski later said that he was in a sort of trance for a while, overwhelmed by the abundance of impressions and bewildering contrasts that a strange metropolis provides. Olga's former artistic association with the city had made her familiar only with the Academy of Music, the rehearsal quarters, and a few mansions of opulent friends. As the wife of the glamorous new arrival, she had to face the neighborly campaign that was launched to acclimatize the Stokowskis to their new home. The sun-filled skies of those October days added pleasure to the interest of sight-seeing.

In the beginning they were barraged by invitations to see the most striking places. They were shown City Hall, with its thirty-foot bronze statue of William Penn on its tower; the post office, graced with a statue of the seated Benjamin Franklin; and the Customs House, designed by William Strickland, America's leading architect, and modeled after the Parthenon of Athens. They also saw Strickland's ecclesiastical works: St. Paul's Episcopal Church and St. Stephen's Church. But the most historically significant was Christ Church, the colonial edifice whose design was by Dr. John Kearsley and whose steeple was planned by Benjamin Franklin. The Stokowskis were awed to see the pews of Washington and Franklin, and in the churchyard the graves of Franklin and Francis Hopkinson, lawyer, poet, the first known American composer, inventor of a metronome, and a signer of the Declaration of Independence.

Then, of course, the Stokowskis had to see what is perhaps the most famous of all American historical monuments—Philadelphia's Independence Hall, designed by Andrew Hamilton, where the second Continental Congress met in 1775, where Washington was chosen commander in chief of the Continental army, and where the Declaration of Independence was adopted on July 4, 1776.

Philadelphia had been the most important city of the thirteen colonies, commercially, politically, and socially. The very first bank in the United States was opened there in 1780, and a dozen years later, the first mint for the coinage of U.S. money was established in the city. Philadelphia served as the national capital from 1790 to 1800. The first Shakespearean performance in the United States was probably in 1749 in Philadelphia, which also boasts the oldest playhouse in the nation, the Walnut Street Theater, built in 1808.

There were numerous institutions of learning, which further enlarged and enhanced the cultural aura of the city. Most important among these was the American Philosophical Society, founded by Franklin in 1743, the first and most famous academy of science in America. Women were accepted in the educational milieu, as was evidenced by the existence of Bryn Mawr College and the Woman's Medical College, the first chartered school of medicine for women to confer the M.D. degree.

The focus of musical culture in Philadelphia was the Academy of Music, where Abe Lincoln had spoken and Jenny Lind had sung. Acoustically its concert hall is one of the most flawless and renowned in the world, and to this day it remains structurally exactly as it was built.

The young blond Apollo with the power and the purpose surveyed this gold mine of cultural potential, and said to Olga, "This is a great city. It must have a great orchestra."

At the very first rehearsal Stokowski was shaken to discover that the orchestra was anything but. He knew its brief history under the direction of Fritz Scheel, when the ensemble had gained high critical acceptance in Philadelphia and elsewhere. On its first visit to New York in 1902, *The New York Times* wrote, "The Philadelphia orchestra is one of uncommon excellence . . . brilliant and flexible . . . rich and warm. . . . There is very little in its playing to indicate that it is of such recent establishment." The famous Eugène Ysaÿe, after playing a Bach violin concerto with Scheel's orchestra, was reputed to have declined to play the same piece with Gericke and the Boston Symphony, remarking, "Not after the Philadelphia Orchestra will I play the Bach concerto."

Richard Strauss and Felix Weingartner were comparably extravagant in their praises when Scheel invited them as guest conductors. The acme of the orchestra's artistic achievement came in 1906, when it was invited to the White House to perform a concert for President and Mrs. Theodore Roosevelt and four hundred guests. The occasion was a total triumph.

No sooner had Scheel fully established himself as a distinguished asset to the orchestra and to the city, than tragedy struck. He unfortunately became the victim of a complete breakdown, mental and physical, and died within a year. The bereaved members of the orchestra association began a frantic search for a worthy replacement. It was a difficult assignment, and they made a few false starts. Within the year, however, they found a successor to Scheel who appeared to have many of the same qualities. Karl Pohlig, a Bohemian-born conductor, was highly recommended, auditioned in Europe, and engaged in 1907. He was forty-nine, the same age as Scheel; sported the same severe handle-bar mustache; and boasted an equally proficient German training under great teachers.

From what one can gather, the resemblances stop there. His early years in the Reich had turned him into a heel-clicking martinet with the arrogant confidence of an undefeated general, almost entirely bereft of charm. Before Philadelphia he had been director of the king of Württemberg's court orchestra in Stuttgart. "When he left," said violinist Carl Flesch, "there were no tears in anyone's eyes."

At first, Pohlig's Philadelphia concerts received encouraging reactions from local reviewers and audiences, and though his programs were criticized for being too long and too heavy, his competence was unquestioned. Nevertheless, he was mercilessly clobbered by the press in the second month of his tenure when he took the orchestra to New York. The *World* termed the proceedings "provincial," and the *Sun* raised its eyebrows in wonder that "so rough an organization should have been brought all the way across the State of New Jersey." In Philadelphia, he was rapidly getting to be a bore and a boor, and the calls for his dismissal were growing ever more insistent.

Pohlig had his champions, however. They pointed to his undeniable musical integrity, his flawless memory in conducting without score, his broadening of the orchestra's musical horizons with contemporary scores, and his expansion of the season to an annual total of eighty-six concerts (including tours) from sixty-two in Scheel's day.

Herbert Kupferberg, in his delightful book *Those Fabulous Philadelphians,* states that "perhaps Pohlig's most lasting contribution was his invitation in 1909, to Sergei Rachmaninoff to guest-conduct the orchestra in his Symphony no. 2 in E-minor and Moussorgsky's *Night on Bald Mountain.* This was the great Russian pianist-composer-conductor's first appearance on an American podium and also the beginning of his long and warm association with what he was later to call 'my very favorite orchestra.' "

Finally, Pohlig's unpleasant disposition and behavior so antagonized the orchestra, so alienated the audiences and provoked the press, that the board, with whom he was at loggerheads anyway, sought a means of getting rid of him. Their poorly kept "secret negotiations" with Stokowski did the trick. Pohlig had no choice but to resign in return for the entire annual fee that would have been due under the terms of his contract.

Few regretted his departure. Philadelphia deserved more and demanded more. When Pohlig resigned, the board cabled Stokowski in Munich the official invitation to be their conductor, effective immediately. Although Stokowski did not yet know it, the Philadelphia Orchestra at that point was virgin soil, waiting for the young firebrand who was to strike the spark of unmatched greatness.

The excited welcome that had marked the arrival of the Stokowskis gradually cooled to a certain formality, a polite curiosity. Olga felt that the Main Line was saying, in effect, "Very well, now we've done our bit. You're nicely settled in a comfortable, spacious house in the suburb of St. Martin's, and Maestro has taken a pied-à-terre in town. Now let's get down to our daily lives and work."

Stokowski had made it immediately clear to Olga that it would be quite impossible for her to continue her career and also fulfill the role of the conductor's wife in so important a city. Her admirers were as incensed to hear of this request to stop playing and performing as they were to learn of Olga's agreement to devote herself completely to the furtherance of her husband's musical career.

She worked exclusively for him with incredibly selfless enthusiasm for almost three years. Olga was an artist, but not a prima donna. She tackled every chore and responsibility that arose in a totally generous spirit. Her life with Stokowski in Philadelphia, despite many pleasant and rewarding experiences with a few cherished friends, was a severe discipline for Olga. As she began to realize how much she had taken on, how much was expected of her, she was aghast, but undaunted. "I just tightened my corset strings and pitched in," she said, her eyes flashing in grim remembrance. She became a one-woman social and cultural institution, in which role she is still remembered.

Of course, she had expected to attend luncheons, teas, and after-concert suppers, but she was also expected to be a walking calendar, remembering exact dates and the events connected with them. Mainly, she was expected to ingratiate herself with the women's committees, those precious groups so instrumental in making an orchestra flourish or perish.

Although Olga spared nothing in the effort to be helpful to, and cooperative with, the orchestral community, one thing became clear to her: "The female inhabitants of the City of Brotherly Love were disinclined to turn that emotion into sisterly love, especially toward the wife of 'their Stoki.' " It also disappointed her to learn how few knew or cared about music. "So many of these well-born ladies were basically uneducated," she observed. "They subscribed to the symphony for sociability and for prestige, but the concerts themselves were merely events at which their conversation was being constantly interrupted."

Stokowski had turned a sober face toward his interests. "It had taken him even less time than it had taken me," said Olga, "to recognize and face the fact that Philadelphia was no bed of roses. There was an awful lot to do, and *we* had to do it. We had much to learn, and we were impatient to start."

A curious situation existed in Philadelphia in the first decade of this century, and it was important for them to understand this. Some wanted a Philadelphia Orchestra. Others maintained that a series by visiting ensembles such as the one given by the great Boston Symphony "quite sufficed" for the musical needs of the city. The "Montagues and Capulets of musical Philadelphia," as Olga described them, were still waging war when the Stokowskis came upon the scene. For a time, Stokowski himself had to face the open disfavor of the "antis." Olga overheard someone assert heatedly, "The only reason that man Stokowski conducts without the notes is that he can't read a score!"

Stokowski's bitterest recollections of those first stormy years in Philadelphia were of the many battles he had to wage on every front not only to establish the foundations of a good orchestra but also to inculcate a sense of respect and justice in its officials toward music and musicians. He started immediately to protest against whatever prevented good artistic results; he wanted to fire all but perhaps a dozen members of the orchestra, and he insisted on the improvement of the inadequate conditions of the dingy rehearsal room on North Broad Street.

In hundreds of conversations and interviews, Stokowski invariably answered the question "What was the Philadelphia Orchestra like when you got there?" with the same response: "It was no orchestra at all: very disappointing. It had a stiff rhythm, hard tone, and no flexibility or imagination. Everyone played meaningless notes. Everything was terribly mechanical. There were only four first-class performers, Anton Horner, the first horn, Otto Henneberg, third horn, a remarkable timpanist, Oscar Schwar, and the concertmeister, Thaddeus Rich. [Stokowski sometimes varied this, naming only the first three players.] So I had to rebuild that orchestra, get good players in each choir, and strong leaders to head the sections. It was very difficult. One can't fire everybody. Without a job, they would all starve. It had to be done gradually, but it had to be done."

From Oscar Schwar, a fellow faculty member at Curtis who became my friend, I heard the details of Stokowski's first contact with the orchestra. He would never forget, he said, that Monday morning of October 7, 1912, when an amazingly young and handsome Stokowski, wearing a light blue shirt open at the neck and gray flannel trousers, sprang onto the podium of their depressing and overcrowded rehearsal room. At a prearranged signal the orchestra rose simultaneously. Having heard of Stokowski's Olympian detachment, they themselves had decided to remain formal and silent. As they stood there, somewhat awkwardly, a look of surprise and a forced smile appeared on Stokowski's face as he gestured for them to be seated. They were to start the rehearsal with Brahms's Symphony no. 1 in C-minor. After a few seconds of reflection, he raised his ice-blue eyes and said crisply, *"Guten Tag*. Brahms! First *mooment."* Then, almost instantaneously and with a slashing stab, down came his baton.

The unexpectedly swift downbeat caught most of the players unprepared to begin that monumental opening. When two or three straggled in late, Stokowski stopped them. Bending slightly forward, fixing them with blazing eyes, the baton held aloft like a sabre, he gave the downbeat again in a lightning stroke. This time, all the players involved came in like one man.

"But how they came in," Schwar recalled. "I could hardly recognize the men I had been playing with or the music that we thought we knew so well. It was as though we had been given some magic potion. Of course, in a way we had, for none of us had ever experienced such authority and vitality before. This man went straight to the heart of the music. He formed and molded every phrase and with almost no physical effort. Everyone had heard that Nikisch achieved maximum precision with a minimum of bodily motion and that he was Stokowski's idol. It was immediately obvious. With almost invisible indications, Stokowski led us through that famous movement in a way that made it seem like a new piece. With hardly a word of explanation, with no more than the twitch of a wrist or an eyebrow, he extracted the most from every player. Only his facial expressions became more intense and his shoulder muscles more contracted as his burning eyes and curled fingers coaxed us to ever greater expressivity and sonority. At the end of the movement, having played our hearts out in response to the man's irresistible sweep, having been interrupted only a few times by some gentle suggestion or helpful comment, we were all filled with new hope and excitement.

"But our joy was short-lived. Before breaking for intermission, Stokowski said, 'Gentlemen, we must do better, much better. We are too far from an acceptable performance.' Almost the entire rehearsal time was devoted to the four movements of the symphony, the central work of the first program. The reason we had been subjected to comparatively little detailed criticism became painfully clear. Stokowski was not going to waste time or energy or instruction on a group of musicians, most of whom he had already decided would not be members of that orchestra one minute more than necessary. There was no use teaching or scolding, for it was not unwillingness, but sheer inability of all but a few musicians to meet the standards of our new leader."

Meanwhile, until the desired conditions could be brought about, Stokowski patiently worked on, preparing for his debut at the end of the week. He drilled the orchestra incessantly, and the musicians improved tremendously with each rehearsal. It is a testimony to Stokowski's ability to inspire that this also was true of those who knew that their "number was up." Stokowski was in absolute control. He never lost his temper with the orchestra, never raised his voice. On the contrary, he would lower his voice for a subtle rebuke or a sarcastic comment.

Schwar recalled Stokowski saying, "Second clarinet, don't play notes—sing them." To the first violist, he said, "Make up your mind. Either you must ask the orchestra to tune to your A or you must learn to play in tune with theirs. You are always sharp. Not your mind—just your intonation!"

"I'll try to do it your way," said a cellist after Stokowski had made a suggestion. "Don't do anything for me," Stokowski answered. "Do it for music. That's what I'm doing it for." His musicians, whether or not they agreed with his musical ideas of a work, first had to give themselves completely to his concept. Then, he encouraged them to attain it in their own way. He did not "conduct" his players. He actually "played" them. That is perhaps why he rarely called his "instruments" by their names or even bothered to learn more than those of a few favorites.

Stokowski never wasted time or words, but he was always willing to work as hard or as long as a musician needed if the player was capable of carrying out a suggestion. If a player was not, he was dismissed. No sooner had Stokowski begun rehearsals, than he started weeding them out in his mind. Within the year, he had fired thirty-two.

I remember him saying, "When I got there, I was astonished to discover that the orchestra was not comparable to what I had left in Cincinnati." When I told this to Schwar, he said, "We were all aware of that. He made no secret of his feelings."

But it took more than poorly prepared musicians to throw Stokowski. Looking ahead was always one of his strongest traits, as was his ability to blot out the past. His tenure in Cincinnati had been brief but brilliant. It was already a blurred memory when he began to express his primary frustrations and dissatisfactions with the Philadelphia personnel and that indefensible rehearsal room on North Broad Street necessitated by the Academy's constant bookings. As Olga described it, in her book, *An American Musician's Story*, "The orchestra completely filled this room, the ceiling was low and there wasn't space for sound projection. The orchestra could practice notes under such conditions but no idea of tonal balance could be obtained. At the rehearsal [the soloists] played on an upright piano placed in the far corner of the room! [They] couldn't hear the orchestra and the orchestra couldn't hear [them] at all."

"The conditions cannot be imagined," said Stokowski. "In that room, everything above a mezzo forte sounded like menacing thunder." Despite the difficulties and the shortage of time—four days of rehearsal with an orchestra that, with three or four exceptions, Stokowski called "deplorable"—his debut program was characteristically impressive. He offered, in addition to the mighty Brahms symphony, three other challenging works: Beethoven's *Leonore* Overture no. 3, Ippolitov-Ivanov's *Caucasian Sketches* (an American premiere), and Wagner's *Tannhäuser* Overture.

"During the arduous days of rehearsal for that difficult program," said Schwar, "Stokowski never grew angry or disturbed. He gave confidence, he inspired us to play way beyond our ordinary capacities. On the day of the concert, he stepped onto the podium in front of an orchestra he had literally rebuilt in less than a week. The concert was a sensation. At its conclusion, the huge and excited audience and a grateful orchestra gave Stokowski an unprecedented ovation. Sounds like this had never come from that stage before, and our eyes were moist with happiness."

The reviews were glittering and impressive, as indicated by the *Philadelphia Public Ledger* of October 12, 1912:

Leopold Stokowski made his debut yesterday afternoon at the Academy as conductor of the Philadelphia Orchestra, in the opening concert of its thirteenth season. Every seat was taken and the extra chairs had been placed within the orchestra rail. There was much enthusiasm, manifesting itself at the beginning in prolonged applause as Stokowski came forward with bowed head, evidently pondering the content of his musical message. Those who went forth to see a hirsute eccentricity were disappointed. They beheld a surprisingly boyish and thoroughly business-like figure, who was sure of himself, yet free from conceit, who dispensed with the score by virtue of an infallible memory, and held his men and his audience from first note to last firmly in his grasp. . . . There is, from first to last, no languor or slackened moment; he directs with a fine vigor and intensity that mounts to ecstasy yet does not lose its balance or forget its sane and ordered method.

Also attending that first concert was Arthur Judson, then on the staff of *Musical America,* who wrote, "The reception was not that of an audience merely glad that it had a competent conductor, but wildly enthusiastic because it had discovered a genius." Judson's staunch praise of Stokowski was duly reciprocated, initiating a professional association that persisted for a quarter of a century, starting within two years when Judson became manager of the Philadelphia Orchestra.

Strengthened by his initial triumph and by daily evidences of the ever-mounting appreciation and support of Philadelphia's new claim to artistic fame, Stokowski tried once again to convince the board that first-class musical results were impossible unless the orchestra rehearsed exactly where they performed. The men engrossed in the financial problems of balancing budgets were still not enormously interested in the musical problems of balancing sounds.

Nevertheless, the impression created by Stokowski had sufficiently established his box-office value to effect a compromise whereby most of the rehearsals could be held in the acoustically perfect Academy. This enabled him to attain almost immediately a vastly improved sonority and instrumental variety. The Academy authorities, however, had managed to keep the agreement loose enough so that they could shut the orchestra out if the hall was requested for a lecture or a practicing group. But this occurred so often that Stokowski decided to challenge the administration. One Saturday evening, at a backstage reception after a concert, he called the manager of the Academy aside and once more angrily explained that excellence in orchestral playing could never be obtained without proper rehearsing conditions. "I understand, Mr. Stokowski," the manager said, "but I am powerless to help you."

Stokowski listened a moment, then, tense and cold with fury, in a voice that all could hear, calmly proclaimed, "I must know now whether we can rehearse in the Academy before the next concert. If not, I shall resign."

At that moment a gentleman tapped Stokowski on the shoulder: "I have heard your conversation, and I understand you've been having trouble. What's the matter?"

Stokowski briefly explained the cause of his desperation. The man answered, "I know nothing about music, but I think I see. You want to do a certain piece of work; you need to have the right tools to work with. Am I right? If that is what you ask, you shall have it."

No sooner said than done, for the gentleman was Edward Bok, and the occasion marked the beginning of his deep concern with the destiny of the Philadelphia Orchestra and a close relationship with its conductor. Stokowski described Bok as "a fighter and an idealist" and frequently referred to his invaluable aid. Bok became the moving spirit to insure the permanency of the orchestra and in 1916 made the largest donation (anonymously) to the orchestra's endowment fund.

A pamphlet issued by the board invited public subscription. Addressed "To the Friends of the Philadelphia Orchestra," the opening read: "A friend of the Philadelphia Orchestra Association, who desires to remain unknown, has offered to meet any deficit of the Orchestra for each of five years, beginning with the season of 1916–1917." A following paragraph contained a condition: "That the contract of the present conductor, Leopold Stokowski, shall be extended to cover this period of five years." The terms were yet to be negotiated, but Stokowski's annual fee was eventually to ascend from the initial $12,000 to $110,000 in the last years of his tenure.

It is also well known that Stokowski's ability to control everybody and anything was primarily made possible by Edward Bok and his close friend Alexander Van Rensselaer, who soon climbed aboard Stokowski's bandwagon. As president of the orchestra's board until his death more than twenty years later, Van Rensselaer tendered Stokowski unstinting personal loyalty and solid backing throughout the Maestro's most strenuous fits of capriciousness.

Confidently but philosophically, Stokowski considered his situation. He was well paid and well placed in an important city. He had gained the adulation of the public and the approval of the press. He had powerful friends and supporters who had obtained for him and his orchestra ideal working conditions.

With these objectives achieved, he could readdress himself to the top line, the development of his orchestra. He had yet to find replacements for the musicians he had fired of the caliber needed to build an orchestra "worthy of this city," as Stokowski put it to Van Rensselaer. His benefactor answered, "Go ahead. Hire anyone you need. We'll find the money."

Among Stokowski's greatest assets were an unerring instinct for selecting, and a magnetic force for attracting, the finest available players. But to build an orchestra of such players would take more than money. It would take time and luck, of which there was never enough.

The young conductor was consumed with purpose, with a mystical dream of the oneness of humanity and the power of music. He had to fuse these concepts and combine them with a dramatic orchestral instrument that would bring millions of people together in the thrilling adventure of great music. This could also enable him to direct at least some of man's technological ingenuity toward a humane purpose.

The birth of this century set the scene for a future that would demand an irreversible break with the past. Stokowski recognized this significant challenge and accepted his life-long compulsion to meet it head on. Despite his imperfect scholarship, he always had an insatiable curiosity to know and grasp the scientific principles behind aesthetic phenomena. His restless and inquiring mind took nothing for granted. He never tired of saying, "Tradition is laziness. If something isn't right, we must change it."

These convictions had been first demonstrated in Cincinnati when he began to experiment with moving the sections of the orchestra around and placing some on risers. He once said to me, "Already in Cincinnati, I was able to try out many things with the orchestra that I had long thought about. For example, I said to myself, 'Why should we continue to seat an orchestra just as it was done a century ago? It was formulated and frozen long before the music of our time was written, long before instruments had been improved, changed, and invented. It just makes no sense. Some very obvious principles have been overlooked.' "

He spelled this out specifically in interviews, articles, and in his book, *Music for Us All:*

> The tone of the French horn goes to the right of the player and downward. From the tuba—exactly the opposite. The tone travels to the left of the player and upward. These are facts. . . . From the violin the tone goes upward. . . . If the first and second strings face each other, as they now do in the conventional orchestra, the tone of the first fiddles travels toward the audience, the tone of the second fiddles away from them. The flute's tone goes directly upward from the instrument. . . . Obviously, all these instruments have different directions, quantities, and qualities of tone,

from very light, like the flute, to colossal, like the trombone.

At a concert, the sound should travel from the stage to the audience in the most balanced and effective way. This simply can not be done unless each instrument or family of instruments is placed to maximum advantage.

So I began to experiment, the results were fruitful. I shall keep experimenting with every possible combination of placement and level. I have no system. I shall let the music decide, also the orchestration, the hall, and all variable conditions. For each a different solution may be necessary.

In an interview with Stokowski on these and other of his innovations, Martin Bookspan, then director of recorded music at radio station WQXR in New York, asked, "Have any other conductors adopted these principles?"

"I don't believe so."

"Would it be unfair to ask why?"

With an arch smile, Stokowski replied, "Don't you think that would be a very good question to ask the other conductors?"

Although reseating was one of the important aspects of what is known the world over as the "Stokowski sound," it was only one. Another of his trademarks was his insistence on "free bowing," which accounted for the unbroken songfulness and mellowness of the Philadelphia Orchestra's string sections.

Throughout orchestral history, the string parts of scores have been edited to indicate the preferred position of the bow, up or down, in executing any particular passage. Customarily, the concertmaster checked these signs to determine whether they met with the conductor's interpretative ideas. If not, they were changed accordingly. On occasion, a guest conductor or soloist would bring a premarked set of parts, conforming to their own musical ideas. In any event, all the players were expected to bow identically at any given moment. They were, that is, until Stokowski. He regarded this kind of exactitude as a mechanical effect, admirably suited to such precise chorus-line maneuvers as those made familiar to later generations by the Rockettes in New York's Radio City Music Hall, in contrast to the dancing of a classical corps de ballet. "Mechanism as one part of life is wonderful in an automobile or airplane," said Stokowski, "but not in art, which requires flexible pulsation."

Stokowski was always looking for a continuously flowing melodic line, whether in the top, bottom, or inner voices, to carry the music and the listener's interest along. Free bowing had a simple, logical, premise: A musician is at his best emotionally and technically when he is enabled to play with complete freedom and individuality, in the easiest and most natural way for him to produce whatever effect the conductor demands. When string players are obliged to follow their section leaders and bow up or down in unison, they may attain the greatest precision but also the most rigidity and the least expressivity. There are occasions when this military type of unformity produces just the right spirit, as in a Sousa march, but ordinarily in the symphonic literature it does not produce the smoothest melodic line.

In bowing, string players may have to change the direction of the bow many times within a matter of seconds. At the point of changing, the volume may decrease or actually cease for a fraction of a second, long enough to break the perfect continuity of a flowing melodic phrase, and it was this interruption that Stokowski wished to eliminate.

"But even more than this flowing line," Stokowski said, "the players of classical music are called upon to convey warmth and intensity and poetic passion which cannot be ideally realized when everyone bows together like robots. How to avoid that? My answer was simple. Bow freely, according to your own technical and expressive methods. Then, the sound will not decrease or increase at the identical instant. While some are changing bows, others are bowing freely up or down, permitting a continual stream of rich sound."

Nevertheless, even among those who concede that Stokowski's free bowing method has indeed produced unequaled qualities of continuity and legato, strong objections have been raised. Some prefer greater solidity and homogeneity of tone. Others insist that there can be no acceptable generalization as to the "best method" of bowing: what may be fine for Wagner may well be detrimental to Mozart, and so on.

It is unquestionable, however, that the free bowing not only of Stokowski's Philadelphia Orchestra but of every other orchestra he conducted produced, in expressive cantabile passages, a specific and unique sound of beauty, elegance, and suavity. The string players themselves unanimously ascribed it to Stokowski's admonishments that they luxuriate in the liberating practice of doing what comes naturally, technically and emotionally.

Henry Roth, sharp-eared critic among violinists, suggests that one reason why free bowing has not been accepted or widely attemped is rooted in what he terms "superficial visual cosmetics." "Conductors have been more interested," he said, "in the appearance of conformity or discipline than in any experimentation that may enhance the sound or comfort, physical or psychological, of the player."

What has been much less noted and of equal import is that these problems of continual melodic flow were not confined to string playing. No sooner had Stokowski attained his linear goal with the strings than he began to realize how often their beautiful legato effects were sabotaged in thematic repetitions by woodwinds or brasses when they ran out of breath and necessarily had to disconnect phrases that the strings had stated with flawless continuity.

The bowing problem was solved because there were enough string players to continue sounds while others were changing bow direction. On the same premise, when a solo flute or trumpet had to take a breath in the midst of a phrase that would be more expressive if it were unbroken, why couldn't another player continue it? If two were playing out of a section of four, as in the horns, the other two could enter at the crucial point. And if all the members of a woodwind or brass group were occupied, there was still a characteristically grand Stokowskian solution: He would simply engage extra players.

Stokowski's efficiency as a drill master, his constant innovation, and his ingenuity as a publicist eventually succeeded in attracting a large number of extraordinary talents and artists as applicants for orchestral posts in Philadelphia. But only those were sought and selected who fit Stokowski's preconceived design, who could be woven into the perfect fabric.

Alone with his players at rehearsal, Stokowski was another man. His complete absorption and involvement, more than his grasp of the music, and his imaginative disclosures of its hidden beauties won the awesome respect and slavish cooperation of his musicians. This was the connective bond between him and his orchestra. Each man felt personally responsible for producing the sound that Stokowski's piercing eyes and transfigured face compelled him to create. Sometimes, Stokowski made demands that were foolhardy, even infuriating, but the players were always innately flattered that he asked so much of them. Regardless of their personal feelings toward their conductor and of their frequent disagreements with his interpretations, they were immensely proud to be members of an orchestra for which the impossible was deemed possible.

Once Stokowski found that he had been able to overcome the major obstacles in the creation of his orchestra, he began to tackle others. Heading the list of problems was the provincial concert behavior of the Philadelphia society matrons. Stokowski was infuriated by their late arrivals; by their incessant chattering during the music; by their noisy rattling of shopping bags, some of which they had even parked on the edge of the stage; by their uninhibited sneezing and coughing; but particularly by their determined rush for the exits during the end of the last piece.

Stokowski decided that his Friday afternoon audience, no less than his orchestra, had to be trained. He started plaintively, with gentle hints and appeals, gradually building up a crescendo from mezzo sarcasm to fortissimo diatribe. It worked surprisingly well: From this first year and for almost thirty years thereafter, the adulation of Philadelphia's audiences for their handsome, exciting, and unfathomable conductor was unbounded.

Already at the end of the first season, the music lovers of Philadelphia were falling over one another in frantic efforts to show their gratitude to the boyish genius who had transformed their infirm ensemble into a vital instrument of such pride to their city. Among those who wanted to express their love was a little girl, Sophia Yarnell, who later became Stokowski's closest friend.

Sophia Yarnell was the youngest member of a distinguished Philadelphia family. She was ten years old when the thirty-year-old Stokowski arrived in Philadelphia. Sophia and her older sister, Agnes, used to roller-skate in Rittenhouse Square, through which Stokowski would walk each day on his way to and from rehearsal. "He was the most gorgeous thing you ever saw," Sophia recalled. "Everyday Stoki would stop, not just to say hello but to play with us— usually a fairly strenuous game of cops and robbers." At the end of the first concert season, the two hopelessly infatuated young ladies began to consider what they might send him for the last concert as a token of their adoration. Flowers, of course, were what grown-ups always sent to an artist. But they would outdo the grown-ups. They would make a presentation that Stokowski would never forget.

"We saved up every penny of our allowance money, stole away from our governess one day, ran to the florist's and found exactly what we wanted! How beautiful it was! Fit for a prince! and surely Stokowski was a prince. Our prince!" said

Sophia. That afternoon at the Academy of Music, in the midst of all the wild applause and bravos, the farewell bows and smiles, two ushers walked on stage to present to Philadelphia's glamour boy the most beautiful funeral wreath the city had ever seen! The girls looked straight ahead as their father boomed, "Who in the name of God sent *that* terrible thing?"

Was Stokowski distressed or chagrined, shocked or startled? Not at all. His face beamed. He lowered his head in courtly appreciation as the audience roared with laughter. His two young admirers were ecstatic to see that their wreath had been put on a tripod.

Later that afternoon, following the concert, the Yarnells were having afternoon tea in the living room when the butler entered to announce, "There's a gentleman at the door—Mr. Stokowski. He's here to see Miss Sophia and Miss Agnes." The parents were very puzzled and surprised that he had not come to see them, but they greeted him cordially as he reiterated his request to see the girls, and all went up to the nursery together. Imagine the Yarnells' amazement and amusement as Stokowski thanked the girls profusely and ceremoniously "for that *mogneeficent* wreath" while bowing from the waist to kiss their hands.

In 1914, Stokowski decided that the Philadelphia Orchestra was ready to challenge the supremacy of the New York–Boston–Chicago triumvirate. The Philadelphia's New York debut under Stokowski took place inauspiciously on Wednesday afternoon, January 21, 1914, with contralto Alma Gluck as soloist. The program included Mozart's *Marriage of Figaro* Overture and Blondchen's aria from *The Abduction from the Seraglio,* Brahm's First Symphony, Richard Strauss's *Death and Transfiguration,* and "Depuis le jour" from Gustave Charpentier's *Louise.* Stokowski had carefully calculated a program that would display solid musicianship, imagination, and virtuosity. The showman, on that day hiding beneath a dignified bearing and impeccable restraint, was adjudged "devoid of mannerisms, his attention . . . concentrated on his work."

As an interpreter, he evoked guarded praise. Richard Aldrich of *The New York Times* wrote, "While Mr. Stokowski is not at present to be accounted a great conductor, he is an interesting one and showed unquestionable talent and a native gift that ought to take him far." The orchestra was praised for its "solid, well-knit, and warm quality." Stokowski's full force was yet to be felt in New York.

At the conclusion of the 1914 spring season, the Stokowskis looked forward to a well-earned vacation abroad. The year had been exciting, rewarding, and successful beyond their highest hopes, and it made their voyage from New York to Munich particularly enjoyable. They headed straight for their attractive and comfortable villa on the outskirts of the city, which they now planned to use as their summer home. Olga had a spacious practice room overlooking the garden, and Leopold had a huge bare room in the attic, an arrangement that enabled them both to work in concentrated quiet. Olga permitted her piano to claim her again, at least for an hour or two each day. Life was good; life was peaceful. No one suspected that war was about to explode in the face of an unprepared world.

In Munich, good neighbors and old companions were waiting for the Stokowskis, and the first month passed quickly and happily. Late in June, the heir to the Austrian throne and his wife were assassinated. It was lightly treated as just another killing in Sarajevo. One night in July they heard that Austria had declared war on Serbia. Two nights later, a German friend, a government official, told them that a state of emergency had been declared in Germany, which guaranteed the internment of any British citizen as an enemy alien. World War I had erupted in their back yard.

Packing immediately and leaving behind whatever could not be stuffed into two knapsacks, they fled, with the gigantic score of Mahler's *Symphony of a Thousand*. Theirs was the last train to cross the border before it was shut tight for four years.

Upon his return from Europe, Stokowski set about planning the next season, resolved to build a solid tradition of orchestral virtuosity and imaginative programming. That year, 1915, he acquired American citizenship. He also initiated a series of "Pop Concerts" in a repertory— replete with fireworks—by Chabrier, Johann Strauss, Weber, Wagner, Saint-Saëns, Bizet, Rimsky-Korsakov, and early Stravinsky that revealed him as a born man of the theater. The concerts were singularly successful in selling Liberty Bonds, as were those of an army band from nearby Camden, New Jersey, which Stokowski organized and conducted. This unequaled ensemble enticed audiences to travel from other cities to hear it. A born eclectic, Stokowski enjoyed conducting the army band as much as he did his symphony orchestra. He leaped from one idiom, period, and nationality of music to another, totally different, with utter ease and freedom.

In the second decade of our century, the musical world was on the brink of revolutionary changes. Its modernism nowadays is ancient history. We know all of its masterpieces and its failures, many of both written by the same composers. Stokowski conducted everything, without judging it. Judgment, he believed, was the public's job. His obligation and goal was to make available to the largest audience as much contemporary music as possible so that it could be evaluated. In the 1915–16 season he played contemporary works of the utmost diversity: the orchestral suites from Stravinsky's *Firebird* and *Petrushka,* Richard Strauss's *Alpine Symphony,* Scriabin's *Poem of Ecstasy,* and Schoenberg's Kammersymphonie no. 1.

This last, very cerebral work, although not atonal, proved unbearably dissonant, and the Academy's audience loudly voiced its displeasure during the performance. I was told that in the middle Stokowski strode off the stage in a fury. When quiet was restored, he returned and started it again from the very beginning. At its conclusion an intimidated audience, fearful of a third repetition, offered some dutiful applause.

Stokowski programmed the Schoenberg Kammersymphonie at a performance in New York at the Ritz-Carlton Hotel sponsored by the Society of the Friends of New Music. Richard Aldrich reviewed it perceptively in *The New York Times:* "The *Kammersymphonie* did not yesterday show the prescience of a master, the vision of a seer into unknown realms of beauty. . . . Will our grandchildren see it and smile indulgently at the bewildered listeners of 1915? The question is not really important: bewildered listeners of 1915 can only listen for themselves. Mr. Stokowski conducted an admirable performance of this difficult and complicated work with apparent enthusiasm and belief."

During the fall of that war-torn year of 1915 Stokowski dropped his own bombshell, the announcement to the board of directors of his intention to present the American premiere of Mahler's Eighth, the *Symphony of a Thousand,* which had shared his narrow escape from Munich. In 1910 he had heard Mahler himself rehearse and conduct its premiere in Munich and had since obtained permission to conduct its first American performance in Philadelphia.

Though many urgent requests had been sent to the Viennese publishers from other eminent organizations eager to present the American premiere, the distinction had been conferred upon the Philadelphia Orchestra. Stokowski modestly disclaimed any personal credit. His plan for the production required three choruses—a main one of 400, a second one also of 400, a children's group of 150—an augmented orchestra of 110, and 8 vocal soloists, making it Stokowski's *Symphony of 1,068.*

The monumental project was to be produced in March of 1916, and rehearsals would begin in October of 1915. Stokowski suggested a minimum of three performances in Philadelphia. The Society of the Friends of New Music had offered to sponsor a New York premiere at the Metropolitan

Opera House and had allocated $12,000 to transport the entire Philadelphia cast for the one performance. Stokowski confidently stated that these gala events would make musical history and could possibly recoup all the expenses, which he estimated at approximately $14,000.

The board gasped. Fearful that the unknown work would prove unpopular and unprofitable, they wanted to drop the whole idea. Stokowski convinced them, however. The daring and scope of the project, as he explained it, the possibility of it bringing Philadelphia international musical significance and fame, carried the day. With the unanimous consent of the board, the Philadelphia Orchestra Association proudly announced the performances in Philadelphia and New York.

Once the news broke, the box office was flooded with ticket orders from all over the eastern half of the country. In both cities people lined up for tickets in subzero weather, and scalpers were reported to have sold 50-cent tickets for $100.

The choruses were selected in the spring of 1915, and rehearsals began in October, Stokowski himself training the first chorus, with choral conductor Henry Gordon Thunder rehearsing the second. Frances Wister notes, "Singers who were inattentive or who skipped rehearsals were not retained, and towards the end everybody was overworked and wrought up to a pitch of excitement."

On March 2, the day of the premiere, lucky holders of tickets for the unreserved sections waited in an icy drizzle from midafternoon to curtain time for the good seats. From seven until eight o'clock a steady stream of automobiles stopped at the Academy doors, while all society and a Who's Who of musical America streamed into the building.

Attending the performances were the Ossip Gabrilowitsches, Josef Hofmanns, Ernest Hutchesons, and the Ernest Schellings, Albert Spalding, Kurt Schindler, Harold Bauer, and Artur Bodanzky.

While the critics received the work with restraint, the performance won a spectacular reception. At the end, the orchestra rose while the audience cheered and waved handkerchiefs and gloves. "The performance," wrote Daniel Webster in his perceptive obituary of Stokowski in the *Philadelphia Inquirer,* "brought the kind of success Stokowski wanted for himself and his orchestra. The report of it crowded news of the Battle of Verdun off the front pages of Philadelphia newspapers." The board presented Stokowski with a bronze laurel wreath offered by its president, Alexander Van Rensselaer, who said, "This premiere marks an epoch in Philadelphia's musical history to which no other event is comparable."

Samuel Lacier, in the *Philadelphia Public Ledger* (March 3, 1916), captured the excitement of the occasion:

Every one of the thousands in the great building was standing, whistling, cheering and applauding, when Leopold Stokowski, his collar wilted, his right arm weary, but smiling his boyish smile, finally turned to the audience in the Academy of Music last night.

He had scored, so famous musicians agreed, the greatest triumph of his career, the greatest triumph the Philadelphia Orchestra has known in its sixteen years of life and he had done it on a stupendous scale with the American premiere of Gustav Mahler's Eighth Symphony. He carried along with him to triumph an orchestra numbering 110 pieces and a chorus of 958 singers, to say nothing of the city's music lovers and scores of musical pilgrims from other cities."

The demand for seats was so great that six extra performances were given in Philadelphia before the entire cast and staff numbering 1,200 people, journeyed to New York by private trains.

The performance at the Metropolitan Opera on April 9 was inspired, and the audience thrilled. Again the house was studded with musical luminaries, including Ignace Paderewski, Alma Gluck, Efrem Zimbalist, Pablo Casals, Rubin Goldmark, Frank Damrosch, Victor Harris, George W. Chadwick, Mischa Elman, Emma Eames, Leopold Godowsky, Rudolph Ganz, Percy Grainger, Alfred Hertz, Frank Kneisel, Josef Stransky, Marcella Sembrich, Antonio Scotti, Fritz Kreisler, and Ernestine Schumann-Heink.

The distinguished William J. Henderson writing tongue-in-cheek in the *New York Sun* (April 10, 1916) said:

> If Philadelphia believes that Mr. Stokowski is essential to her musical development, let her decline to permit him to conduct great concerts in New York. This is a piece of perfectly disinterested advice.
>
> The *Sun*'s musical chronicler would be delighted to see Mr. Stokowski a New York conductor. He has personality, force, authority, temperament, scholarship and imagination. His conducting of the Mahler Symphony was masterly. He would be a valuable factor in the musical life of New York.

At last Stokowski had gained unqualified recognition in America's musical capital. His predictions for the success of the occasion materialized, and the memorable event even came out with a small monetary profit, made world news, and began a progressive movement of Mahler performances that has, over the past sixty years, made this formerly neglected composer as popular as Brahms.

The significance of the event to the orchestra itself was well stated in Webster's obituary of Stokowski:

> The Mahler performance was the single event that boosted the orchestra onto the top rung of American orchestral life and into international renown, and it made Stokowski a national figure. His coup came as other major orchestras faded. Boston had slipped after firing Karl Muck. Chicago was routine under the long tenure of Frederick Stock. New York's two orchestras were struggling under uninspired leadership.

Stokowski had taken Philadelphia to the summit.

5

FROM THE BEGINNING, STOKOWSKI was all that he was to become. The glory that accrued to the orchestra, however, was remarkable when we realize how firmly placed at stage center were America's idolized opera stars, whose positions were so much more favorably advanced and promoted by the recording companies. But in the wings, about to capture the spotlight, were three conductors, Stokowski, Toscanini, and Koussevitzky, who would see to it that the symphony orchestra would shine as luminously as the opera.

The first professional effect of Stokowski's Mahler triumph was a carte blanche invitation to record for the Victor Talking Machine Company, whose appealing picture of Nipper, the little dog listening acutely to "His Master's Voice," remains one of the most winsome illustrations of America's promotional genius.

Stokowski's first reaction to working for Victor was an unequivocal no. He had little respect for the phonograph and its limited possibilities. For about a decade after its invention by Thomas Edison in 1877, it had crawled along lamely as an amusing sound-reproducing gadget. Two early instruments, equally poor, competed for public approval: One reproduced sounds from a wax cylinder that was a sequel to Edison's device, and the other, from a flat shellac disc invented by a

German-American, Emile Berliner. Their preliminary uses were as dictation machines, as commercial entertainment gadgets that played a ditty on the insertion of a coin, and as a trendy device for recording songs or poems at home.

In 1901, the Gramophone Company of London, the first recording company to hang out its shingle, chose the flat shellac disc. Its Russian subsidiary evidently had a staff of visionary music lovers, for it immediately accomplished the revolutionary transformation of the phonograph into a genuine musical instrument and recorded the celebrated stars of the Imperial Opera House in St. Petersburg. One year later, the Italian branch took the cue by signing and recording a young Italian tenor, Enrico Caruso, who had made a sensational debut at La Scala in Milan. The phonograph record was in.

It took many years to expand beyond this point, for the voice was the only musical instrument that early recording techniques were capable of reproducing with any degree of fidelity. Foreign vocal records became the rage. The Gramophone Company then produced an improved disc, a prestigious line called the Victor Red Label. Caruso's records set new standards of artistic excellence and commercial profit. The next year, his records were released in the United States, where Victor's success soon instigated formation of a powerful competitor in Columbia Records.

The expansion and extension of both the medium and repertory were inevitable, but until the electrical method of recording was perfected in 1924, all attempts beyond vocalism were unsatisfactory to the musically sensitive. Still, the Victor executives would not accept Stokowski's rejection. They came to his home again and again to argue that the record business was booming, that Victor had more than ten thousand dealers in America, that the art of every great performer must be preserved. To an ever-larger public, owning a record collection had become a status symbol. "The greatest music of the greatest conductor of the greatest orchestra in the world," they said, could only be adequately reproduced on the Victor Red Seals.

Stokowski pointed out that the few attempts to record orchestras in Europe had revealed that the acoustical recording and reproducing techniques were not equal to reproducing the rich range and volume of an orchestra. The sound distortion of acoustic recordings was too harsh, too grating, too undeveloped. There was nothing further to discuss.

When the Victor executives left, Olga tried again to persuade him. He responded by playing a few Victor recordings on a machine the company had sent him. First, they heard a violin solo by Fritz Kreisler, which was all but drowned out by the raucous surface noise; then, a performance of Paderewski's on which the piano sounded like an out-of-tune harp; and finally, a salon orchestra in a Strauss waltz that sounded as limp and sleazy as a dishrag.

Coincidentally, one year before she had met Stokowski, Olga had met Thomas Edison when she was engaged to play a recital in the inventor's home in New Jersey. Thereafter they became friends, and she was astounded to discover that the celebrated inventor was far from being either a practical businessman or a music lover. "He was congenitally destined for the laboratory," she said. "He had become quite deaf and asked me to play for him while he sat with the tips of his fingers on the piano, getting the vibrations that his ears were hearing only a little or not at all."

Edison used to show Olga around his workroom, and one day he said, "I often wonder what all this is going to mean to musicians." He did not realize to what degree his cylinder mechanism had outgrown its preliminary uses and become a musical instrument.

One week after Stokowski's last rejection of Victor's offer, company representatives requested another conference. Confidentially, they told Stokowski and Olga that many important experiments and developments were in progress and that their technicians had been working day and night and were on the verge of solving many irksome problems. They assured Stokowski that his extraordinary knowledge would further the entire cause of recording. They would welcome and adopt any suggestions that he offered in the process of making records. He could involve himself in every stage of the enterprise and would be giving new impetus to exploitation of the greatest potential in musical history. Records would create ever larger and more sophisticated audiences, and they would promote the cause of immortalizing musical performance.

To this, Stokowski reacted immediately and enthusiastically. He responded not only to the long-range goal of excellence, to the opportunity to make the music of the Philadelphia Orchestra available to millions, but especially to the prospect of working in the laboratories with engineers as well as on the podium with musicians.

Olga broke open quite a few bottles of champagne that day. Stokowski proposed the last toast: "To our records! When do we start and what should we do first?"

"As soon as possible" was the unanimous decision, and the repertory was entirely up to the Maestro. In October and November 1917, at Trinity Church in Camden, New Jersey, Stokowski and the Philadelphia Orchestra made their initial acoustic recordings: Brahms's Hungarian Dances nos. 5 and 6, the "Scherzo" from Mendelssohn's *A Midsummer Night's Dream,* and the "Dance of the Blessed Spirits" from Gluck's *Orfeus and Euridice.*

The musicians had to crowd and crouch, tightly huddled under the huge recording horn. No possible placement enabled the double basses to sound properly, so Stokowski used the tuba to bolster the basses.

The records themselves were the heavy, breakable 78-rpm variety, limited to four and a half minutes of playing time. "The sound was horrible," said Stokowski. "The surface noise killed every subtlety; the distortion was unbearable. I hated those records, but I did not regret my decision to go ahead. The important thing was to keep on working and experimenting no matter how painful the process. Yet those records were praised by critics and wonderfully accepted by the record-buying public. Artistically, I refused to be discouraged because I knew that eventually, American technological genius would come through."

Despite the remarkable success of these experimental records, a great many people were still rejecting "canned music." "I wouldn't have a phonograph in my house," said one director of the Philadelphia Orchestra to Stokowski. "I'm glad that the orchestra makes records, as the royalties reduce the deficit, but I refuse to listen to them." Comments like this spurred Stokowski to assist the new technology to a point where it would not only preserve faithful performances for posterity but would eventually produce a sound obtainable only in the finest concert halls.

Stokowski's association with the Victor Company was the start of the significant role that he was to play in the history of sound recording via records, radio broadcasts, and sound films. It has always been a matter of considerable conjecture as to how much he actually knew about this complex field from a scientific and technical point of view. No matter. His curiosity, interest, and tireless experimentation led to new concepts and methods of sound reproduction, right up to the anticipation by several decades of stereophonic techniques.

There was a long road ahead, full of unpredictable hazards. Even recording repertory, apart from popularity or length, posed problems in those tense days. Stokowski had been asked to choose four short works. Three out of the four were by German composers. By 1917, a feverish antagonism had arisen throughout the United States against everything German and Austrian. The works of composers from enemy countries were naturally banned on concert programs. "But that did not satisfy the war fanatics," writes Olga in *An American Musician's Story*.

"Despite the fact that London audiences were capable of calmly enjoying *Tristan und Isolde* during an air raid, some violent elements in the United States felt that listening to Mozart was unpatriotic. . . . When the question of banishing all German and Austrian music from symphony programs became acute, Clara Clemens Gabrilowitsch [the daughter of Mark Twain] and I decided to undertake a little diplomatic mission of our own. I had known Col. Edward House all my life. President Woodrow Wilson was visiting the Houses near Boston. Clara and I laid the matter before the President and Colonel House. We returned armed with the official verdict that it was not necessary to extend current warfare to composers long since dead nor to deprive our audiences of the musical masterpieces that belong to the world." Olga and Clara successfully settled the matter, at least for the two orchestras conducted by their husbands.

The summers of the war years from 1916 were spent on the Maine coast, since the Stokowskis naturally could not return to Munich at this time. They took a house in Seal Harbor, which along with Bar Harbor and Blue Hill, had become a summer colony of many famous musicians. Their neighbors included the Josef Hofmanns, Fritz Kreislers, Carl Friedbergs, Harold Bauers, Ossip Gabrilowitsches, Leopold Godowskys, Walter Damrosches, and Ernest Schellings. The social atmosphere was established by the John D. Rockefeller, Jr., and Edsel Ford families.

At the beginning of each summer fifty grand pianos would arrive at the Seal Harbor dock. From every house came the sound of pianos, and of harps, too, for the great Carlos Salzedo had also arrived with a flock of six female pupils, most of whom he married and divorced within the next few decades. To men like Salzedo and Stokowski, divorce was the future tense of marriage.

Stokowski had as good a time as possible for a man who was temperamentally allergic to large groups. He was a loner and a romantic, a classicist and a modernist, and none of these. The sure way to total frustration for Stokowski's inti-

mates was to attempt to clarify or reconcile his constant contradictions in statement or action.

The difference between this ambivalent man's caprices and
passions was Oscar Wildean; the caprices lasted longer. In
order to get along with him, one needed to adopt an utterly
impersonal attitude. One never knew from one minute to the
next whether he would be humorous or grave, ironic or
sentimental.

In the summer of 1918, Olga, Harold Bauer, and Ossip
Gabrilowitsch, all of whom had been engaged by Stokowski
to appear as soloists with the Philadelphia Orchestra in one
of Bach's concertos for three claviers and orchestra, formed
a piano trio. Taking full advantage of the unusual opportunity for numerous and leisurely rehearsals in Seal Harbor,
they "liberated" four pianos and put them all in the huge hall
of the Gabrilowitsch estate. The fourth piano, serving as the
orchestra, was played by Stokowski.

For two months they slaved and fought over every single
detail of what was later called "the perfect ensemble" by the
papers in Philadelphia, Baltimore, Washington, and New
York during the season 1918–19. The concert was repeated
in Detroit with Gabrilowitsch conducting from the piano, for
the dedication of the new Orchestra Hall built for Gabrilowitsch's Detroit Symphony Orchestra.

Olga's relationship with Stokowski became increasingly
distant during the next months. Once the war was over, she
began performing again and recording for RCA Victor.
Since 1916 Olga had gradually slipped back into playing,
because of demands for her services and the pleas of the
Philadelphia Orchestra's manager, Arthur Judson. In between times, she vacationed in the Bavarian Alps with Geraldine Farrar, shopped on the rue de la Paix with her mother,
went everywhere, and saw everyone but obviously *sans* Stoki.
Therefore, it came as a shock to read in 1921 that Olga
Samaroff Stokowski had given birth to a baby girl, Sonya

Maria Noel. Stokowski was always the object of gossip, and for several years his name had been linked to several attractive Philadelphia debutantes. His every move, his colorful character, his clothes, his apartment furnishings were avidly chronicled by the press. Romances had been "covered" by innuendo; scandals remained under the carpet. Consequently, the town was rocked on its heels in 1923 when Olga sued for divorce, using the routine, unexciting grounds of "mental cruelty." Everyone felt cheated of the juicy details.

"When it became certain in 1923 that unclouded domesticity was not to be my lot," Olga wrote, "I decided to take up my winter residence in New York City and spend my summers in Seal Harbor, Maine, in the house which royalties on the Victor records had enabled me to acquire."

After the Stokowski divorce, the gentlemen of the press could remain gentlemen and still keep the fascinated community supplied with the delectable items of Stokowski's amours, which was quite a relief for the journalists who had endured a decade of professional frustration. Now there were no holds barred. The years between Stokowski's marriages were those in which he and the press were freest to keep his public informed and titillated.

The first item concerned Stokowski's move from his little flat on Locust Street to 1716 Rittenhouse Street, where he occupied the second and third floors of a fossil of a house. Although the apartment was gaudily painted in every imaginable color, the furniture and furnishings were incongruously plain, comparable to the digs of an indigent student. There was a tiny kitchenette and a bathroom; the bedroom had the few minimum necessities. Only the bed was capacious. On the top floor was a chartreuse studio–living room dominated by a small grand piano and a stunning fireplace designed by Stokowski himself.

When visitors came, Stokowski was apt to greet them in lounging pajamas in some shade of red or yellow set against socks or slippers in vividly contrasting colors.

When he was alone, complaints were made by residents of the Barclay Hotel across the way that when they stood on stools in their rooms, they could see Stokowski sunbathing on his terrace with nary a stitch on!

"Bouvier Street, the narrow thoroughfare behind the Barclay," wrote Daniel Webster in the *Philadelphia Inquirer,* "was the favorite haunt of those eager to know Stokowski's last love. The traffic there was a complex of wives of orchestra members, actresses, society belles and debutantes." And as of 1924, there were also students from Curtis Institute, which by the time I had joined the faculty two years later had come to be known as the Coitus Institute. I heard all about Stoki's amours from a few talented and lovely students, all then in their late teens and all of them having an affair with Maestro. Stokowski never at any time mentioned any of his affairs. But most of the women with whom he was intimate were hardly that circumspect and spoke of their sexual escapades with positive braggadocio, even though this high-strung man was sporadically impotent.

Stokowski had a name for women with whom he had non-platonic relations. He called them "nurses." When I once asked why, he said, "Very simple. Nurses are lifesavers, no? They are angels of mercy who rejuvenate us." Once, when a friend heard of Stokowski's affair with the wife of one of his orchestra men, he asked him point-blank, "Haven't you any conscience?" Stokowski answered, "None. Conscience is that which hurts when everything else feels marvelous. The percentage is against it!" Concerning adultery, he once said to someone else who chided him, "Look, freedom of action has always been perfectly understood between me and my wives. That was the strength of our relationships."

Although Stokowski's three wives were extremely striking, his interest was not confined to beautiful women. He needed women—beautiful and beautiless, tall and short, fat and skinny, rich and poor, bright and dumb. There is nothing amazing about that. A lot of men need a lot of women—and vice versa. The astounding thing is that a man who studied mountains of scores old and new, conducted so many rehearsals and concerts and recordings, maintained a huge correspondence, gave interviews, made speeches, and auditioned would-be orchestra members and soloists could make so much time for so many women.

Not once did Stokowski indicate the slightest interest in what people thought, wrote, or said about him. This was one of the ways in which he seemed to be secure. But one can never know. His second wife, Evangeline, once asked me, "I wonder if you realize the extent of this man's feeling of inferiority? It is indescribable."

The key to this aspect of Stokowski's character is perhaps that he was a perfectionist, virtually incapable of satisfying himself in anything, and so he was naturally and eternally doomed to the pursuit of an ever-receding horizon. No matter how successful a concert or a conquest, the next had to be better. It became his all-consuming passion.

6

SINCE 1920, I HAD REGARDED THE PHILADELPHIA ORCHESTRA as "my orchestra." On my seventeenth birthday, I received the most exciting gift of my life, a subscription to the Tuesday night series of Carnegie Hall concerts by the Philadelphia Orchestra under Stokowski. For two long years since inauguration of the series in 1918, I had dreamt of a time when I would be able to buy a ticket for even one of those evenings, which had become events rathers than concerts. But no one could buy a ticket for the Philadelphians, not for love or money. Subscriptions were completely sold out. They had virtually become something you had to inherit. Someone had to die before anyone else could acquire one, and that is just how I got mine. A kind musical lady who was recently widowed, offered it to me in exchange for piano lessons. Never was I more handsomely paid.

It was the first Tuesday evening of the Carnegie Hall series of 1920–21 when I first heard Stokowski conduct the Philadelphia Orchestra. Late-comers were not admitted until intermission. To be safe, I arrived one half-hour before concert time. In a very few minutes an audience that filled the hall sat in rapt attention, tense with excitement and talking in whispers.

The lights were dimmed and a tingling silence pervaded

the hall. Suddenly, at 8:30 on the dot, out of the wings sped
Stokowski, crowned with golden hair, a study in impeccable
black and white. With hardly a nod to the audience he
jumped upon the dais and, with a vicious forward stab with
his baton, launched into a full-speed-ahead performance of
Wagner's *Ride of the Valkyries.* What an act—this tall, imperious figure sculpting the shapes of phrases, punching with the
left fist for entrances, curling expressive fingers, stretching
hands and chin to the heavens.

Such theatrical razzmatazz I had never before seen from
anyone, anywhere. Yet, the tumultuous music, the man's
power, the virtuoso performance, and the flashes of tonal
lightning from the orchestra left everyone mesmerized. At
the final crashing climax the audience sat spellbound, not
applauding for an astonishing length of time. Then the
whole house burst out screaming and clapping hysterically.

Whether one agreed or disagreed with Stokowski's interpretations, one could not listen to him and the Philadelphia
Orchestra with a dispassionate ear. I do not recall any performance of his to which I—or anyone, for that matter—
could listen with indifference.

In the mid-twenties he hit his full stride, making headlines
with all the "isms": ultramodernism, futurism, dadaism, and
the rest. He performed Stravinsky's works, including the in-
accessible ones, though Stravinsky was severely critical of
Stokowski's liberties with his scores. To Stravinsky, the conductor's first obligation was to carry out the wishes of the
composer to the letter of the score, to refrain from anything
remotely resembling "interpretation."

When Stokowski's audiences stopped kicking about Stravinsky's music, he turned to Arnold Schoenberg. First he
premiered *Pelléas and Mélisande,* which one critic termed
"one interminable moan" and which the audience slept
through. Stokowski decided to wake them up at another concert with Five Pieces for Orchestra, op. 16, which achieved

the desired result. Everybody got angry. Music-lovers wrote indignant letters to the newspapers, critics wrote stinging reviews. Stokowski was in seventh heaven.

When Schoenberg struck out, Stokowski's next pinch-hitter was Edgar Varèse, whose *Amériques* featured a fire siren that blasted the unsuspecting matrons out of their seats into their limousines, and monopolized newspaper columns.

In his headline hunting, Stokowski did not always depend upon sheer volume. His superb showmanship produced one of his greatest triumphs in the Philadelphia premiere of *Bolero,* Ravel's seventeen-minute orchestral crescendo on one banal theme. The American premiere went to Toscanini and the New York Philharmonic and was an instantaneous success. A few weeks later, after a Friday afternoon concert at the Philadelphia Academy of Music, Stokowski acknowledged his warm applause with an "encore," the *Bolero,* and the audience went crazy.

The newspaper critics had all left the hall, and so once again word of mouth had to prove its efficacy, for at the Saturday night concert, after the last number, the audience applauded with unusual fervor and would not let up. Time and again Stokowski came out to bow and returned to the wings, while the applause grew deafening. They knew what they wanted, and so did Stokowski, but he remained deadpan. Finally, he walked to the front of the stage, signaled for silence, and with baby-faced innocence asked quietly, "Would you like to hear it?" All hell broke loose. That is the story of the Philadelphia premiere of Ravel's *Bolero.*

Stokowski's theatricality was also evident in his ad libitum use of unusual instruments such as Javanese gongs, Indian temple bells, Chinese drums, the tam-tam, and the Thereminvox (which produces so-called ether music) if they served his purpose. He once brought a pagan icon to a rehearsal of Henry Eichheim's tone poem *Bali,* placed it full of burning incense in front of the orchestra, and proceeded to rehearse the work in what he conceived to be the proper psychological atmosphere. One is again confronted with two Stokowskis. Both account for the radiance and afterglow of his orchestra, but it is not easy to differentiate Stokowskian stagecraft from Stokowskian musicianship.

At almost every rehearsal, some time was taken to try out some new work. The mood that prevailed was always one of respectful and contemplative attention, all very relaxed, whereas the rehearsal of a work scheduled for performance or recording was another story. Then Stokowski, looking like one suddenly possessed, would conduct with fiery intensity and relentless determination, soon driving his players beyond their capacities. On their faces one could see joyous excitement over some subtle nuance, some incredible sonority that he would extract from them by a spontaneous twist of the wrist or twitch of an eyebrow. Stokowski was evidently and constantly being renourished by the music. Despite spurts of grueling labor over one passage or section to attain accuracy and understanding, spontaneity was never entirely absent in rehearsal or performance.

His superb orchestra, he once told me, enabled him to yield to what seemed like an occult power that filled him and his orchestra with a prodigious energy. He would then conduct with maniacal abandon, emerging from the platform wringing wet and feeling like a lion released from a cage. The effect on the audience was invariably electric. He said, "In such moments I feel as though I have attained universalism. I feel at one with everything and everybody."

What was often mistaken for posturing was Stokowski's occasional facial impassiveness. When he listened to his orchestra, he summoned every last iota of nervous coordination so tightly adjusted that the slightest distraction would disturb it. That too contributed to the impression of arrogance and remoteness, when all the while his whole being was wrapped in artistic concentration.

Prior to performances, Stokowski would prepare himself in his dressing room mentally and spiritually, with great care.

Totally alone, totally silent, he would do deep-breathing exercises to summon maximum concentration. If someone said, "Good evening," or merely brushed passed him when he was on his way to the stage, he would wheel around and return to his room to restore his former degree of concentration. Famous for starting on the dot, on such occasions he was compelled to keep audiences waiting fifteen minutes. This preparation was no act, but his theatrics were so innate that they constantly exposed him to critical allegation.

Stokowski abandoned the baton in 1925 when he made a sudden, strong accentual beat with his "baguette," as he used to call it, and the stick collided with his left hand and broke in two. Stokowski grew impatient with anyone who asked when that happened, invariably saying something to the effect that "time is too valuable to remember such things." Yet "hand-made music" became a Stokowski trademark, one of the most characteristic and eloquent means and manifestations of his art. No aspect of it induced more comment or controversy.

At the beginning of the 1926 season, subscribers to the Philadelphia Orchestra concerts found the following insertion in their programs:

> The great conviction has been growing in me that the orchestra and conductor should be unseen, so that on the part of the listener more attention will go to the ear and less to the eyes. The experiment of an invisible orchestra is for the moment impossible—so I am trying to reach for a similar result by reducing the light to the minimum necessary for the artists of the orchestra to see their music and the conductor.
>
> Music by its nature is remote from the tangible and visible things of life. I am hoping to intensify its mystery and eloquence and beauty.
>
> LEOPOLD STOKOWSKI

Stokowski ordered the house lights extinguished and allowed only infinitesimal lamps over the orchestra stands,

while a huge spotlight played upon the conductor from below so as to project mammoth shadows of his flashing, expressive fingers and hands onto the walls and ceiling of the
stage. There was no denying that his striking profile, graceful movements, sweeping gestures, and pantherlike lunges
provided a fantastic ballet and reams of newsprint, pro and
con, as Stokowski's fingers became ten mobile batons.

Then as today, Stokowski's musicological status was a matter of unceasing, biting debate. His critics pounced upon this
latest experiment as peacockery and accused him of having
violated more than any musician's share of musical canons
but conceded the potential fruits of his "indomitable adventurousness" in the constant effort to extend the scope of
orchestral playing.

Not until I had been at the Curtis Institute for about two
years and had worked around and with Stokowski almost
daily did I grasp particular elements of his art and his methods. All I had known were his unique achievements in creating artistic wholeness out of highly personal convictions, in
making the orchestra sound ever greater each time in
rhythmic vitality, transparent tone, velvety sonority, and in
the ability of each section to shine radiantly and not obscure
the playing of any other section. I tried to discover to what
extent the science or art of logic related to these results.

How it was done is a problem perhaps only partially explic-
able. But perhaps it would be better to tackle the question of
what was done. One of the commonest queries still asked by
the most musical laymen in our sophisticated orchestral age
is, with such great players today, does an orchestra really
need a conductor?

From time to time, a conductorless orchestra will appear
and quickly disappear, though never quickly enough for me.
Through the basic struggle merely to keep together musically, their resultant metronomic rhythm is lifeless. Furthermore, such groups have a kind of historical innocence about
the baroque and rococo repertory, thinking that it must be

played strictly "in time." The inflexible treatment of music that the most superficial investigation would disclose as swinging, dancing, improvisational, and expressive is utterly inexcusable. Metrical accentuation belongs to the performance of military marches at a parade. All other music, from the rhetorical baroque style through the dramatic art of romanticism and the free forms of twentieth-century music, demands spontaneity. Without a conductor, a symphonic repertory would emerge in a straitjacket or in chaos.

Even the earliest instrumental or choral groups invariably elected a leader from among its members. As musical organizations increased in size, as music became more complex, the necessity of a conductor became ever more obvious. On the most basic level of ensemble, a conductor is essential. Moreover, in order to assemble a homogeneous group, a conductor must assume the responsibility of selecting players who will blend to produce his tonal ideals. The conductor must also select the repertory; convey interpretative intentions; and determine tempi, dynamics, and balances so that one instrument or section does not overpower another.

In order for an orchestra to function successfully, it must have a conductor with a profound historical, stylistic, and instrumental knowledge of a huge repertory. The conductor must also know the nature and technique of every instrument. He must understand human elements (the varying responses of each player), time elements (how long it takes to make each instrument "speak"), bowing and breathing characteristics and lip tensions—all that is involved in assuring the punctual entrance and maximum effect from every instrument. No wonder that the conductor, this musician who does not play a note, is the most valuable and most highly paid member of an orchestra.

Moreover, not all of the conductor's activities are confined to the podium. The conductor also has associative, intellectual, and civic obligations. He must establish workable relations with his board of directors, members' committees, audiences, and, most important, his orchestra. If, in order to maintain his artistic integrity, he runs afoul of someone, he must handle it according to his own resources and ego, but handle it he must. He is also one of the most influential personages of the cultural community. He has the artistic obligation to encourage the deserving composers of his time and to nourish young and talented performers. He can be of inestimable value in animating the financial support of the orchestra.

One of the most vital roles of a conductor is as the messenger of the composer. As such, he galvanizes and unifies his orchestral forces, using them as his instrument to project not only the work but also his conception of it. In the presence of a conductorial genius, music becomes more than music—it takes on the dimensions and drama of life itself, the air is electric with excitement, and familiar music shines with a new and blinding light for orchestras and audiences alike.

The reverential quality bestowed by the entourage of genius has also inspired egotism of hilarious proportions. After an exceptionally exciting Boston Symphony performance by Serge Koussevitzky of Tchaikovsky's *Pathétique* Symphony, a woman came backstage bathed in tears. Emotionally overcome, she sank to her knees in front of Koussevitzky saying, "You are God." Lifting her up gently, he answered, "I know, my dear. It is a great responsibility."

During the early twenties, it was clear to all of us who heard the Philadelphians regularly that with each concert Stokowski's conductorial mastery was growing and that his orchestra was moving forward at his pace. In those pre-Curtis Institute days, he had maintained a worldwide and perpetual search for musicians who would enable him to develop the greatest orchestra the world had ever heard. In 1927, three of his fastidiously chosen musicians paid me the compliment of joining my classes at Curtis in compositional analysis, and through this association flutist William Kincaid, oboist Marcel Tabuteau, and trumpeter Saul Caston became my closest friends and associates in Philadelphia.

All of them asserted that from the moment of their first rehearsal with Stokowski's orchestra, they were astounded by the Maestro's omniscient or psychical ability to draw super-human powers from his players. They also held in special admiration Stokowski's remarkable restraint in not overre-hearsing his players, leaving room for them to indulge in individual freedoms of expression in the inspiration of the moment. Of all conductors this autocratic disciplinarian gave certain favorites among his first-desk players the greatest opportunity for self-expression, musically and technically. With Kincaid, Tabuteau, and Caston this leeway extended itself to personal liberties that they alone enjoyed and ac-cepted as their due.

Daniel Saidenberg, the orchestra's first cellist during the twenties, told me, "Stoki's ability to exert discipline was occa-sionally matched by a sense of humor. After a concert at which I had played the Saint-Saëns A-minor Concerto, one of my buddies said, 'Watch your step, Danny. All through the second movement, Stoki was looking at you with fire in his eyes.' I hadn't noticed anything, but sure enough, the manager came over, saying that Maestro wanted to see me. Now came the confrontation. 'Saidenberg, why didn't you look at me during the concerto?' Stoki asked. 'Where were your eyes?' I was nonplussed but decided that it would be better to tell the truth than to make up some story. 'Well, Maestro,' I said, 'I was looking at my new girl friend, who was sitting in the second row.' With that Stoki smiled, patted me on the rear, and said, 'I can well understand that, but don't let it happen again.' "

In Halina Rodzinski's book *Our Two Lives* she describes how on the very first day Artur Rodzinski came to assist Stokowski in 1929, his boss immediately restyled his hair without a part and combed straight back from the brow. "That's how a conductor should look," said Stokowski, pointing Rodzinski at a mirror in his dressing room at the Academy. Mrs. Rodzinski continues, "Artur accepted this without question for the rest of his life. But other things he acquired from Stokowski he did his best to eliminate. Once, he told me, his four years in Los Angeles were largely spent in divesting himself of what he considered Stokowski's bad musical habits and platform mannerisms—except for one: he always stood with his feet close together, never parting them even when his gestures became expansive . . . in climactic moments. Artur was unfailingly grateful to Stoki throughout his life for what his senior had taught him in those Philadelphia days. But he was not uncritical of the man."

Stokowski's ability to inspire musicians was sometimes balanced by the ability to turn them off. Saidenberg alerted me to a remarkable violinist who quit the Philadelphia Orchestra and went on to become America's greatest authority on constitutional law. "Raoul Berger was a wonderful violinist in the Philadelphia Orchestra. One day at rehearsal, Stoki stopped the orchestra and pointed to him, shouting, 'You, what's your name?' The reply came in a small voice, 'Berger—Raoul Berger, sir.' 'Well, play in tune,' said Stoki. The next day in precisely the same spot the same incident took place. The third day in precisely the same place the incident was repeated. Berger couldn't stand it any longer and, turning on Stoki, said, 'On Monday you asked me my name. On Tuesday you asked me my name. Now it is Wednesday, and you're still asking my name. What's wrong with your memory? Haven't you learned it yet?' Stoki fired him."

From what I had heard and read about Berger he was evidently an extraordinary musical talent who had won some impressive recognition. I asked him what relation there was between his decision to abandon his musical career and his association with Stokowski. In response Mr. Berger sent me an article that he had written for the Harvard Law School *Bulletin* of October 1962 and a few pages of recollections, from which I quote.

In Berger's youth, when music was his only goal, "there was nothing for it but the orchestra. When the Curtis Institute opened in 1924, I was awarded a scholarship with Carl Flesch and entered the Philadelphia Orchestra to pay my way. Fresh from the Institute of Musical Art and the class of Franz Kneisel in New York, where all was dedication to the music, I was dumbfounded to behold in Stoki a man so in love with himself as to be oblivious to the duty he owed to the giants at whose shrine he should have worshipped. It was Stokowski all the way, the Jovian thunderbolt, the spotlight on his golden hair, etc. I used to think that his talent was corrupted by his vanity, but it ran deeper than that; today we call it narcissism.

"In rehearsal Stoki was given to the methods of a marine drill-sergeant, brutal and insulting. In those days he was accustomed to make sweeping changes every season, so that those who were dependent on their jobs lived in fear and trembling.

"He had his good qualities—a rich, voluptuous sound, great precision and vitality. In music that called for fire and sensuality he was at his best. His 'Danse Infernale' from Stravinsky's *Firebird* was truly demonic, etched in biting rhythms. He rose to sensual ecstasy in the *Afternoon of a Faun*.

"Unlike Walter and Mengelberg, Stoki indulged in no long-winded 'explanations' of the music in literary images. All was addressed in terms of how to do it, as it should be. Consequently rehearsals were short, not a minute wasted, often only half the length of the average rehearsal. He knew where the weak spots were and rehearsed them. . . . Not a little of the 'mesmerism' of which some of his players speak grew out of the fact that the men were not wearied by long, boring rehearsals, that we had fewer concerts and rehearsals than most major orchestras, that often they had not had a chance to play a work through, and therefore fell on it with ardor at the concert.

"Then too, he had his matchless players—Tabuteau, Kincaid, and Caston. When he once adjured Anton Horner to play a passage softer, Horner, after several tries, rose, brandished his horn and said, 'There are sixteen feet of pipe in this, and if I don't blow in, nothing comes out.' That closed the matter."

Berger was never in that position: He lost all desire to be.

"What lingers in my mind," he concludes, "is Stokowski's indifference to the duty he owed to the greats whose music he was performing, strutting like a cockerel, unaware that he was at the feet of the masters. I chanced to see his last television interview in England just before his death. There was the same old comedian, sporting the same phony accent in his native English, the same bag of tricks, only now larded with pious tributes to his 'colleagues.' When I think of him across the gap of fifty-four years, which should serve to blur personal resentment, it is with undiminished contempt."

But if there were contradictory opinions among colleagues (as there certainly were), it must be acknowledged that the public loved Stokowski. The week's highlight for every Philadelphia music-lover who was unable to obtain or afford an orchestra subscription was the Saturday night concert series, for which several dozen unreserved seats were made available at fifty cents. Saturday after Saturday, year after year, lines formed in the late afternoon, soon winding around the block of the Academy of Music. Weather made no difference, for there was a protective cover above that stretch of sidewalk. But neither rain nor sleet would have kept the devotees from taking appointed places at strategic points that would insure a seat. Everyone knew everyone else and held places for each other. Every hour or so, a drugstore attendant would come by, selling sandwiches, fruit, and hot coffee.

Exactly at 7:30 lights were flashed on and the standees

poised themselves for the assault on the box office. Then, the fortunate recipients bounded up the stairs to the "peanut gallery." A few moments before the concert was to start, doors were shut against the late-comers, the orchestra finished tuning, lights were lowered, hearts beat faster, and a deathlike silence prevailed. Then Stokowski would spring out of the wings, sprint to the podium, jab at his men, and the heavenly sounds would begin.

The same sort of magic that Stokowski exerted on adults extended to young people. He never understood the concept of the "generation gap." Consequently, nothing was ever closer to his heart than young people's concerts. Started in 1921, they embraced his greatest loves—music and youth. Although youth concerts were not Stokowski's innovation, they took on an entirely new dimension under his imaginative direction. A perennial adolescent himself, Stokowski always had a fabulous affinity for youngsters and vice versa. If there were any secrets to his longevity, this was one of them. Inevitably, each youth concert had some picturesque surprise, some colorful and imaginative angle that wowed the kids and made Stokowski their hero.

Among the most memorable moments occurred when the program featured the *Carnival of the Animals* by Saint-Saëns, in which the widely known Philadelphia pianist, composer, author, and teacher Jeanne Behrend, participated as a child. "Just before we started to play the fifth section entitled The Elephant," said Jeanne, "two elephants walked on stage! Stoki had collected a live menagerie to illustrate the famous composition. On another occasion, the featured work was Prokofiev's *Peter and the Wolf.* Stoki was said to have searched high and low to have a real wolf appear but had to settle for a German shepherd."

It was small wonder that adult Philadelphians tried to crash the children's concerts. A rule was finally adopted that grown-ups were not allowed unless they were chaperoning no fewer than ten children. Even at that, all sorts of dodges were attempted to gain admittance. One prominent Philadelphia couple attempted to sneak in by having the wife dress up in Mary Janes and hair ribbons and the husband pretend to be her father.

Viola B. Marshall of Medford, New Jersey, who for fifty years has taken all the children of the family to the Philadelphia Orchestra's children's concerts, recalls, "One morning Stokowski had his little daughter Sonya, who was then about two years old, sitting on the podium beside him. During the music the little girl fell off and began to cry. Without missing a beat, Stokowski continued to lead the orchestra with his right hand while he leaned over, picked up his daughter, set her down again, wiped her tears away with his handkerchief, and held and comforted her, all with his left hand."

Stokowski's feeling for youth and interest in musical education found a specific focus in 1922. In that year, Mary Bok, daughter of Cyrus Curtis and Louisa Knapp and wife of Edward Bok, conceived the Curtis Institute of Music. Although she invariably said humbly, "I have merely spent the money my father earned," her own contribution to the cultural life of Philadelphia was immeasurable. Her father, the influential publisher, had named Louisa editor of his first acquisition, the *Ladies' Home Journal,* which soon won the largest circulation of any semimonthly magazine. The purchase of the weekly *Saturday Evening Post* and several newspapers followed, out of which grew the Curtis Publishing Company. Eventually, Edward Bok, a young Hollander whom Louisa had met in New York, where he had made himself a fine journalistic name, succeeded her as editor of the *Journal,* and in 1896, he married the boss's daughter, Mary. He encouraged her musical solicitude and she persuaded him of the need for a great music school where gifted people without the means and opportunities to develop their talents might flourish under the tutelage of preeminent musicians.

Two years before its inauguration, Mary Bok began discussions with Stokowski and Josef Hofmann, calling upon their guidance and participation in implementing her all-consuming dream of building the ideal music school, a tuition-free institute for young musicians who sought professional careers. "The support and promotion of music and music education" was the stated objective of the charter, signed according to Mary Bok's graceful plan, on Stokowski's birthday, April 18, 1924.

A distinguished advisory committee chose a faculty comprising many of the world's foremost musicians and musicologists. Artistic director Josef Hofmann let it be known that the school was on the alert for superior talents. Hundreds of the most gifted found their way to Philadelphia, where scholarships, accommodations, pianos, and generous assistance awaited all who were accepted. The reputation of the institute spread like wildfire throughout the entire musical world. The first classes were held on October 1 in three handsome homes off Rittenhouse Square, recently purchased and altered. Success came rapidly. Students of genius, or at the very least of extraordinary talent, came from all over.

For the first quarter of this century the Philadelphia Orchestra drew its players almost entirely from Europe. Since that time the personnel has been almost completely American-born or -trained, virtually every member of the orchestra having come out of the classrooms of the Curtis Institute. The Curtis Symphony Orchestra gathered for the first time in 1924. Stokowski had assigned the teaching of all but the string instruments to the principal players of his orchestra: Daniel Bonade (clarinet); Saul Caston (trumpet); Philip Donatelli (tuba); Walter Guetter (bassoon); Anton Horner (horn); William Kincaid (flute); Oscar Schwar (tympani and battery); Gardell Simons (trombone); Marcel Tabuteau (oboe); and Anton Torello (bass). These artists participated in all the rehearsals seated beside their students. Throughout the distinguished musical life of the Curtis Institute, its student orchestra has given many notable performances, not only in the school's auditorium but also in the concert halls of great cities. It has also participated in numerous broadcasts for the national radio networks. Everyone who has been associated with the Curtis Institute takes pride in the astounding number of its students who have attained international renown.

Shortly after the orchestra's formation, Stokowski wrote, "I have always dreamed of an ideal training method for our orchestra—at last it is come—in the student orchestras of the Curtis Institute. I can develop completely trained young artists fully equipped for every school of symphony playing—an opportunity of the highest value to our orchestra."

Although Stokowski was only able to serve as teaching conductor for three years, it was sufficient for him to establish an orchestra worthy of the Curtis Institute's reputation as one of the world's foremost musical institutions. Throughout his life Stokowski remained closely associated with the school and continued to draw upon the reservoir of artists that it developed.

7

MANY OF STOKOWSKI'S most memorable musical achievements were interlaced with the activities of the Curtis Institute. The years 1926–36 were also the years of my teaching tenure there, and I have always considered it among the luckiest of my many good fortunes.

At that time a few legendary figures of the faculty began to supplement their private lessons with group projects. Whenever I could possibly arrange for a stolen hour from my own schedule, I was the fascinated auditor at operatic coaching-ing classes of Marcella Sembrich and Emilio de Gogorza, lecture-recitals on ancient harpsichord music by Wanda Landowska, solfège classes of Renée Longy Miquelle, Curtis Quartet rehearsals coached by Leopold Auer or Efrem Zimbalist, harp ensembles of Carlos Salzedo, and rehearsals of the student orchestra under Stokowski and Fritz Reiner.

In the Curtis classrooms of those years one found Gian-Carlo Menotti, Samuel Barber, Leonard Bernstein, Sylvan Levin, Jorge Bolet, Henri Temianka, Rose Bampton, Boris Goldovsky, Shura Cherkassky, Jeanne Behrend, and many more en route to distinguished careers.

Again, Stokowski conjured an orchestra out of thin air, this time a student orchestra that music critic James Felton later termed, in the *Philadelphia Evening Bulletin,* "nothing

116

less than a junior-league version of the Philadelphia Orchestra itself."

Stokowski was exacting with the young musicians, neither kind nor humorous, but an impressive teacher. He got his results through the intensity of his own dedication—by example, not preachment. He was only testy and impatient with a lack of attention or effort.

Each rehearsal sustained his reputation for toughness, but he was toughest on himself in enforcing self-imposed standards of excellence. His zest for hard work was equaled only by his readiness to act against convention and boldness in tackling anything new and promising.

After working with the student orchestra he would sprint breathless into the Curtis Institute Library to pour over the rich collection of orchestral scores we were acquiring and then to hear the newest recordings that had arrived. The librarians scurried about in response to his polite but sharp requests.

It was evident, particularly during these days, that he was a man who lived to capture the moment. He slept only six hours a night, he practiced yoga, he generally ate and drank sparingly. He strove constantly for perfection and power, which in turn would yield the approval and love for which he had a voracious appetite. For him, variety within unity was the primary principle not only of art but also of life.

Although he was hard and demanding of himself and his students, he was gracious to his colleagues but never effusive. Whenever Stokowski was asked pointedly for an opinion about a specific composer, composition, or performer, if he could not be complimentary, he almost invariably clammed up. He rarely criticized and rarely praised. Through the years I cannot remember more than a handful of solo artists whose performances he mentioned as memorable. He singled out Kreisler's inspiring interpretation of Brahms's Violin Concerto, Szigeti's of Beethoven's, Zimbalist's of the

Mendelssohn E-minor, and Hofmann's of both Chopin piano concertos. Another highlight for him was a harpsichord recital by Wanda Landowska "playing Bach with incredible freedom and passion, yet with iron rhythmic control."

I remember him being visibly moved whenever he recalled cellist Emanuel Feuermann's recording with him of Ernest Bloch's *Schelomo,* which he said had "the warmest colors and purest phrasing I ever heard on that instrument."

A curious favorite of his was Bela Babai, "the most erotic gypsy-style violinist" who played in New York night spots and whose records he bought for worldly women who agreed that Babai was the "hottest" fiddler they ever heard.

Stokowski spoke of Rachmaninoff with special affection and appreciation. In the performances of his works, Rachmaninoff's flexibility and endorsement of Stokowski's suggestions, from slight alterations to radical changes, fortified Stokowski's own convictions about taking liberties. He insisted that his modifications of a composer's work were not comparable to "painting over another's canvas." The original remains for all to see and hear, Stokowski contended.

Among the conductors who welcomed and furthered contemporary music, none understood the composer's economic plight and aesthetic problems better than Stokowski. He was an essentially practical man, acutely aware that there were very few composers after the age of patronage able to make a living from their work, with the exception of those who wrote music for the theater, all of whom grew very rich and died of indigestion. He was always mindful that his century, like every previous one, was producing its share of masterpieces, so many of which he spotlighted.

In 1931, when Stokowski introduced Shostakovich's First Symphony, he invited the orchestra's president, Alexander Van Rensselaer, to a rehearsal. Afterward Van Rensselaer seriously urged him to "explain this complex music" to his audiences, especially to the Friday afternoon ladies. At the next concert, before performing the work, Stokowski addressed his audience: "Mr. Van Rensselaer has asked me to explain this music that you are about to hear. He thinks you won't understand it, and has also asked me to tell you why I play it. I play it because it is great music. If you don't understand it enough to discover that, I'll play it right over again, but I won't try to explain it." The performance received wild applause. The audience was taking no chances.

After the first year at Curtis, Stokowski began to find his schedule overdemanding. Running his orchestra was a full-time job. Running the Curtis orchestra was time- and energy-consuming. He was set upon from all sides. Recordings were another drain and musically only partially rewarding. He was invited to perform and give a commentary on radio broadcasts by every network. They would require preparation for which he had no time. He was also anxious to try performances of opera in concert form, especially since Curtis was full of gifted and attractive young singers, only a few of whom he had had the opportunity to hear.

Stokowski obviously had an unfulfilled ambition to conduct opera. For the moment, concert versions were the obvious outlet. Whatever he conducted sounded as it never had with any opera orchestra, and he "staged" everything with compelling dramatic effect.

This accounted for his intense interest when in 1925 he was invited to join the League of Composers in New York to conduct some contemporary opera premieres. An appointment was arranged with Claire Reis, founder of this most prestigious and active group for the promotion of new music. In her splendid book, *Composers, Conductors, and Critics,* Mrs. Reis recalls the meeting:

We had made an appointment to meet at the home of a music patron, where he was staying temporarily. . . . I waited for him in a charming Victorian drawing-room. . . . At a slight sound I turned to find that Stokowski had entered the room so silently that I barely heard him. He made quite a picture, dressed in a magnificent Japanese kimono of deep blue, his bare feet thrust into native sandals. I had certainly not expected to meet him at four o'clock in the afternoon in such exotic attire. Actually it helped to put me at ease, forgetting for the moment the usual superbly tailored and dramatic figure of the podium whom I had always looked at with awe.

Mrs. Reis immediately unfolded the League's plan to present Manuel de Falla's marionette opera, *El Retablo de Maese Pedro*. Stokowski got right to the point. Had they secured all the necessary performing rights? When she affirmed this, he asked, "Will you then relinquish the rights and let me perform it with my friend Edgar Varèse's society, the International Composers' Guild?" At this she was dumbstruck, for he had named the League's arch competitor, at a time when they were at the height of their intense rivalry.

At the risk of jeopardizing any future liaison with the great man on the League's first contact with him, Mrs. Reis rejected his suggestion and held her ground firmly. Needless to say, the conference led to nothing. But unpromising as it was, it opened the door to several brilliantly successful collaborations within a few years.

In 1928, a young man named Sylvan Levin applied at Curtis to study piano with Moritz Rosenthal and conducting with Rodzinski. He was in his early twenties and looked even younger. From his eleventh year, he had been active in every phase of vocal and instrumental music, classical and popular, as a scholarship student at the Peabody Conservatory of Music. He seemed to have heard and read everything. After his second week of lessons at the school, Rodzinski ran over to Josef Hofmann's studio saying, "Put this boy on the faculty. He's remarkable."

"Teaching what?" Hofmann asked.

"Anything," said Rodzinski. "Right now we're in greatest need of an opera vocal coach."

"Will six thousand a year be all right?" Hofmann asked. Later, Sylvan said he had never dreamed of so much money.

In no time Sylvan became invaluable and extremely popular. When a vexing question arose, the byword was, "Ask Sylvan—he'll know." And he did. His reputation spread rapidly. Stokowski heard of him just when he had tracked down the original version of Mussorgsky's *Boris Godunov* and decided to conduct a concert version. It is ironic that Stokowski, so frequently attacked for tampering with music, should have been the first to restore the original version of a work that almost every musician, from Rimsky-Korsakov up and down the ladder, felt it a positive duty to "correct." Stokowski in 1929–30 did what it took the Metropolitan Opera another forty years to do.

To the practical Stokowski, first things came first. Where would he get the time to find the right singers, and who would handle all the other details? Perhaps this Sylvan chap could be useful. When the score arrived, Stokowski sent for Sylvan. Together they opened it. In five minutes Sylvan had caught three misprints in the French horn parts. That did it, and he became "Stoki's man" in an evermore loyal association that lasted almost twenty years.

Boris became Sylvan's first assignment. Stokowski had asked him to keep his eyes and ears open for an ideal cast and for suitable candidates for future productions. This, of course, suited Sylvan perfectly because he could then be as valuable to the institute's cause as to Stokowski's. Sylvan would spot the important singers of the student body and recommend them to Stokowski, who almost invariably accepted them and gave them their first break.

Whenever Stokowski had singers to deal with, he seemed to become malevolent, possibly to counteract the enormous emotional appeal to him of "the voice, the most beautiful of all instruments." He often recommended totally unknown singers (mainly from among the Curtis students) to fill important roles both to circumvent the traditional temperamental displays that some stars exhibited and to eliminate any question of his authority over cast as well as orchestra. Most times it worked and brought glory to all concerned.

Natalie Bodanya, one of Curtis's most accomplished singers, told me of her early encounters with Stokowski: "I came to Curtis to study with Marcella Sembrich. A notice on the Curtis bulletin board announced that Stokowski was producing a concert version of Mussorgsky's *Boris Godunov.* Ivan Ivantsov was to sing the title role, and Sophia Breslau, the role of Marina. Auditions were scheduled at Curtis to fill three remaining leading roles—the Prince, Princess, and Nurse. The vocal department was agog with excitement." All but Natalie Bodanya, who flatly announced that she would not audition for Stokowski. She had heard how "impersonal and impossible" he was.

The trouser role of the Prince went to Irra Petina and the Nurse's to Rose Bampton. No one applied whose voice and appearance suited the Princess.

"Is it possible," Stokowski asked Sylvan, "that there's not one singer at Curtis who can do it?"

"There's one," said Sylvan, "but she won't."

"Why?"

"Doesn't like you," Sylvan said.

"What's that got to do with it?" Stokowski asked. "It's a fine chance for her, and she shouldn't throw it away. I'd like to hear her."

Sylvan told this to Natalie, adding, "Of course, you must do it. Let me say you'll sing for him tomorrow."

Natalie saw the sense of this and showed up the next morning "looking like a slob," she told me when she recalled the incident, "wearing bobby sox and without any makeup."

Stokowski rose gallantly as she entered. "How do you do, Miss Bodanya. How *wahnderful* of you to come," he said in his most seductive accent. "What do you wish to sing?"

"Oh, how about 'Musetta's Waltz' from Puccini's *La Bohème?*"

Stokowski nodded. After she sang, he asked, "Could you sing some Mozart?"

"I've no Mozart ready. Besides, why should I sing Mozart for a chance to sing Mussorgsky?"

Sylvan glared and shook his head disapprovingly. Stokowski smiled, turned to Sylvan and said, "Yes, she *is* perfect for the Princess. Thank you both. See you at rehearsal."

Things went well. Natalie got along with everyone and became not only a Stokowski fan but also an admirer of Sophia Breslau. At the third rehearsal, they were working on a section starting at letter *B*. Suddenly, Stokowski turned around and said, "All right, now to letter *M*." His right hand shot out, and the orchestra made the cruel jump to a man. Of course, Sophia had not, and she was still searching for her place when Stokowski stopped the playing and in a voice loaded with sarcasm said, "It would be helpful if some of you could take a course in sight-reading and solfeggio." Breslau blanched. "On behalf of that wonderful woman," Natalie told me, "after rehearsal I walked into her dressing room and said, 'I know it's none of my business, but I hope you'll accept our apologies for what happened. Believe me, you have the sympathy and admiration of everyone in that hall. Stoki behaved abominably.' 'Thank you, my dear. Sometimes, Stoki's a very naughty boy, but he's a genius,' said Breslau, with characteristic dignity."

Natalie went on to tell me, "After that outburst all the other rehearsals went marvelously. He called me 'Lollipop' and treated me like a real princess. What floored me was his handling of the chorus, which started out sounding like a polite and polished British ensemble. At the end of the first rehearsal, you wouldn't have recognized them. Stoki had them hollering like drunken Russian peasants. They scared me. It was a fabulous transformation.

"The morning of the dress rehearsal I walked out on the stage, in my regal costume. I could just feel Stoki's incredulous eyes following me and could almost hear him saying, 'No. It can't be. It can't possibly be that snotty kid, that sloppy Lollipop who auditioned for me.' During the first performance, the eyes again pierced right through me. Backstage, Stokowski came over to me and said, 'Lollipop, I'm taking you home tonight.' 'Oh, thank you, Maestro, but it's not necessary. I'm a tough kid from New York; I can take myself home fine.' 'Not tonight,' said Stoki. One of the orchestra men standing nearby came over and drew me aside, saying, 'Listen, stupid, he doesn't want to take you home to *your* home. He wants to take you home to *his* home.' Walking over to Stoki, he said, 'Natalie lives near us, Maestro. We'll take her home, thank you.' That was that, and since I hadn't actually rejected him, we remained friends and I sang with him quite a few times."

Stokowski was enormously pleased with Sylvan's performance during the *Boris* production. Consequently he continued to delegate to Sylvan ever more challenging responsibilities, from coaching artists to conducting preliminary rehearsals, and at the end of the year named him his assistant conductor. Sylvan became indispensable, sweeping away all the chores that Stokowski had found so irksome.

One of the most familiar and diverting scenes in town was the sight of Sylvan shadowing Stokowski. The swarthy Sylvan, barely five feet tall, looked like an eager gnome running breathlessly alongside the golden-haired, six-foot-two Apollo, both talking like magpies.

Meanwhile, Stokowski had devised a sizable list of great operas he wanted to perform in concert versions, for which he enlisted Sylvan's increasingly responsible assistance. Stokowski was always meticulously correct in his engagement of Curtis students, informing either Mrs. Bok or Hofmann. When Sylvan next spoke to Hofmann, he was told, "Obviously, you and Stokowski work splendidly together. All your choices have been most fortunate. I want to give you full authority to act entirely on your own in the future."

"This," Sylvan told me, "facilitated and strengthened the whole circle of our activities."

Just prior to Stokowski's rediscovery of the original *Boris,* Mrs. Reis again invited Stokowski to join the League of Composers in planning some promising theatrical ventures. He responded warmly and affirmatively, and she was pleased to learn that he had neither forgotten their first talk nor held any grudges. In anticipation of Stokowski's full cooperation, Mrs. Reis introduced to him some young friends who were key figures in the world of the theater. He felt an instant rapport with the noted stage designer Robert Edmond Jones, one of Claire's most intimate friends. They were later to work happily and successfully together.

Stokowski's innate histrionic gifts made him keenly aware that an artistic production demands the synthesis of all its elements, a point he was at pains to prove in rehearsals for his first League production, Stravinsky's *Les Noces.* To design the sets, the League engaged Serge Soudeikine, who had achieved many great successes. Soudeikine immediately assumed that when it came to the stage, Stokowski was a novice. He made no effort to conceal his attitude, while Stokowski made every effort to assert what he thought was his own expertise.

When Stokowski proclaimed, "We must coordinate our lighting with the development of the music," Soudeikine, with a sardonic smile, countered, "I like my work to show off my sets and their costumes to the best advantage." It was the beginning of a feud that never let up throughout the production. Nevertheless, every professional knows the great tradition of show business. When the Metropolitan Opera's great curtain rose on April 25, 1929, it was apparent that everyone had done his job, and superbly. (For the record, the evening was filled out with Monteverdi's *Il Combattimento di Tancredi e Clorinda,* conducted by Werner Josten.)

In the fall of 1929, Claire Reis called on manager Arthur Judson in his New York office to inform him that Stokowski wanted to cooperate again with the League, this time in a production utilizing the entire Philadelphia Orchestra for three performances in Philadelphia and two in New York's Metropolitan Opera House. "And what works has Mr. Stokowski in mind to give us?" Judson asked in a decidedly hostile tone of voice. Claire took a deep breath and said evenly, "He wants to conduct Stravinsky's *Sacre du Printemps.* . . ." Claire took another deep breath before delivering the knockout punch: "And Schoenberg's *Die glückliche Hand.*"

Judson turned white, muttering derisively, "Why, Mrs. Reis, you cannot possibly think that you could fill the Metropolitan with *that* program!"

It is necessary to note that before his tenure as manager of the Philadelphia Orchestra, Judson was a conservatively trained musician and journalist. He regarded all experimental art as anarchy and was convinced of its poisonous effect on the box office. Stokowski considered him "a natural enemy of new music." On this acrimonious subject, the twenty-year relationship between them remained one of armed neutrality. Just as Stokowski was "Stoki" to everyone, so Arthur Judson was "A.J.," but from the moment they met to the end of their extensive association, they were "Mr. Stokowski" and "Mr. Judson" to each other. Personally, Stokowski kept himself completely aloof from Judson, for Judson was not only the orchestra's manager but also the manager of a brilliant roster of soloists and conductors from whom Stokowski wanted to keep a protective distance. Furthermore, Judson was also the "conductor" of a notorious affair with a board member's wife, which was the town scandal. Stokowski resented this as unseemly. Possibly he also resented anyone else enjoying an attractive and wayward wife.

Knowing Judson's history, Claire maintained emphatically

that it was a sensational idea that her board had approved unanimously. Judson said that they would have to see how the Philadelphia board felt about "this Stokowski notion." Claire stalked out and telephoned Stokowski a blow-by-blow account of the first round, leaving the next one to him. Within a week, the board gave its approval.

Actually, the time was long overdue for an American production of the Stravinsky ballet that seventeen years before had become a musical landmark of our century. Finding an appropriate short work to precede it was a knottier problem. After much soul-searching it was concluded that *Die glückliche Hand* by Schoenberg, the other most influential living composer, was a logical choice.

For the Schoenberg opera, Rouben Mamoulian was engaged as stage director, and Robert Edmond Jones was retained to devise sets and lighting. For the Stravinsky ballet, Leonide Massine, associated with the original Diaghilev production, served as choreographer; Nicholas Roerich, the painter and mystic to whom the ballet was dedicated and who had created the original decor and costumes, was invited to recreate his decor; and an exciting young dancer, Martha Graham, was offered the role of the Chosen One.

Schoenberg's atonal curtain-raiser, mimed by Doris Humphrey and Charles Weidman, was described by Jones as "not an opera, but an eerie whimsy." Stokowski once said, "There is little to love about it, but it has the fascination of a jigsaw puzzle." Sylvan Levin said, "It is almost mathematical music, but with Jones and Mamoulian on deck, it made a wonderful stage effect." It never caught on with the musical public.

The Stravinsky ballet was a huge and elaborate production. With the first rehearsal, the clash of temperaments, wills, and egos, began. Stokowski told me that the very first time he attempted to correlate the music and choreography by suggesting a slower tempo, Massine stepped before his corps de ballet with a dramatic gesture and said, "No, Mr.

Stokowski, no. This is *my* province. *My* dancers must move faster, this way," and illustrated his words. Stokowski said nothing, biding his time.

Massine was less than enthusiastic in Stokowski's selection of Martha Graham for the role and began to offer advice. However, she was a decided personality and insisted on expressing her own individuality. Stokowski backed her solidly in her opinions.

"He was wonderful," Martha said. "Stokowski encouraged me in every way. It was an honor to be selected by him, and dealing with the role was made easier by the spiritual support he gave me. I'll always be grateful to him."

Somehow, the tensions and the uproars finally culminated in a common artistic effort. All five performances were sold out and triumphant. In the process, Stokowski became the first conductor to make the cover of *Time* magazine (April 28, 1930). He was also named "musical director" of the Philadelphia Orchestra, with total control of programs, guest conductors—everything.

Apropos, it was not Stokowski, as has been widely chronicled, but Pierre Monteux, the conductor of *Le Sacre*'s world premiere in 1913, who conducted the American concert premiere with the Boston Symphony in January 1924. Stokowski's claim extends only to the American premiere of the ballet.

In 1930 Stokowski's overcrowded schedule compelled him to discontinue all pedagogical duties at the Curtis Institute. To divest himself of still other responsibilities, he appointed Sylvan Levin conductor of the Philadelphia Orchestra Chorus, in charge of all choral productions. Stokowski had learned to rely on his assistant's judgment and advice, and indeed he used both to the hilt when Sylvan dropped the hint that Alban Berg's opera *Wozzeck* might perhaps make an impressive American premiere. Stokowski's 1931 production of that stirring work, a cooperative effort by the Philadelphia

Orchestra, the Philadelphia Grand Opera, and Curtis Institute, stands as a conspicuous milestone in musical history.

There is no more famous Philadelphia story than this. Mrs. Bok launched it with a gift of forty thousand Depression dollars for preliminary expenses. The stupendous production, requiring eighty-eight preparatory rehearsals and sixty on-stage rehearsals, still did not compete in terms of rehearsal time with the original 1925 Berlin production which had needed one hundred thirty-seven. For over six months, the Curtis Institute's faculty and students were embroiled in the proceedings. Virtually all private lessons and classroom work were diverted to some aspect of the opera. Every free moment of the day and night was spent rehearsing, coaching, accompanying, and teaching individual performers and groups of soloists and orchestral players. Those who were not directly involved in the music were commandeered to design, build, and paint scenery; make costumes; gather props; and take care of business and box-office chores. Even the porters exchanged their brooms for paint brushes in order to get the sets finished on time.

Two months before the opening date, Stokowski was scheduled to leave for a six-week tour of Mexico. Before he left, Sylvan Levin played the eighty-eight piano rehearsals, as Stokowski conducted the soloists and directed the stage action. Stokowski seemed to be everywhere at once and drove everyone unmercifully. When he left for Mexico, he put Sylvan in charge, saying, "I am leaving the complete vocal and orchestral preparation to you. However, there's a great deal of on-stage activity such as the fox-trot in the tavern scene. I must forbid you to touch any of this. Also, there are so many details of lighting, cuing, curtain changing—all these theatrical things must be left alone until I return."

"When Stoki returned with only two weeks left for rehearsal," said Sylvan, "he plunged into everything with such mastery you'd think he'd been studying it for years."

I attended his second rehearsal with the orchestra in the pit and the singers on stage. After some twenty minutes of singing and acting, often at sixes and sevens, Stokowski stopped the rehearsal and addressed the principal singers very quietly: "I want you all to understand something," he said. "Get rid of the absurd idea that nothing in this opera matters except what you do individually, and how your voices sound. Don't you understand that you are only part of a whole dramatic entity? You have no regard for operatic integrity. You are vain; you want personal applause. It is all very inartistic, and I will not put up with it. If you can't take this correction, just leave."

Needless to say, no one left. Although the Philadelphia performances of Mahler's Eighth and of Stravinsky's *Le Sacre* had been sensationally acclaimed, neither was comparable to *Wozzeck*'s spectacular triumph on March 21, 1931. Mrs. Bok had been apprehensive about the overabundant publicity surrounding *Wozzeck,* fearing it might arouse critical antipathy. Instead, the occasion immediately established *Wozzeck* as a contemporary classic, the operatic parallel to Stravinsky's orchestral *Le Sacre.* From the opening measures, the audience was thrown into feverish excitement, and at the end of the tragic finale, pandemonium broke loose. Leading critics acknowledged it "a work of genius."

When I congratulated Stokowski at the after-performance reception, he said, "What I find extraordinary is that the disciple of Schoenberg has created the opera which everyone expected of his master. It is the most original work since Debussy's *Pelléas et Mélisande.*"

The parallel was apt, for both works freely use harmonic unorthodoxies whose progressions depend on polyphonic principles and both use many resources in common with older music to which audiences respond emotionally.

The success of *Wozzeck* stimulated Stokowski to investigate the possibility of forming his own opera company, but discouraging associates and the ever-worsening financial condition of the country killed the idea. He had to wait for almost thirty years to conduct opera on a regular basis. Instead, he accepted the League's invitation to conduct a few scaled-down, but highly imaginative, productions that enabled him to work with Robert Edmond Jones, who had become a staunch ally and favorite collaborator.

In 1931, the Philadelphia Orchestra board reported the first deficit since the endowment had been set up. With it came the implication that Stokowski's frequent absences and his debatable programs when he did assume his duties were exacting a heavy toll. Without his knowledge, the board sent a prospectus to the subscribers announcing the decision to eliminate all ultramodern music until a more propitious time. When Van Rensselaer told Stokowski, "The board instructs you not to play any more experimental music," the Maestro was infuriated and said, "Tell them I don't take 'instruction' from them and I'll play whatever I please!"

Stokowski led off the next season with what amounted to a contemporary festival. Anton Webern's Symphony for Small Orchestra was so ferociously hissed that Stokowski stalked off the stage, only to return and play all eight minutes of it through again from the beginning. The audience walked out in droves. At the next concert, the subscribers' ears were assailed by Mossolov's *Soviet Iron Foundry*. This time the board of directors screamed with anger at Stokowski's open defiance.

After completing his fall stint, Stokowski's next step was across the gangplank of a ship leaving for the Orient, "to undertake some special studies." Judson, with whom Stokowski's relations were growing ever more strained, had engaged Toscanini as guest conductor for a few weeks, but one week before Toscanini's first concert, a cable arrived expressing the Maestro's regret that a severe attack of bursitis necessitated his cancellation. Judson seized the opportunity to offer a highly endowed young conductor he had taken under management his "big chance."

Thirty-one-year-old Eugene Ormandy accepted the challenge and over the weekend thoroughly mastered and memorized the difficult and stunning program that Toscanini had scheduled. The critic of the *Philadelphia Record* wrote: "An audience that was genuinely pleased to hear a program of beautiful music . . . accorded Eugene Ormandy an enthusiastic welcome yesterday. . . . If he had cunningly chosen a program which would contrast with the cacophonous effusions sponsored by Mr. Stokowski last week, he could not have shown to better advantage." Throughout twenty years in Philadelphia Stokowski had faced many crises, but this review sounded an unfamiliar and prophetic note, for Ormandy eventually took over and remained over forty years.

Upon Stokowski's return, he demonstrated that his advocacy of modernism was matched by his showmanship and pragmatism. Both asserted themselves in the dawning realization that in such troubled times people have a desperate need for music that will bring them spiritual and emotional sustenance and inspiration.

Sylvan Levin's background had made him keenly aware of music as an entertainment, and he was influential in encouraging Stokowski toward more accessible programs that would bring the masterpieces to an ever wider public, starting with a fresh batch of great operas in concert form.

Stokowski, with his quaint sense of humor, began to address Sylvan as "Maestro" while referring to himself as "Maestrino":

May 12, 1935

CARO MAESTRO ILLUSTRE,

Now that you have not a thing to do!!!!! Do you think you would have time to do me a favor and time the whole of *Parsifal* without cuts? I suggest you do this alone and without your orchestra; otherwise, the tempo might be too fast!!

Also the same afternoon could you look through *Carmen* noting the places that are rich cream, those that are just milk, and those that are mainly water? Because we may do next season a very much abridged version of *Carmen.*

I cannot think of anything else to do that afternoon except perhaps you would invite me to tea so as to fill out the time! (Yes, lemon meringue pie.)

Always,
MAESTRINO

Stokowski was moving more and more toward what is recognized as his most significant achievement—the broadening of popular interest in serious music. He developed a firm conviction that radio, recordings, and films would inevitably be the most effective instruments in bringing aesthetic understanding into everyone's life. It explains his immediate acceptance of a broadcasting series on NBC in 1932, which made Stokowski a household name. It also gave rise to an embarrassing incident that spurred him to acquire a more solid technical background.

I was told by Bill Thomas, formerly of Young and Rubicam's radio department, that before the series began, NBC officials gave Stokowski the grand tour of the original Fifth Avenue studios. Pausing before a control room, Stokowski observed a man manipulating a panel with rows of dials and galvanometers.

'Who's that?" Stokowski asked.

"He's the engineer who controls the sound."

"Do you propose to have one on *my* programs?" Stokowski demanded.

"Oh, yes. He's necessary on all programs."

"Not on mine. No one controls Stokowski's sounds but Stokowski." And he marched off.

This put NBC into a real quandary. They patiently explained the facts of broadcasting to Stokowski but to no avail.

He remained adamant. Faced with a crisis, they gave in and reluctantly built at huge cost a portable glass-enclosed control room on rollers for him to operate.

As Stokowski rehearsed, he practiced on the dials while the program staff suffered. He would wave his hands and then suddenly reach down to twist a knob, often the wrong way and invariably too much or too little, for he was unable to gauge the blended sounds as heard in the control room. Inevitably, the first broadcast was a sonic disaster.

For the next broadcast a bright engineer had an inspiration. "Let's use *two* control cubicles," he suggested, "a well-screened functioning one, and a disconnected play-toy for the conductor." They built another, and the scheme worked just fine.

No one knows who tipped off Stokowski, but about the third rehearsal, he strode right past the glass monster and never looked at it again.

Around this time, the Moore School of Electrical Engineering at the University of Pennsylvania invited Stokowski and me to work as a team on a series of acoustical experiments on the nature of sound. Stokowski, of course, had a considerable amount of experience in acoustical development as applied to the techniques of recording. Now he was intent on learning the principles and terminology involved in all reproduction of sound, as was I. My assignment was to assist in a scientific analysis of the relation of piano touch to tone. Stokowski's was in the far-reaching directions of what became known as frequency modulation and stereophonic reproduction. We worked resolutely for four months with Professors Harry Hart, Walter Lusby, and Charles Weyl— professor of mathematics as well as physics. Weyl had an excellent technical background in electrical engineering, and his hobbies were music and acoustics. He represented the best of two cultures and contributed enormously to Stokowski's eventual achievements.

Stokowski's activities at this time were prodigious, and it is proof of his intellectual curiosity that throughout he remained tenaciously devoted to the project and never missed one session. For him the electronics field ceased being merely an interest and became his newest passion, a field he resolved to master. He showed boundless curiosity, asked pointed questions, and made meticulous notations of the answers for future use. He would not, as do many musicians, leave the problems of recording to technical experts. He was constantly experimenting in the placement of men, instruments, and microphones.

Charles O'Connell, RCA Victor's artistic director, was Stokowski's admired associate during the years 1926–38. He always said that "it was a joy to work with Stokowski" and insisted that the unique excellence of the Philadelphia Orchestra's recordings has been "attributed to almost every circumstance except the really causative ones." O'Connell, like everyone, fully appreciated the magnificent acoustical properties of the Academy of Music. But he emphasized the special resonator designed for recordings by Stokowski, his understanding of every phase of the mechanical aspects of recording, and especially his improvisational conducting technique, so ideally suited to any recording system. Stokowski's revolutionary experiments with the placement of the various players and their instruments were paying off handsomely.

His ever-increasing fund of electronic-mechanical knowledge was, of course, the greatest bonus. Once confident in the production staff and satisfied with O'Connell's microphonic plan, he left the details entirely to them. (Such ideal circumstances were rarely available.)

"In his last several seasons with the Philadelphia Orchestra," wrote O'Connell in his book *The Other Side of the Record,* "we had become so completely *en rapport*—even to the extent that I would use an extra microphone to pick out details in the orchestra that I knew he would want to hear—that we could go through a recording session from start to finish, from *ppp* to *fff* without the necessity for the recording engineers to touch their instruments. I have never worked with any other musician who could do this."

Inevitably, Stokowski had his share of failures, but he was mostly powerless to prevent those that occurred within the recording apparatus. The industry was still plagued by surface noise, insufficient fidelity, and the constant interruption of major musical works every four minutes, the standard side-length of 78's. Sales had plummeted from 100 million in 1927 to 6 million in 1931. RCA determined to produce a long-playing record. Stokowski, of course, was put in musical charge. He chose Beethoven's Fifth, played through without interruption by using two alternating recording machines. The performance was one of his finest, but the resultant quality of sound was constricted, the records deteriorated quickly after playing because of the heavy tone-arm, and the discs required prohibitively expensive phonographic machines. He recorded other works in this process, but the experiment failed and died quickly. Although the industry had to wait almost twenty years for Peter Goldmark's invention of the more practical LP Microgroove disc for Columbia Records, Stokowski's experiment must undoubtedly be considered yet another "first."

Stokowski risked constantly, convinced that in order to realize success one must be willing to risk failure and to take chances against all the odds. The orthodox Toscanini admired this aspect of the young innovator. In 1931 when I visited the Italian maestro in New York, some of his orchestral associates were there and the conversation included a reference to Stokowski's recent and frustrating long-playing record experiment. One of the musicians, wanting to ingratiate himself with Toscanini, made some disparaging remarks about Stokowski's "fancy experimental failures." Toscanini's temper flared, and he said, "He's right! If you don't fail you don't do anything. Acoustical recordings are horsecars. They must be improved."

One of the riskiest artistic ventures Stokowski undertook was the open competition with Toscanini in 1930 when a two-week exchange had been negotiated, whereby Toscanini would conduct the Philadelphia Orchestra and Stokowski would lead the New York Philharmonic. Toscanini's daughter Wanda Horowitz, who attended Stokowski's performances, relates that after he had given a stirring reading of Borodin's "Polovtsian Dances" from *Prince Igor,* an excited music-lover seated near her jumped up shouting, "Bravo, bravo! Stokowski is great—Toscanini or not—Stokowski is a great conductor!"

His companion tugged at his sleeve and pointed, alerting him to Wanda's presence, whereupon the man clapped his hand over his mouth in embarrassment. Wanda walked over to him and said, "Don't be embarrassed, I agree with you, and so does my father."

So did most of the critics. Disagreement was to be found mainly among the members of the Philharmonic. Rarely did Stokowski have any trouble with his musicians, but during that two-week association, real trouble broke out with the orchestra that George Szell later dubbed "Murder, Incorporated. They were always out to prove the superiority of their idol, Toscanini."

Now in addition, they were all set to prove the absurd suspicion that Stokowski "could not read music." Unwittingly, he played into their hands in selecting for his first rehearsal Stravinsky's thorny *Le Sacre du Printemps.* The mere choice of such a difficult and relatively unperformed work guaranteed hostility at the outset. Hostility turned to open resentment as Stokowski jumped onto the podium without a greeting. "Four bars after *G,*" came the command, and the downbeat. Utter chaos ensued. "Take it easy, buddy," quietly suggested a viola player. "Relax, Maestro," said the irrepressible first oboist Bruno Labate. "Give us an upbeat before the downbeat."

Stokowski was miffed but said nothing. Later in the rehearsal he became furious when several woodwind players utterly refused to follow him. Stokowski imperiously banished one offending clarinetist from the rehearsal. Instead of offering an apology and a plea for forgiveness, as Stokowski expected, the player merely said, "Thanks, I haven't had a free Thursday evening in years." The orchestra guffawed, Stokowski froze, and it was uphill all the way.

"I prefer not to talk about it," Stokowski told me. "It was one of the most shocking experiences of my life." He resolved never to return, but we all know the fate of resolutions.

It is difficult for me to blame Stokowski on his approach to these instrumentalists, since my own experience with him was so positive, personally as well as musically. The most revealing aspects of his methods were made apparent to me when I played the premiere of my Second Piano Concerto with the Philadelphia Orchestra under his direction in March 1933. Then I learned that in working on a score which he had not previously conducted, he did not prepare a completely analyzed interpretation. He allowed himself to react emotionally and intuitively to the music as it went along and then attempted to bring out his personal feelings in the performance. There was no set Stokowski interpretation for any composition. The orchestra was always ready for him to mold a work not only at rehearsals but at the concert, or rather at each concert at which it was played.

Still other features of his approach to a new score were revealed during rehearsals. At the first one, as I walked to the piano I was surprised to find Stokowski's assistant, Artur Rodzinski, on the podium; Stokowski was sitting in solitary elegance in one of the gilded red-plush seats in the center of the hall. I had known that on the "first reading" of a complex score by an avant-garde composer, the orchestra was usually taken through its initial paces by Rodzinski. Evidently, my unexperimental, even romantic, score was also scheduled for a first reading—à la Schoenberg or Webern.

What I did not know until I was on stage was the existence of a complicated arrangement of green, red, yellow, and blue lights on top of the conductor's desk, which Stokowski manipulated from his seat to flash directions to Rodzinski to start, stop, play softer or louder, slower or faster. Rodzinski's observable reaction to those bewildering gleams of light was sheer desperation. Afterward, he confided his resentment of this "traffic-light system," calling it the most sadistic procedure he had ever endured.

That is how Rodzinski, the orchestra, and I rehearsed for a solid hour. At intermission, Stokowski came up to me and said, "I trust you understand that I rarely conduct the first rehearsal of a work new to me. I first listen so as to know what I want to do with it—if I want to at all. I have definite ideas about your score. I don't think you wanted everything that you put down. Do you mind if I change a few things here and there? And perhaps try out some things I think you wanted?" I said that I could only be grateful.

As the orchestra began to tune up, I returned to the piano. Then there was a sudden hush; the side curtains parted; and Stokowski, blue shirt open at the throat, flew in, sprinted to the dais, and in a high voice delivered some mumbo jumbo to the orchestra that completely passed me by. It was all run together and sounded something like this "Chasins cunsharto firs' mooment faw meshes affer letter *J*—no, make it tree." Down went the saberlike hands. I, the composer and soloist, was completely lost and had to scramble like mad to find the right place in time for my entrance, although the orchestra members came in precisely to a man.

It was not long before Stokowski called a halt. Completely immersed in the music, he called out with hardly a trace of an accent, "Second trombone, you be quiet here for eight measures. Third horn, I want you to play the first two measures and then nothing. All right. Letter *P*." The section emerged with a totally unexpected clarity, and all I could do was smile my gratitude at Stokowski's questioning face as he turned toward me. Later on, he stopped again and said, "That isn't what you mean. I think this is. Boys, you know that flutter-tongue effect? All right, let's go." There it was, just as I dreamt it, and so it continued right to the end of the work. Stokowski realized a dozen things for me that I had been unable to realize for myself. A conductor like that is not by accident called an interpreter. He actually becomes a partner of the composer. This is one of the many reasons why Rachmaninoff regarded the Philadelphia as his favorite orchestra. He once remarked, "Stokowski has created a living thing. He knows what you want, he puts it in, and he infuses vitality into every phrase."

8

THE DEPRESSION was partially responsible for Stokowski's instigation in 1933 of Philadelphia youth concerts at a seventy-five-cent top to attract audiences from age thirteen to twenty-five. The conductor and his orchestra contributed their services without pay, offering five or six Saturday afternoon concerts a season. It was a long-term educational project, unique in every respect. Stokowski had in mind not only the influential effect of music on young people but their subsequent musical influence on their parents.

It brought Philadelphia's young people to the concert hall in droves. They chose their own music, wrote their own program notes, designed their own brochures, and painted their own posters. The standard repertory was naturally featured, but Stokowski found something to say about almost every work, and each concert featured a piece that everybody could sing. The audience was invited to submit original compositions, and several piano pieces were orchestrated by Stokowski and performed. The soloists for the most part were young artists, some selected from competitions. Others were Jascha Heifetz and Kate Smith.

The members of Stokowski's audience—3,000 strong—became more than auditors: they organized themselves into a Youth League with elected delegates. They held committee meetings at "Stoki's apartment," and informal groups would gather outside his house to socialize and sometimes to sing. This was Stokowski's milieu—young people were his people. They became deeply involved with the entire orchestra and constituted a very tangible force in the city. When Stokowski was at war with his board of directors, they took up the battle cry and supported him ardently.

The town was startled when Stokowski told the youngsters in his audience to learn the words of the "Internationale," as they were going to sing it at the next youth concert. The outraged hundred-percenters dubbed Stokowski a "Red" and demanded an explanation. Stokowski said quite simply that he thought it was a good piece to sing, and sing it the youngsters did, effecting a cockeyed compromise à la Stokowski, by translating the Communist anthem into French! Uncle Sam survived.

For a self-centered artist, Stokowski had an unusual sense of social and civic responsibility. One spring morning in the dark days of the Depression, I walked through Rittenhouse Square to find him in shirt sleeves conducting two hundred unemployed musicians. His objective was not only to uplift their spirits but also to call attention to their plight and to assist their immediate needs, as their children and wives passed the hat. The strains of band repertory such as operetta potpourris, Strauss waltzes, and Sousa marches loosened the pockets of entranced passersby.

The fabulous woodwind and brass sections of his orchestra would naturally account for Stokowski's interest in bands, and during the Depression he seized the opportunity to utilize their power to uplift the spirit. But a Stokowski does not conduct a "brass band": He organized a remarkable group that he called the Band of Platinum. Characteristically, the paradoxical Stokowski had them play the symphonic literature and made them sound like a major orchestra. They toured, filled auditoriums, and got rave reviews, even one from that inexorable judge of classical music, H. L. Mencken, who reported with amazement in the *Baltimore*

Sun, "Stokowski has converted a brass band into a first-rate musical instrument." Stokowski was merely running true to form. In Philadelphia, he built a superb police band, this time the Band of Gold. Again the results were astonishing.

Eventually, Stokowski wanted to remove himself from the strenuous schedule of a specified number of annual rehearsals and concerts. The opportunity of bringing music to the largest available audience via mass media strengthened his resolution. He wanted to be at liberty to make one musical film each year, conduct several significant broadcasts, record important compositions with renowned orchestras, and guest-conduct internationally.

Stokowski believed that he could accomplish many constructive things by signing a contract with CBS for a nightly, fifteen-minute radio show commercially sponsored. He was attracted by its insistent format of five times a week and by the fact that it would be the first time that an established orchestra was commercially sponsored for a nationwide symphonic series.

The ever-increasing bickering with the orchestra board on programs and policies was becoming unbearable. Stokowski suggested a tour of the Orient with the orchestra, which the board rejected. A Russian tour was probed, but that too was rejected. He requested Bruno Walter and Wilhelm Furtwangler as guest conductors during his absences—also rejected.

During 1934, the antagonism between Stokowski and Judson was becoming progressively worse, the manager claiming that no matter what topic arose, Stokowski would take the diametrically opposite position and could not be budged. Unwilling to submit any longer, Judson announced his intention to resign within the year.

To complicate matters, the Metropolitan Opera Company, which had established a series in Philadelphia, canceled the season, having become a casualty of the Depression. On the advice of Judson and with the support of Curtis Bok, president of the board and an ardent opera devotee, the Philadelphia Orchestra stepped into the breach and did the Met one better by announcing a formidable repertory. Naturally, they invited Stokowski to conduct. He refused flatly, in retaliation against their utter indifference to his plans to form an opera company following the triumph of *Wozzeck*. An ambitious but impractically administered series of ten productions led to a financial disaster, completely dissipating the orchestra's arduously acquired surplus of $250,000.

The board had delayed in appointing a successor to Judson, which made it still more difficult for Stokowski to plan for the coming season. One reason behind the board's inactivity involved Miss Esther Everett Lape, whom Bok had brought from New York to administer his philanthropic projects. Stokowski strongly supported Bok's efforts to effect her appointment as manager. The board balked, certain that this would surely be relinquishing complete control to Stokowski and Bok. The matter was dropped.

Stokowski exploded in an eight-page letter to the board, listing all his grievances and accusing the members of "running the concerts as social affairs for the affluent." In conclusion he stated that there was but one solution: "to elect in the near future a new board," as the present directors were "too elderly and too conservative." Otherwise he would tender his resignation. Once again Stokowski was on the front pages, and the town buzzed with conjectures.

When he appeared on the platform before his usually staid Friday afternoon audience, the Main Line ladies applauded "until their bonnets shook with enthusiasm," according to one newspaper, and the orchestra rose to honor him. Stokowski interrupted the unprecedented tribute to say, "I have sent my resignation to the orchestra's board of directors because of deep underlying differences. I am hoping that some day we will find a way to continue, but it looks impossible to me now."

Once the morning papers came out, the orchestra office

was swamped with phone calls from indignant subscribers. The musical community bordered on hysteria. Mass meetings were held at hotels, and musical supporters paraded down Broad Street, demanding a reconciliation. The orchestra's committees adopted resolutions requesting Stokowski to remain and the board to be retained. Mary Bok got up at a meeting and said, "Philadelphia can't let Stokowski go."

The Youth Concert Committee sprang into action. The most emotional climax came at the last concert of the year, a week after Stokowski's dramatic announcement, when the young people jammed the Academy and unanimously voted that he remain and the board abdicate. They wrote and mimeographed a song of praise and entreaty to Stokowski to the theme of the "Pilgrims' Chorus" from Wagner's *Tannhäuser.*

In the midst of all this turmoil, Stokowski was calmly coordinating a performance of Bach's monumental B-minor Mass to be presented at his annual Christmas concert and at the inauguration ceremonies of the new campus and buildings of the Westminster Choir School in Princeton, New Jersey.

Curtis Bok arranged a board meeting, calling for its resignation, which would enable him to select a new board with "more inner understanding and awareness" of what Stokowski was trying to do. The board declined, whereupon Curtis and Mary Bok resigned. The board issued an announcement, emphasizing the need for "a thorough reorganization in the operating methods of the orchestra, and the scope of the functions and personnel of the board itself." To effect this, the board appointed a committee to meet with Stokowski in an attempt to resolve their points of contention. This committee was evidently strongly influenced by the public outcry, indicating that it was ready to acquiesce to Stokowski's every wish.

The board was reduced from twenty-four members to fifteen, merely seven of the former group remaining. Dr. Thomas Gaites of the University of Pennsylvania became the new president. Added to the board was an elected delegate from the orchestra and a representative from the youth concerts. Judson was allowed to resign.

Stokowski attended the first meeting of the new board and consented to cooperate wholeheartedly. He was pleased at the announcement that Reginald Allen had been chosen as Judson's successor. Allen, scion of a distinguished Philadelphia family, had formed a friendship with Stokowski while working as a promotion executive for Victor Records.

The crack was patched over, but the patch wore thin, and in 1936 the final break came. Stokowski submitted his resignation, to become effective in 1938. By then the board wanted him out no less than he wanted out. Philadelphia needed him and appreciated him but could no longer stand him. Part of the deal with the board was the firm commitment to realize, in 1936, his primary and perpetual dream of taking the Philadelphia on the first transcontinental tour ever made by a major symphony orchestra.

Stokowski had accomplished a brilliant stroke of strategy in first confiding the plan to Thomas Joyce, director of Victor Records' publicity activities, who seized upon the concept as a sensational promotional opportunity. Gaining Victor's financial and musical support virtually guaranteed the board's final approval for the tour.

Early in the spring a special ten-car train left Philadelphia. Aboard were one hundred twenty men and three women, embarking on a six-week tour of thirty-eight major American cities from coast to coast. It was the hope of its conductor that this tour was only the first lap of a worldwide journey "to make the best possible music and to bring it to the greatest number of people everywhere."

The itinerary demanded seven concerts a week, almost every one in a different city. In order to maintain so exhausting a schedule, Stokowski conducted only five concerts a week; the sixth was assigned to his associate conductor Saul Caston, and the seventh, to Charles O'Connell, who originally went along to produce Stokowski's records for Victor.

Stokowski was never more joyous or proud than he was throughout this tour, which from the first to the last concert was unsurpassed in conveying the mastery and inspiration of the conductor and his superlative orchestra. Yet two of those concerts stood out above the rest, according to every one of its players, and these were the two concerts performed in Hollywood. At the final rehearsal, Stokowski addressed his men: "The position that this orchestra holds in the esteem of this great country has been shown to you night after night from the Atlantic to the Pacific. We have no soloists. None is needed, for each of you is incomparable, supreme on your instrument. These concerts must be our best, for our programs are a synthesis of a monumental era of music."

True, but in featuring the favorite flowers of his repertory —Brahms's First Symphony and his own transcriptions of Bach's D-minor Toccata and Fugue and of excerpts from Wagner's *Tristan und Isolde*—Stokowski had much more in mind: to become a movie star and to make musical history in Hollywood. He did both. He had long felt that compensation for musical artists was unjust and inequitable. He thought he was entitled to rewards comparable to the stars of screen and sports. Money was always a thing with Stokowski.

In Philadelphia, Stokowski had been the luncheon guest of Josef Hofmann at the elegant Barclay Hotel, and more recently, I had invited him to dine with me in my Philadelphia apartment at the Chateau Crillon. In reciprocation he invited us both to luncheon one weekday afternoon. We gathered in the entrance hall at Curtis, and Stokowski began to walk us toward Broad Street while he launched into a severe criticism of people's eating habits. "I'm taking you," he said, "for a really nourishing luncheon." Suddenly, he steered us into an automat. Changing a bill at the cashier's window, he handed Hofmann and me ten nickels each and with a lordly gesture, said, "Get whatever you want."

Everybody stared, but Stokowski was completely oblivious —except when he carefully picked a table next to one occupied by two attractive girls with whom he exchanged wide smiles and, before luncheon was over, telephone numbers.

Joseph Sharfsin, Stokowski's lawyer and friend, told me, "Stoki had a reputation for being cheap as hell, even stingy. But I remember sending him bills and getting checks by return messenger." The ambivalent Stokowski could be stingy with pennies but generous with dollars. His tyrannical nature was sometimes matched by largesse when compassion was called for. Before the days of hospitalization insurance, one of his musicians had a long siege in the hospital. Throughout it all the man's salary never ceased, and he received round-the-clock nursing care in a private room. Only his attorney and the hospital cashier ever knew that each week it was Stokowski who, on his way to visit his ailing colleague, stopped by her office to pay the whole staggering bill.

A common Stokowski trait was his reluctance to forget or forgive. One example involves the request of a violinist to be excused from the orchestra on Yom Kippur. Stokowski refused and fired him. Years later Sylvan Levin asked Stokowski to reengage the man, who was a fine artist and a good friend. When Stokowski heard his name, he said, "I want nothing to do with this man." Sylvan knew Stokowski too well to interpret this irrational attitude as anti-Semitism, but it hurt deeply. Who knows why he wouldn't take the man back? Possibly Stokowski had a vague memory of something unpleasant between them; possibly he felt that not showing up for one rehearsal was a mark of disloyalty—but the real reason will never surface.

"This is what Stoki could do to people," said Sylvan, "but he never did it to me, so I can't fault the man, except for one thing. In his last days he burned most of the letters he had received from the great people, like Stravinsky. He didn't want any record of himself." This man of the future wanted no part of the past, not even his own.

During the last tumultuous years of Stokowski's tenure in Philadelphia (from 1934 on) he grew increasingly frustrated and restless. With few exceptions, he disliked his orchestral associates. His closest friends were dead, and his social interests virtually nil. To his worshipful public—except for the youngsters—he was unapproachable. Caesar himself at the summit could not have been a more formidable figure to his legions than Stokowski was to his audiences, hardly any member of which ventured backstage to express the appreciation and affection he craved.

Beneath his supercilious exterior, Stokowski was a very dependent and lonely man, always in need of love and assurance. Fortunately, his imperious personality incited not only opposition but also support. These are the circumstances that account for the significance Stokowski attached to his "youth league," which became a cult devoted to its charismatic leader.

Among its most ardent and active members were two girls about thirty years younger than Stokowski who were to play consequential roles in his life. Natalie Bender was an ambitious composer, whose first name Stokowski Russianized to "Natasha." Feodora Chabrowska was a student physicist, whose name Stokowski perversely de-Russianized to "Faye Chabrow." When they met Stokowski in 1928, both were about eighteen and were pupils in the dance class of Mary Binney Montgomery, a tall, lovely young Philadelphian who was a good friend of Stokowski's and a noted member of the avant-garde of society and the arts. She and her dance company appeared quite frequently with Stokowski at the Academy, at the Robin Hood Dell, and also with the Philadelphia Opera Company.

A friend said that almost from the moment that Mary

Binney introduced the two girls to Stokowski, "their entire existence consisted of working at their jobs and devoting practically every spare moment to Stokowski's needs." This was an exaggeration only until the end of Stokowski's last marriage, when the girls were able to assume more constant and comprehensive responsibilities. Of course, in connection with the youth concerts, they and Mary Binney were always the first to write and circulate petitions and protests and to organize rallies. Domestically, they were always ready to cook a meal or to perform any chores at Stokowski's apartment or theirs.

Whatever I say about Faye and Natasha is secondhand, for I do not remember ever meeting them, although we must have been together in the same place at the same time on many occasions. If so, they were never pointed out to me. I considered this extremely strange until Stokowski's second wife Evangeline told me that she had never met them either before she and Stokowski were divorced, although she knew that the girls had entered Stokowski's life fully six or seven years previously.

It was a long time before I realized that no one, not even Stokowski's most intimate associates or his wives, ever knew where he was, with whom he was, or what he was doing an hour before or after they had been with him.

Gradually it became apparent that few could get near Stokowski who were not in the good graces of his two hand-maidens. Even within the inner circle there were fears and jealousies. Time and again, people for whom Stokowski had professed deep love and loyalty said that they had written and telephoned him repeatedly but received no response whatsoever. Almost without exception, and over a span of forty years, these people have said, "Stoki could not have been so false and faithless a friend, nor could he have grown so old and forgetful. The messages never got through. The girls didn't want us around. It's as simple as that."

"Stoki had warm and enthusiastic relationships," said Joe

Sharfsin, "and sudden breakups. He clung to those who served his momentary needs. The moment they didn't, he was through. Every inactive friendship was a closed chapter."

Those of us who worked around Stokowski and Sylvan agree that their long association was filled with mutual respect and achievement. Sylvan's deepest sorrow was in the mid-forties after their prestigious collaboration at the New York City Center. In some totally unexpected and inexplicable way their relationship was severed when Sylvan found it absolutely impossible to communicate with Stokowski. He made no bones about there being but one possible explanation: the most cherished relationship of his life had been deliberately destroyed, he said, "by the girls." One is mystified why Stokowski never made the effort to inquire what had happened to Sylvan. I have, of course, no basis for judgment in this matter, as he mentioned it only recently.

Those who observed the girls when they occasionally accompanied Stokowski on his tours recollected many conflicts within the trio. Obviously there was a good deal of emotion generated in their relationship. A pragmatic explanation was forthcoming when Sophia Jacobs once asked Evangeline to explain why Stokowski, who could be so capricious, had maintained a relationship with "those unattractive girls" for so long. "Oh," said Evangeline, "there is nothing Stoki liked so much as service for free." When I challenged Sophia to explain the longevity of her close friendship, she said, "I never asked him for a thing." On the contrary, she was the soul of generosity throughout their sixty-five-year friendship. But, one might ask, what did he actually consider "a friend"? We will probably never know.

9

AT NO TIME WAS THE PUBLIC ever less interested in Stokowski the man than in Stokowski the musician. If the premise of his friendships was bewildering to them, the premise of his marriages was even more so. The liveliest rumor of 1926 was that Stokowski, then forty-four, had jilted his favorite companion (a Philadelphia debutante of nineteen) to marry Evangeline Brewster Johnson, fifteen years his junior, a handsome, widely traveled, effervescent woman of heroic stature.

Evangeline and Stokowski met at an after-concert party given by Marie Dehon, then Mrs. William Polk, in January, in that same New York home where twenty years before she had arranged for Stokowski and Olga to meet.

Evangeline had been invited to meet Stokowski on several previous occasions by a mutual friend of theirs, the inventor John Hays Hammond. Each time she declined. "You see," she told me, "I had subscribed to the Philadelphia Orchestra for years and considered Stokowski the greatest conductor in the world, but I had no interest in hearing how much he hated spinach!" She had been assured that Stokowski was not coming to Marie's party. When she got there, she found that not only had Stokowski been invited but he had been seated next to her at the supper table.

"I had just come back from Egypt," she related, "and had become intrigued by Coptic music and had been studying

152

something about it. As soon as Stokowski sat himself down, he turned to me and said, 'I hear you've been to Egypt. Would you mind telling me something about its music?' Whatever I said seemed to interest him. Then we got onto yoga—in which both of us were intensely interested—and then to philosophy, art, and food. Three weeks from that night we were married."

Shortly after, they spent one entire day exchanging their "inner ideals" and then drew up statements of their credos. Stokowski wrote:

To REACH up to EVER hipher plANES
of physical AND INNER life

———

To Gε —
FRANK, simple, clEAN (especially
inside)

———

To WORSHIP —
BEAUTY, STRENGTH, LOVE,
NATURE, SUN, MOON.
FIRE, WATER, AIR

Evangeline responded:

To find ever more direct avenues to God.
To give back to the World.
To have Compassion.
To be aware of the Value of Time.

Evangeline

Evangeline's father was a chemist who established the widely known pharmaceutical company of Johnson and Johnson. When Evangeline announced to her conservative family that she was going to marry Leopold Stokowski, her brother demanded, "Who's he?"

"He's a conductor," Evangeline replied.

Drawing himself up, her brother said, "In this family, one doesn't marry conductors."

"Darling," said Evangeline, "not a streetcar conductor!"

In Philadelphia, there was no great love lost between Evangeline and the ladies of the Main Line. They were stiff and uppish; she was liberated and humorous, talked with a booming voice, and was considered eccentric. The ladies of Philadelphia had evidently read the considerable publicity that constantly attended her. One of the first women to fly a plane, she committed the outrageous sin of shunning a skirt in favor of pants. In 1914, it made her so angry to have to wear stockings when she went swimming in Palm Beach that she printed incendiary leaflets condemning the stupid custom and dropped them from her plane all over the beaches.

During the war, being too young for foreign duty, she served as a New York Red Cross ambulance driver and plunged headfirst into political and sociological causes. As a friend of President and Mrs. Woodrow Wilson, she became an ardent worker for the League of Nations. Although the intimate of presidents and kings, she refused to be "a society figure." Always, she was a fiercely independent thinker, a born rebel, and an instinctively militant protagonist of women's rights—a one-woman liberation movement.

Olga and Evangeline, who became good friends, during the latter's marriage to the Maestro, were as different as any two women imaginable, an indication of the enormous range of Stokowski's needs and demands when it came to selecting a mate. Olga, the professional musician, was willing to give up a successful career to be the power behind the throne. Evangeline was not a professional, but she was dedicated to her own activities. She maintained her identity staunchly, and this contributed to the gap between her and the Philadelphia ladies. (Evangeline was unaware of their feelings toward her and consequently did nothing to change them.)

Stokowski admired this maverick streak in her (it was certainly convenient that she was often busy traveling when he wished to pursue other romantic interests), and their marriage became an interesting and quite avant-garde relationship. Of course, it helped that money was no object. They had an arrangement throughout the marriage whereby each of them put $10,000 annually into the kitty for basic expenses. Evangeline assumed everything over that. She was a magnificent manager and organized their several homes, children, secretaries, and servants with virtuosity. And she handled her own private life as well as their life together. She told Stokowski when they married that because of her many responsibilities and obligations in New York, she would have to spend at least half her time away from Philadelphia. "That's great!" said her husband. "The trouble with most marriages is that people are together too much."

They had two daughters: Gloria Lyuba in 1927 and Andrea Sadja in 1930, both of whom are known by their middle names. The birth of Lyuba showed Stokowski once again to be decades ahead of his time. Today it is not uncommon for a husband to attend the birth of his child, but fifty years ago it was virtually unheard of. Evangeline told me that whenever she had a labor pain, Stokowski would lay hands on her and the pain would lessen. First, he would breathe deeply and his face would reflect intense concentration. "Perhaps it was his yoga training," she said, "but it was a sort of miracle." Shortly before Lyuba was due, Stokowski asked Evangeline whether his presence at the birth would help her. "If you'll be there," she told him, "I'll take the absolute minimum of any drug offered me." He was present every minute, and she had a very easy birth without anesthetics.

Prior to the birth, he kept his Friday afternoon ladies up to date on his domestic drama, alerting them to the possibility of his being called to the Lenox Hill Hospital in New York. The Friday after the blessed event, he regaled them with a blow-by-blow account, not omitting one graphic detail. They never stopped buzzing over that one.

When the children were little, the Stokowskis spent some of their summers in New Milford, Connecticut, and some in Santa Barbara, California, where they had built a simple but roomy house almost with their bare hands. "Stoki was neither a disciplinarian with the children," Evangeline explained, "nor too permissive. He trusted me to supervise their development. I gave them much freedom, encouraged them in drawing and painting, sculpture, horseback riding. To a great degree they really devised their own lives. Their father was away much of the time and when he did have some hours, he adapted to them and tried to reach their level by playing physical games. I sometimes felt that he got the children so excited with their antics that it was difficult to quiet them down. That's my only criticism!"

When I said to her, "Obviously, he was not the usual father," she replied that he never wanted to be. "His job was the orchestra," she said. "He thought that I was doing a good job with the children." Indeed she did. Both are accomplished women leading interesting lives with husbands and children. Brown-eyed and auburn-haired, Lyuba's primary interests are painting and literature. Sadja, towheaded and blue-eyed in her father's image, is a physician specializing in family planning. Evangeline also became a second mother to Sonya, Olga's daughter, who spent at least half of each year with the family in a close and devoted relationship. Blue-eyed, with whitish blond hair, she became an accomplished actress, married William Thorbecke, and became the mother of four children.

Stokowski took an almost year-long leave of absence in 1927–28 and he and Evangeline saw India and Bali together, where Stokowski was fascinated with the exotic sonorities and complex rhythms of their exquisite music.

His next trip two years later "to study the art and wisdom of the Far East" was astutely timed to avoid competition with Toscanini's extraordinary ascendancy in New York. When Stokowski returned, it was to a fervently grateful Philadelphia, as well as New York, which had greatly missed his particular magic. Bathed in a new international aura, he was inundated by offers of all sorts, including the exciting prospect of conducting several theatrical premieres for the League of Composers. As these offers were being implemented, however, the Stokowski name was splashed across the newspapers for other than musical reasons.

A threat to kidnap the Stokowski children horrified the nation. Evangeline had received menacing telephone calls saying that unless a specific sum of money was dropped at a specific place and time, the girls would be abducted and held for ransom. Stokowski, naturally, was out of town conducting when the harassment began, but Evangeline handled the situation with her usual self-possession. The police provided alarms and protection in New York and Connecticut. Armed guards accompanied the children everywhere. Finally and fortunately the threats ceased. The would-be kidnappers were never found. For years thereafter Stokowski carried or kept within easy reach two 45-caliber Colt revolvers.

Evangeline influenced Stokowski's life tremendously. Her wide interests, wealth, and organizational ability reinforced his professional independence, freedom of action, and the opportunity to travel when and where he wished, for pleasure or for professional purposes. Her companionship made traveling rewarding and exciting, and there were few corners of the world that they did not get to know in the most advantageous way. They lived in high style, met the crème de la crème everywhere, and were lavishly feted.

In 1929, leaving Lyuba in the charge of friends, they took off for Europe. Before leaving, they had accepted membership in an American-Soviet Intellectual Cooperation Committee. On their first evening in Moscow, they were invited to hear Mussorgsky's *Boris Godunov*. Stokowski noted that several parts of the opera had been altered to include Soviet propaganda.

Invited to an after-opera reception backstage, Stokowski was asked to speak. He got up, his face scarlet with anger, jumped on a table, and in German denounced the production. "Don't you realize that you are committing a crime against art?" he stormed. "Musical art is the reason for your being here tonight. How dare you pervert this occasion and performance by introducing a political issue into a great work of art? You should be ashamed of yourselves!"

A translator repeated the speech in Russian. Evangeline, who had visions of their being shipped off to Siberia on the next train, was relieved to observe that a few members of the company, especially the elderly artists, were nodding vehemently as tears streamed down their cheeks. The majority, however, looked bitterly hostile and shook their fists at Stokowski. Tugging at Stokowski's coattails, Evangeline said, "Let's get out of here!" They left without another word. Later in the trip, however, they felt warmly welcomed and safely on artistic ground when they met Shostakovich, Prokofiev, and other Soviet musicians.

In France they met Ravel; in Finland, Sibelius; in England, Vaughan Williams. And from each composer, Stokowski extracted the promise of a premiere.

The Stokowskis visited Vienna in 1931, and so did I, though we did not meet. I had the privilege of attending a luncheon with Sigmund Freud at the Austrian Club. It was suggested that Dr. Freud might be interested in hearing about some of the eminent faculty members of the Curtis Institute. I mentioned some names I was sure he would know, but Freud's face remained immobile until I mentioned Stokowski, when, with a quizzical expression, he said, "Tell me about *him*."

"The musician is fascinating," I answered, "but the man is perplexing. He's really two men."

"Only two?" he asked in a surprised voice. "That's very fortunate for a man with such an eruptive temperament."

I told Freud a little about Stokowski's fascination for and with women, explaining his candid "arrangements" with his wives and their mutual understanding.

Freud thought a while and then said, "Your country is so surprised at your 30 percent divorce rate. Living together in marriage is often very difficult, and the surprise should be that so many people endure quiet desperation, even acute misery. It is remarkable how many thwarted egos tolerate tension and frustration without exploding in some form of appropriate reaction. What I have called the human *id* cannot tolerate tension for long; it requires release and relief. This part of us is selfish, very demanding, and quite irrational. Fortunately it has the power of fulfilling its desires by imagination and fantasy. The id is the spoilt child of the personality. It doesn't think; it only acts and reacts. The admirable thing is that so many people who feel repressed by others are able to control their feelings. The Stokowskis seem to be mature people."

One cannot know whether Freud was simply being polite, but we must acknowledge that in fact the Stokowskis coped with whatever difficulties they may have experienced in their marriage.

After the children arrived, Evangeline, like all Stokowski's wives, became a mother figure to him—the symbol of purity to whom he could no longer be a lover. Extramarital relations were not only understood but, as Stokowski had put it, "were the strength of our relationship." The marriage became "an arrangement" and a most advantageous one. Though Evangeline was not his bed companion, she was his wife in every other way. She supplied financial stability, sound advice, intellectual stimulus, and contacts. She chose his clothes and kept after him to replace them when they wore out. She administered their domestic obligations in New York, Palm Beach, New Milford, Santa Barbara, and Saint Martin. She had nothing to do with Stokowski's Philadelphia studio apartment or his later-acquired California house, which she rarely visited. Part of her skill was the ability to delegate authority to assistants in every department of their lives, and part was to deal calmly with Stokowski's eccentricities.

In the early thirties, several film studios began tempting Stokowski with highly seductive offers. He was more than interested, particularly because of his increasing dissatisfaction with conditions in Philadelphia. His Hollywood career started in 1936. Stokowski's first two films were hugely successful: *The Big Broadcast of 1937,* with a cast including Jack Benny, George Burns, Benny Goodman, and Ray Milland; and *One Hundred Men and a Girl,* with Deanna Durbin. The insatiable showman loved the public adoration he received as a movie idol, and as he settled into the California life-style, he craved more exposure, more money, and more "action." He even purchased property and built a small house in Beverly Hills. As a sun-worshipper, nudist, and fruit and vegetable enthusiast, Stokowski was attracted to the physical characteristics of southern California.

He found a soul mate in Greta Garbo. When he met the solitary Swede, her classic beauty was already internationally famous. She was easily the most glamorous screen star in the world. Although their romance did not ignite instantaneously, the press pounced upon their association, every stage of which provided juicy gossip for well over two years. When they sunbathed or exercised, they were spied on; when they sampled restaurants, they were mobbed by fans. Despite their struggle for an essentially secluded existence by avoiding virtually all public events and large parties, they continued to make headlines. One tasty morsel concerned Stokowski painting his front steps blue and gold—Sweden's colors.

The next year, they took off whenever possible for trips abroad, but the Europeans, Middle Easterners, and Orientals gaped and stared no less than the Americans. They spent much time in Italy, where journalists failed to make them talk. The most Garbo ever said was, "My friend [Stokowski], who has seen much and knows about the beauty of life, offered to take me and show me these things." Stokowski said, "I never discuss my personal affairs."

Once, when reporters followed Stokowski in his automobile through the hills, he stopped, wagged a long index finger at them, and said, "I know, I understand. You have your work to do." Thereafter, Il Duce obligingly forbade the Fascist press to invade their privacy.

Everywhere, the famous pair made absurd efforts to disguise themselves, with wigs, hats, and makeup, which merely made them all the more conspicuous. Whenever they ventured out, they were trailed by gangs of derisive kids.

In Rome, Stokowski enlisted the cooperation of Massimo Freccia, the Florentine-born conductor. Freccia was guest-conducting in Rome, lodged at the Hotel de Russie, when Stokowski telephoned from London, saying he could not get proper accommodations in Rome and would appreciate assistance in getting a hotel suite. "The city was jam-packed," said Freccia, "and at that time Stokowski was not well known in Italy. I managed to get him a room, no suite. When he arrived, he immediately told me that the next day he was expecting 'a charming lady-friend from Munich, a Miss Gustafson,' assuring me that I would adore her." As no further accommodations were available, Freccia offered his suite in exchange for Stokowski's single room.

The evening before "Miss Gustafson" arrived, Freccia invited Stokowski to dinner. Suddenly, Stokowski turned to him and asked, "Do you have the score of *Die Walküre* with you?"

"Of course not, but I'm sure I can get it for you tomorrow, after my rehearsal."

"To late," said Stokowski, "I need it now."

They finished the meal hastily, and Freccia got busy on the telephone. Naturally, every library was closed, but finally he reached an operatic coach who had the score. Could he possibly bring it over? "When my guests leave," he said.

"At the unconscionable hour of midnight," Freccia related, "my obliging and perspiring friend arrived, dragging three heavy volumes. Stoki nodded his thanks and started thumbing through each volume, occasionally stopping for no more than a moment. Then, snapping the third volume closed, he said, 'Just as I thought—it *is* B-flat. Well, it's two-thirty. I must sleep. Good night. Thank you.' My friend was stunned at being so summarily dismissed. This was behavior he couldn't understand. Nor I, frankly. But he had met a giant, he could not deny that.

"The next afternoon, Stokowski walked in with 'Miss Gustafson.' They made quite a contrast. He was dressed gaudily in a light blue suit, yellow gloves, and pink socks. She wore dark glassses, a trench coat, and a slouch hat. I didn't recognize Greta Garbo until we had been together several hours. Even then I didn't reveal that I knew who she was until the news services tracked her down the next day and let the cat out of the bag. On her first afternoon, I'll never forget her walking over to her one suitcase and opening it. Instead of a black lace negligee, or something equally exotic, out came two bunches of carrots—yellow and red—on which she proceeded to munch."

They did not know Rome or speak Italian and wanted to see and do everything possible in a few days. So Freccia drafted friends "who were delighted to disrupt their schedules for the good cause," he said.

"When they left for the tranquillity of picturesque Ravello, which I had suggested, I and my friends who assisted them were frankly relieved. Though they were gracious and always full of apologies for 'imposing,' their presence was demanding."

Ensconced in a rocky retreat at the Villa Cimbrone, the couple were assigned armed carabinieri and police dogs as personal guards to keep the curious throngs at bay. Charming tidbits were fed to the fascinated public by observant and eavesdropping gardeners and servants. Each morning they were seen performing Swedish setting-up exercises in the garden, while Garbo was heard saying,. "Vun, two, vun, two —Mees-terr Sto-kovf-ski, vy can't you keep time? Vun, two." A waiter at a nearby restaurant who served them their luncheon of carrots, beets, and lettuce said, "He certainly must love her to eat that stuff. Before she came, he used to eat plenty of meat and spaghetti."

Stories of their liaison spread to New York. A record salesman told me that the public suddenly had a new regard for the Maestro. One day a Southern belle came into his shop. "Ah'm havin' dinnah tonight with some music-lovin' friends," she said, "and ah'd appreciate a little help, 'cause ah don't know a thing about classical music."

"How about Beethoven's Fifth Symphony?" suggested the

salesman. "There are versions by Toscanini, Koussevitzky, Stokowski, and others. Which do you want?"

"Ah don't know any of those gentlemen," she said.

"Oh, but surely you must know of Stokowski!" he insisted. "Didn't you read that he and Greta Garbo are in Italy together?"

"Is that so!" the woman exclaimed. "He *must* be good. Ah'll take him."

In the fall of 1937 rumors of their impending marriage circulated even before Evangeline got her divorce in Las Vegas, Nevada, on the standard grounds of "extreme cruelty." Besieged by the *paparazzi,* Stokowski telephoned his attorney, Joe Sharfsin from a phone booth in Italy. "What *ees* going on? What *ees* happening?" he pleaded.

"I'll tell you what's going on," Joe said. "The Philadelphia Orchestra board is about to fire you, and the Hollywood studio is about to fire your lady friend."

"How can I get rid of these photographers and the people that surround this hotel and keep us prisoners?"

"Come home," Joe said, "and come alone. I'll meet you at the dock. Just let me know what boat you take."

"I met him at the boat," Joe said, "along with a hundred reporters, whom I had told that he would only answer questions relating to his musical activities. When we got back to Philly, everything indicated clearly that the City of Brotherly Love didn't have any to spare for Stoki. Stoki's authority, power, and popularity were on the skids simultaneously."

When Garbo returned, rumors of their marriage had not abated and were fed by Stokowski's presence when she again set sail aboard the Gripsholm for her home in Sweden and he was in New York to bid her bon voyage. Again reporters plagued them with The Question. She said, "We are very good friends, but marriage to him would not be possible."

Stokowski's intimates have said that Garbo was the only woman he ever loved. Apart from the world's susceptibility to romance, it is undeniable that Garbo was the only woman he ever actually pursued across hills and dales and oceans. It is also apparent that Stokowski's home life with his wives eventually provided something less than domestic bliss. Despite his marital status, Stokowski was a sex symbol of the twenties and thirties. The sophisticated women who knew him, however, say that he could not wholly satisfy himself or anyone else sexually. He had that terrible inferiority that was the root of an inner struggle he would never win but would never stop waging.

The private life of public idols is hardly ever private, even or especially when they are the exotic Garbo and the dashing Stokowski. But social decorum was no small matter in those days. It still loomed large and took its toll on Stokowski's marriage. When I asked Evangeline about it, she said, "I was not upset in the usual way. Perhaps something is wrong with me, but I have never felt jealousy. You don't own yourself completely, so how can you possibly own another person? You can't. Both Stoki and I believed that true love expresses itself through one's concern for the other's happiness, not one's own. That's how individual love merges with universal love. That was always our understanding.

"Stoki's greatest love was always music. It was my conviction that if a conductor wants to endow Wagner's *Tristan und Isolde,* for example, with its true passion, he should be in the throes of the excitement of a new love affair."

Evangeline smiled. "I remember that early in our marriage, Stoki was conducting it in Philadelphia, and someone brought a note from him to my box. It read: 'All this music is for you—and so is all the music in my heart.' I wish I had kept that paper," she said pensively. "Although we both led our independent lives, I realized that Stoki's life in Beverly Hills was rejuvenating him and changing his whole life. After the children and I returned to New York and resumed our normal routine, Lyuba, who was then nine, said, 'Mother, tell me about Greta Garbo.' I asked if she'd been reading the gossip columns. 'No,' she said, 'my classmates say that Daddy is having a love affair with her. What are you going to do?' I answered that I was thinking about it, but how can you want anyone who doesn't want you?"

When Evangeline next saw Stokowski a few months later in New York, she told him, "If you can't be more of a father to your children and more of a husband to me, I want a divorce."

"You can't mean that," he said. "You agreed that my romances were good for my music. I won't consent to a divorce. We have the perfect marriage. You have your complete freedom, and so have I."

"Yes," she said, "but going on your own and with all this notoriety, the children are involved. Our paths are separating, moving in different directions."

Evangeline related, "I then told him that regardless of the law, I didn't want a thing from him. Moreover, I said that the children were coming into adolescence and that they needed at least a few years of a normal home life. They had already begun to say that when they grew up, they would never get married, and were crying a great deal. I felt that it would be best to terminate our marriage."

The inevitable divorce was effected, yet Evangeline and Stokowski remained on good terms and enjoyed an amicable relationship the rest of his long life. In fact, she always spoke so well of him that once one of the girls teased her, saying, "If you think he's such a wonderful person, why did you divorce him?"

Through the years his daughters saw him anytime he or they wanted. He came to visit their homes overnight or for a week at a time in New York, New Milford, and Palm Beach, and he occasionally visited Lyuba's home in Geneva, Switzerland.

Everything considered, his relationship to Evangeline appears to have been the most constructive and durable influence of his entire life.

10

WHILE THE DEPRESSION was rocking most of the country, Stokowski was being warmed by the California sun and by the atmosphere of plenty created by the public enthusiasm for "talkies," which carried the film industry right through the thirties.

Directly after the triumphant appearance of the Philadelphia Orchestra in Los Angeles, Stokowski, attended by his Mexican houseman, José, had a small one-story red-stucco house in the Pueblo style built for him high above the lights of Hollywood, and it served as his West Coast headquarters for a decade. Surrounded by a tiny yard filled with cacti and succulents, the house had no pool, no garden, and no neighbors. A garage housed a Rolls-Royce and an Oldsmobile, which he hardly ever drove.

Here Stokowski's professional life took on a new, but totally predictable, direction. His sensational performances had served to remind filmdom that he had long been one of the musical gods of America. But now he wanted, and felt he deserved, a greater kind of public acclamation, and he knew exactly how to go about achieving it. Always assuming a photogenic gesture or posture, on or off stage, Stokowski kept himself in the headlines. Long before his eventual departure from Philadelphia was a certainty, he had received a few lucrative film offers. Now they began to pour in from every leading studio and ranged from writing musical scores and scripts to straight acting roles. He even contemplated a film based on the life of J. S. Bach, in which he would not only arrange and perform the music but also play the title role. Hollywood also beckoned him to play Richard Wagner. Fortunately, these ideas and several others equally unsettling never materialized. Stokowski's first film, *The Big Broadcast of 1937,* presented him briefly as the Philadelphia Orchestra's conductor in his transcription of Bach's *Eine feste Burg* chorale prelude and the Little Fugue in G-minor. The next film, *One Hundred Men and a Girl,* was musically more representative, including performances of Wagner's Prelude to Act 3 of *Lohengrin,* Berlioz's *Hungarian March,* Liszt's *Hungarian Rhapsody no. 2,* and the finale of Tchaikovsky's Fifth Symphony.

When called upon to act, Stokowski emerged as an awkward and insufferably pretentious character. Nevertheless, *One Hundred Men* became a box-office smash and rescued Universal Pictures from bankruptcy. Although Stokowski conducted a specially assembled orchestra in this film, audiences assumed it was the Philadelphia and consequently the sales of his Philadelphia Orchestra discs skyrocketed.

About this time, Walt Disney, after a hard day's work on his first full-length animated feature, *Snow White and the Seven Dwarfs,* was dining alone at Chasen's Beverly Hills restaurant and saw Stokowski at a nearby table dining in equally solitary splendor. "Why don't we sit together?" he called out, extending a welcoming hand. Stokowski smiled his assent and moved over.

"I've been hoping for years," Stokowski said, as he sat down, "for you to do a full-length animated musical picture in which the dramatic and dynamic range of great music would be coordinated with the unlimited freedom of your cartoon imagery. What a magical *fanta-zee-ah* that could be!"

"If you'll conduct it, we'll do it," said Disney.

They talked for three hours after Disney confided that he was negotiating for the rights to make an animated short around the story and music of Dukas's *The Sorcerer's Apprentice*. Stokowski assured Disney that he was enchanted with the idea, but he tactfully refrained from mentioning his own far more ambitious hopes for an extensive production on which he could lavish the utmost resources of his orchestral forces around a pictorial spectacle, all reproduced with the most advanced technological facilities.

Stokowski and Disney took to each other immediately. Both had limited academic educations and fertile genius; both were loners who craved the spotlight and had the identical mission of bringing pleasure to millions; both had ardent interest in technical innovation; both personified the American dream of realizing fabulous careers from humble beginnings; and both were eager popularizers with enormous skill and the ability to reach those who knew little or nothing about art.

Destiny had contrived their meeting at that fortuitous point when every movie house of every country had converted to sound. However, sound systems were still primitive and the talkies had yet to produce a film that had the artistic power and beauty of the greatest silent pictures. Now, Stokowski told Disney, the science of reproducing sound coordinated with film images, using first-class music, fine stories, and choreography, could produce an entirely new art.

In a flash, Disney became excited and inspired by the potentialities of Stokowski's concept. Suddenly he realized that in this new field, sound would dictate every other element of a picture and that the microphone would match the camera in importance. Stokowski made Disney aware that of all famous conductors, he alone had taken the time and trouble to make a thorough study of audio reproduction and projection.

Stokowski was alone among musicians in being capable of explaining musical matters to film producers and to the bankers who dictated their policies. What Stokowski had in mind would require vast sums, and only he could pry loose the huge amounts of money, time, thought, and labor needed to realize the project that would eventuate from his casual meeting with Disney that evening. They agreed to meet again as soon as possible. Meanwhile, Stokowski headed east to rejoin his orchestra and Disney dug in to complete *Snow White.*

Their intentions and attitudes are revealed in two letters. Disney wrote to his New York representative on October 26, 1937: "I am all steamed up over the idea . . . and believe that the union of Stokowski and his music, together with the best of our medium, would be the means of a great success and should lead to a new style of motion picture representation." Stokowski wrote to Disney on November 2: "I am thrilled at the idea of recording *The Sorcerer's Apprentice* with you, because you have no more enthusiastic admirer in the world than I am." In this letter, he added his agreement to make some preliminary recordings to give an idea of his tempi and a warning that these recordings would not be "so brilliant or colorful as those we can make on film by the new method I am developing." Stokowski as usual was doing his homework well in advance.

The transition of *The Sorcerer's Apprentice* from a Mickey Mouse cartoon based on Dukas's nine-minute tone-poem into *Fantasia,* the superlatively animated large-scale film in which great music was performed, recorded, and reproduced with unique brilliance and fidelity, merits more pages than we have here.

Put as briefly as possible, the unprecedented success of *Snow White* when it was released late in 1937 altered the philosophy and policies at the Disney studios, caused the demolition of the Silly Symphony cartoons, and cleared the way for the historically significant collaboration between Stokowski and Disney.

There was never a question as to the suitability of Disney's

Stokowski at age sixteen in 1898

Stokowski with bride Olga Samaroff on their honeymoon in 1911. *Courtesy Solveig Lunde Madsen.*

Photograph of "Stokovski" from *The Musical Courier*, 1911

Leopold Stokowski (in long ringlets) and Josef Hofmann at Mary Bok's birthday party in Camden, Maine. The theme of the party was "Mary Had a Little Lamb." *Courtesy of the International Piano Archives, University of Maryland.*

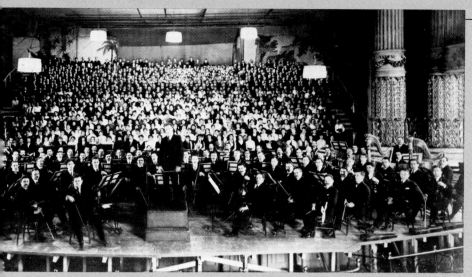

Mahler's *Symphony of a Thousand*, Stokowski and the Philadelphia Orchestra at the Academy of Music, March 2, 1916. *Courtesy Leland Lowther.*

Stokowski in 1926 when the author met him

Evangeline Stokowski with daughter Lyuba and Olga's daughter, Sonya, in 1927. *Courtesy Mrs. Evangeline Merrill.*

Evangeline with daughters Sadja and Lyuba in New York, 1933. *Courtesy Mrs. Evangeline Merrill.*

The Beverly Hills home Stokowski had built for him in 1937. *Courtesy Marguerite C. Friedeberg.*

Stokowski with Lyuba and Sonya in 1927

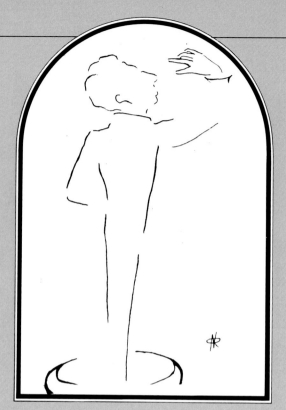

A caricature of Stokowski by Olga Naumoff Koussevitzky.

From "The Big Broadcast of 1937." *Courtesy Paramount Pictures.*

From *100 Men and a Girl*. Photograph by Ray Jones, Universal Pictures. Courtesy of Adrienne Fontana.

Benny Goodman with Stokowski. A publicity shot taken during the filming of "The Big Broadcast of 1937," in which they both performed. *Courtesy Paramount Pictures.*

Stokowski consults with Disney animator John Lounsbery during the production of *Fantasia*, 1940. © *Walt Disney Productions.*

Stokowski and Walt Disney consult on sketches, 1940. © *Walt Disney Productions.*

During the filming of *Fantasia* at the Disney studio, May 1940.
© *Walt Disney Productions.*

Mickey Mouse shakes hands with Stokowski. © *Walt Disney Productions.*

Stokowski at a New Year's Eve party given by Basil Rathbone in Beverly Hills. *Courtesy Mrs. Bernadine Szold Fritz.*

BELOW: Stokowski and his orchestra celebrate the mayor's birthday in Atlantic City, 1940. *Photograph by Lou Shumsky. Courtesy Elizabeth Waldo.*

The rehearsal in Atlantic City, 1940, for the first tour of the All-American Youth Orchestra. *Photograph by Fred Hess & Son.*

On his return from the first AAYO tour. Left to right: Elizabeth Waldo; Franklin D. Roosevelt, Jr.; Eleanor Roosevelt; Stokowski. *Courtesy Elizabeth Waldo.*

In rehearsal with Ralph Hollander and the American Symphony Orchestra. The Maestro signed this photograph. *Photograph by Dr. Jack Fein.*

With members of the ASO ball team. *Photograph by Hans Weissenstein, Whitestone Photo. Courtesy Stewart Warkow.*

Stokowski and Glenn Gould at the recording of Beethoven's Piano Concerto no. 5. *Courtesy CBS Records.*

Stokowski and Gloria with sons, Chris and Stan, 1952. *Photograph by Philip A. Hitchfield. Courtesy Dr. M. L. Berliner.*

The Maestro ca. 1970. *Photograph by Dr. Jack Fein.*

The Maestro ca. 1970.
Photograph by Bert Corman.

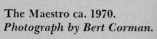

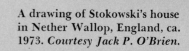

A drawing of Stokowski's house in Nether Wallop, England, ca. 1973. *Courtesy Jack P. O'Brien.*

ABOVE: At a recording session in London. Left to right: Paul Myers, Stokowski, Roy Emerson, Sidney Sax. *Photograph by Clive Barda.*

BELOW: Stokowski's ninetieth birthday party at the Hotel Plaza, New York City, April 18, 1972. Right to left: Seth and Jason Goldsmith (Sadja's sons); the birthday boy; Laila Dexitre (Lyuba's daughter); Lyuba; Richard Rhodes; Sonya. *Photograph by The New York Times.*

Recording in London.
Photographs by Clive Barda.

The headstone in Marylebone cemetery
reads: 18 April 1882–13 September 1977.
"Music is the Voice of the All."

original choice. The venerable fable of the sorcerer's apprentice had a rich literary history dating back to a second-century legend by the Roman Lucian, and it was no less than Goethe's poetic version of the tale that provided composer Paul Dukas the inspiration for his brilliant score. The original piece is short, but Stokowski had suggested the possibility of writing an overture on its themes and of expanding it through various other compositional devices.

Continuity was prepared, visualizations were submitted by the studio's most imaginative animators, and by mid-November 1937, Disney wrote Stokowski, "Honestly, I have never been more enthused over anything in my life . . . we are anxiously awaiting your arrival."

Stokowski's response contained a surprise: "May I make a suggestion which perhaps is impractical? . . . What would you think of creating an entirely new personality for this film instead of Mickey? A personality which could represent *you and me*."

Disney showed what he thought by totally ignoring the suggestion. Stokowski finally arrived in Hollywood early in January 1938, lugging the annotated scores and orchestral parts of a sizeable portion of his repertory. The Maestro had plans of his own. For the first seven days, he was shown a visual continuity on film synchronized with a rough test track of the music. At this point he asked to hear and see everything else, from the story continuity to the animations. Finally, possible alterations, cuts, and extensions of the music were discussed throughout a grueling week at meetings that sometimes went around the clock.

The recording sessions were scheduled to start the next week at the Selznick studios, where there was enough room for a large orchestra of the top musicians of Hollywood. They were selected by Philip Kahgan, a principal violist of the Los Angeles Symphony who was also personnel manager for Paramount Pictures and who had worked closely with Stokowski on the Durbin picture. At Selznick's, together with

William Garity, technical head of Disney, and with Edward
Plumb and Leigh Harline, musical heads, they spent all day
Saturday and Sunday making tests, checking balances, and
planning orchestral seating. The first actual recording began
on Sunday at midnight, running into the early hours of the
next day.

Each section of the orchestra, divided into seven choirs,
was enclosed in a three-sided partition, one each for the
violins, violas, cellos, basses, and so on. The open sides faced
Stokowski, who was to conduct the "cartoon frames" that
composed the Disney films. He was assisted by earphones
that beat a quiet tempo to fit each motion on the screen.

This click-track, as it is called, enables the musical score to
be tailored to fit the motions of the eventually completed
films. The unvarying rigidity of the click-track upset Stokowski frightfully, since his own conducting marked a flexible rhythm, which naturally conflicted with the mechanical
beat. The partitions, which did not enable the musicians to
hear each other, diminished their impeccable standards. After a few attempts to reconcile and adjust himself to the
unbearable situation, Stokowski irritably tore off the earphones saying, "I can't use these things to follow the screen
motions. I can work better without them." The department
heads assured him that everything sounded fine in the recording booth, but to no avail. The engineers were desperate. After Stokowski left, one of the orchestra musicians
picked up the click-tracks and rerecorded the whole score.
Garity stayed up all night cutting the recorded tracks, reporting that he was extremely disappointed in the overall results
of the session and upset about "the poor ensemble" and a
disagreeable mechanical noise emanating from the string
sections! Later, Stokowski returned to rerecord the piece.

A Disney staff member was not overly impressed with Stokowski's perfectionism. In a letter to the Disney business
manager, Walt's brother Roy, he wrote, "Though Stokowski
considers our recording satisfactory, Bill Garity and Leigh
Harline and many others are not satisfied with it."

The costs of the production mounted astronomically. Despite every effort to hold down the overhead, Ben Sharpstein, the production supervisor, recalled, "When it was finished we realized that we would never get our money back on it. . . . But Walt, always alert to opportunities, came up with an idea. We had to merchandise the film so it would make money. Quality came first, and box-office would follow quality. This was the birth of a new concept."

An extravaganza with appropriately great music was the plan, stimulated by Stokowski. Now, he emphasized that whereas the element of repetition is strong in music and welcome to the ears, it is both boring and tiring to the eyes. Consequently, he cautioned the animators and cameramen to avoid using the same shots and angles when the music is recapitulated. They followed his advice (to good advantage) and won great praise.

Stokowski's recording successes through numerous experiments gave him the confidence to try anything, when possible. At Disney's, he often wanted to handle the controls, mixing, balancing, adjusting, and coordinating sounds. He could only be kept from fiddling with the dials and blasting the ears off the sound track by being told by Disney that the union forbade his touching them.

His incredible ability to sail through everything was most effectively demonstrated at the story conference of November 8, 1938, when the Bach-Stokowski Toccata and Fugue in D-minor was being discussed. This was the first composition to be heard in what a sorcerer named Stokowski had somehow transformed from a Mickey Mouse cartoon into a huge "Concert Feature" named *Fantasia*. The project would also include excerpts from Tchaikovsky's *Nutcracker* Suite, Stravinsky's *Le Sacre du Printemps* (excerpts), Beethoven's *Pastoral* Symphony (abridged), Ponchielli's *Dance of the Hours,* Dukas's *The Sorcerer's Apprentice,* Moussorgsky's *Night on Bald Mountain,* and Schubert's "Ave Maria," with soprano Juliet Novis and chorus. Also scheduled was Debussy's "Claire de Lune," which was later discarded.

The transcript of that meeting surprised me greatly. I found it shocking that Stokowski, Disney, and a staff of other famed experts in their specialties talked on a level that could only be called elementary and full of oversimplification.

When Disney asks, "What does the Toccata and Fugue represent?" Stokowski answers, "It is a motif or decorative pattern which gradually develops more and more. Finally, it becomes perfectly free. The theme, which comes at the beginning, develops more and more, with more and more voices and instruments. It is a growth like a tree growing from a seed." Disney then suggests, "We might use Stokowski's face . . . let the lighting effect and color change as the music changes. I feel that there is a theme in the background in the music, there, with something into the foreground and covering it up." Whereupon Stokowski says, "That is counterpoint." This inane talk went on and on.

I was totally puzzled until the real nature of this conference was made clear to me by David Raksin, one of filmdom's finest composers and a professor of music at the University of Southern California. "Perhaps you don't realize that with one or two exceptions, Stoki was talking to men who knew nothing about music. Walt was scared to death by the very name of Bach, so that Stoki was in the double role of teacher and salesman. He was not talking to musicians—he had to explain the work to people who couldn't really understand. What he says makes sense in a rudimentary way. Of course, Stoki had a lot of malarkey in him, and he knew that a musician of his caliber had to do a certain amount of hocus-pocus in order to maintain his stature and power. If he tried to tell them about the nuts and bolts of music, they'd run out on him, but if he maintained his magnificence, wore impeccable white tie and tails, and fluffed his hair, and all the rest of that jazz, it would do wonders for the budget.

"Stoki was trying to convince Disney and his staff that they could use Bach's Toccata and Fugue and that if it were compelling and colorful enough it would be acceptable even to those who would ordinarily reject it. He was right—he was supremely right, and he did a tremendous service to music.

"Stoki always had a way of saying things that were easily subject to criticism. For example, how obvious it is to us when he says to the Disney crowd, when they are getting over their heads, this almost innocent thing: 'In the fugue when there is counterpoint; in the music there should be counterpoint on the screen. It will be very easy to follow. The music will explain the picture and the picture will explain the music.' Now, that can be called naïve if one is nitpicking, but Stoki didn't want to put Walt at any disadvantage in front of his own staff. Stoki deserves tremendous credit. There wasn't another conductor in the world who could have sold this artistic and expensive package to the only people in the world who could materialize and market it."

With the handpicked orchestra of Hollywood's top virtuosos, Stokowski recorded *Fantasia*'s entire score time and again while cameras and microphones captured every second of sight and sound. The elaborate preparations and rehearsals were only to facilitate photographing Stokowski, as it was always intended that the Philadelphia would be recording the final score. On hand as musical adviser was composer-critic Deems Taylor, who had returned with Stokowski in September. In response to the desires of Disney and Stokowski to surround the theater audiences with sound, Bill Garity came up with a circular system of four speakers, predating stereophonic sound by decades, whose prohibitive expense compelled a substitute called Fantasound, equally unique. Then, dozens of Stokowski's studio recordings were auditioned, compared, and critically evaluated. Finally, the program was selected and timed, and the cuts and sequences decided upon. Stokowski immediately took off for Philadelphia to prepare his orchestra for the recording sessions on the stage of the Academy of Music, scheduled for April 1939. The basement had to be specially equipped for the complicated system that succeeded in producing a method of sound reproduction immeasurably superior to any ever produced before or since.

In the midst of the *Fantasia* recordings, the complex system was declared a fire hazard by city officials, who ordered it closed. Joe Sharfsin, then the city solicitor and always a devoted music-lover, was prevailed upon to intercede. When the citation was quickly squelched, Stokowski thanked Sharfsin and asked, "Now, what can we do for you?" Sharsfin facetiously confided that he had one secret ambition—to become rich enough to book the Philadelphia Orchestra under Stokowski for an engagement that he alone would hear. Stokowski asked, "How about tomorrow afternoon at two?"

The next day the unbelieving attorney appeared at the stage door of the Academy and was escorted into a completely empty hall except for a hundred men and their conductor, who for the rest of the afternoon played the entire program of *Fantasia*. Stokowski had conveniently neglected to mention that Disney had ordered a special uninterrupted recording of the sound track. In a typically Stokowskian gesture, the Maestro used the session to demonstrate his gratitude.

On that afternoon, Stokowski performed everything except *The Sorcerer's Apprentice,* which had been recorded in Hollywood so many times and so flawlessly that no further take was needed. An amusing postscript is that not one reviewer, including all major music critics, ever noted that the Dukas piece was not performed by the Philadelphia Orchestra nor recorded in Fantasound. Perhaps they were too intrigued seeing Mickey, still clothed as the apprentice, climbing the podium steps to shake hands with Maestro Stokowski. Nobody has ever forgotten that.

Despite the inevitable spurts of strain and stress, Stokowski relished working on what he called "Fanta-*zee*-ah"—and he was constantly infuriated with everyone who "*meez*-pronounced" it. Its unforgettable Broadway premiere created the most startled audience I have ever seen. When the multiple loudspeakers that hung all over the theater produced sounds coming from every direction, the seats actually vibrated. It was an amazing sensation and an audio dream, the result of Stokowski's lifetime pursuit of ways to reproduce music for millions and to do justice to its aural glory. The final product of four years of sonic effort and a million animation sketches opened to decidedly mixed reviews, but has become an ever-increasing success with audiences and at the box office. In 1941, Stokowski, Disney, and their associates received a special award from the Academy of Motion Picture Arts and Sciences for expanding film horizons.

Of course, there is no unanimity of opinion about anything. But most of the best critics have agreed with Virgil Thomson that "Stokowski, whatever one may think of his musical taste, is unquestionably the man who has best watched over the upbringing of Hollywood's stepchild, musical recording and reproduction. Alone among famous musicians who have worked in films, he has forced the spending of money and serious thought by film producers and their engineers toward the achievement of a result in auditive photography comparable in excellence to the results that the expenditure of money and thought have produced in visual photography. Musicians will thank him and bless his name. The integration, phrase by phrase, of music with naturalistic acting and speech is going to produce lots of directorial headaches; but sooner or later it will have to be done. Thanks to Disney and Stokowski, it will probably be done rather sooner than later."

Forty years later, and we are not there yet.

During the completion of *Fantasia,* Stokowski's thoughts turned to other projects, but no other film or sequel appeared in the immediate offing, so he returned east. At a dinner party in Philadelphia during the winter of 1939–40, he found himself seated next to Mrs. Samuel Lyle Conner, a member of the Democratic National Committee from Bardstown, Kentucky, who had long been interested in promoting goodwill in South America.

"Maestro," she said, "why don't you give a South American tour?"

"That has long been a dream of my life," Stokowski replied. He had been frustrated ever since his proposal to take the Philadelphia Orchestra to South America had been rejected by the board of directors. He discussed with Mrs. Conner the possibility of organizing an orchestra of the finest young American talents for such a tour. "What a wonderful idea," she said, assuring Stokowski of her certainty that the State Department was most eager to support any and all efforts to improve official relations with South American countries, which at that time were being courted by the Nazis. They parted that night, both excited by the prospect of an idea so fraught with promise.

As the winter progressed they persevered with the project. Mrs. Conner arranged a series of meetings and parties for Stokowski in Washington, where he thoroughly discussed the plan with National Youth Administrator Aubrey Williams and several influential South American diplomats. Meanwhile, Stokowski had persuaded Columbia Records to share costs in return for recording rights. The All-American Youth Orchestra, as it was to be called, was soon assured of the necessary political and financial backing to embark on the goodwill tour in July 1940.

Now Stokowski was faced with the prodigious task of discovering, organizing, and developing an orchestra of young musicians who had never before played together and in whom he would have to nurture perfection, and all within less than four months. Few conductors, if any, would have attempted it. But once Stokowski had a vision, obstacles that would have daunted other men, melted in the fire of his singleness of purpose, this time fanned by the nagging desire to conclude his personal feud with Philadelphia triumphantly. He also envisioned the orchestra becoming an institution and training ground for its members, who would ultimately return to their own states and foment other orchestras.

From early spring Stokowski held a series of auditions at centers throughout the country. He began in Los Angeles, assisted by Jack Pepper, principal violinist of Philadelphia's opera orchestra, who had appeared under Stokowski many times. When they remet in Hollywood, Stokowski said, "I am interested in starting a youth orchestra of the finest players in the country. What practical method would you suggest for me to find them?" Pepper proposed chamber-music auditions, and Stokowski concurred.

Thirteen or fourteen sessions were organized at the home of a music enthusiast. Although Stokowski found most of his best players in Los Angeles and New York, he traveled widely to attain geographical representation from each state, hearing over one thousand players. Many of the auditions were totally unrewarding.

By June, Stokowski had selected ninety musicians between the ages of fourteen and twenty-five who, with a sprinkling of experienced orchestra players, would form the All-American Youth Orchestra. It included twenty girls, an unprecedented number for that time. Michael Myerberg managed the tours; Saul Caston and John Bitter were Stokowski's associate conductors.

The players gathered for the first rehearsal at the Willard Hotel in Washington, D.C., on June 26, 1940, less than a month before their first concert. They would receive $600 plus living and traveling expenses for twelve weeks of rehearsals and concerts. Stokowski himself received not a penny for conducting.

Directly after the July 4 weekend, Stokowski and his players started rehearsing day and night in Atlantic City. The town's mayor, Thomas Taggart, Jr., had offered the orchestra free accommodations at the city's swankiest hotels. They all knew that at any point, they might be dismissed with

minimal severance pay. At the end of three weeks Stokowski
had combed the group thoroughly, retaining only the superlative players.

The first concert in the ballroom of the Convention Hall to
five thousand sunburned and sweltering boardwalkers was a
resounding success. Music critic Henry Pleasants wrote in the
Philadelphia Evening Bulletin: "Leopold Stokowski has given
America another great orchestra. . . . they played so well,
indeed, that comparisons with the greatest orchestras were
being made during the intermission conversations. . . . There
is vitality and enthusiasm here in an electrifying degree. . . .
The central force of the evening was, however, the pioneering and interpretive spirit of Mr. Stokowski."

What Stokowski accomplished was, and still is, miraculous.
No other conductor has performed a comparable feat. The
mere fact of his presence in front of an orchestra seemed
sufficient to draw out, within days, the synthesized, disciplined, and recognizable "Stokowski sound." The youth orchestra had had, of course, no other master; most of them
had never even participated as members of an orchestra before. The orchestra was unmistakably and in every sense
Stokowski's creation. Nevertheless, once he had chosen
them, his treatment of them was identical to his treatment of
the all-star Philadelphians. The Atlantic City concert, which
Stokowski placed "among the most exciting experiences of
my life," demonstrated beyond doubt that the All-American
was fully ready to represent the United States to the other
peoples of America.

En route they were heard in Baltimore, Washington, and
New York, where Olin Downes wrote in *The New York Times:*

> We are finding out in these days what the youth of Amer-
> ica, directed by authoritative and inspiring leadership, can
> do in music. . . . The boys and girls in Stokowski's AAYO
> did indeed reveal superb capacities as orchestral players.
> They had been selected from the best talents that America
> could offer for Stokowski's purpose. . . . However, without

a man of Stokowski's leadership such concerts would have been impossible. . . . It also refuted the logic of the great majority of musical specialists who had predicted that no orchestra conductor could possibly, in such a short time as Stokowski had at his disposal, give any symphonic body a homogeneous tone and a finished style.

Throughout the long sea voyage they rehearsed four hours a day, finally giving a concert for the passengers in one of the dining halls. At this event Stokowski demonstrated his acute sensitivity to any extraneous sound. In the midst of the opening measures he stopped, half turned, and asked, "What's that noise?" A ship's officer answered, "The air-conditioning, sir." Stokowski said, "It must be turned off. We can't play with noise." It was turned off. Stokowski was ready to begin again. "I still hear noise," he snapped. The officer explained that it was the ship's engines. Stokowski said, "Noise—we cannot play with noise." Incredibly, the engines were actually stopped and for an hour and a half, the ship sat in the Atlantic, gently rocking to the rhythms of symphonic music.

The twenty-one-engagement tour was a complete success. Eight concerts were given in Buenos Aires. One paper reported that after a concert, police had to intervene to clear the theater lobby, which was packed with throngs hoping for one more glimpse of the Maestro.

In accordance with a frequent practice of Stokowski's, his program tactfully included a piece by a local composer, J. B. Massa, entitled *La Muerta del Inca.* The public quickly understood that these concerts were actuated by a spirit of giving rather than of receiving profits. The daily *El Diario de Buenos Aires* reflects the predominant response: "Stokowski is a revolutionist; . . . today music is, principally through the efforts of Stokowski, an art . . . popular not only for the usual select minority but also for the multitudinous masses, a thing never achieved before."

Stokowski was fascinated by some Indian music he heard

played on traditional instruments. At his request, 150 native musicians were taken by bus to participate in the Rio de Janeiro concert. An urban crisis arose when they appeared for the concert mother-naked. A hasty conference resulted in orchestra members rustling up some extra clothes.

The performance supplied a sizable portion of the three hundred recordings of native music that Stokowski supervised and brought home. The dozen and a half All-American discs of standard repertory for Columbia were recorded at the end of the tour.

In September, the orchestra returned home on the S.S. *Argentine* to be greeted at the dock by Mrs. Franklin D. Roosevelt and her son Franklin D., Jr. A triumphant "Welcome Home" concert was given at Carnegie Hall. But the real triumph, for Stokowski, was at the concert three nights later in Philadelphia. After tumultuous applause he addressed the audience: "I am a little sad because I wanted to make this tour with the Philadelphia Orchestra. But when I suggested it, I was told such a tour was impossible. I can't understand that, because we've done it." Although it had been two years since he resigned, and Ormandy had succeeded him, Stokowski could not resist the opportunity to deliver one final blow at his erstwhile foes, the Philadelphia Orchestra board of directors.

Even before the first tour was over, Stokowski had forecast that the All-American Youth Orchestra would become a permanent organization whose playing seasons would be the spring and summer months. The orchestra had temporarily disbanded, but the second tour, this time of the United States and Canada, was already being planned for the following spring.

In the fall of 1940, while I was on a nationwide concert tour, I visited Rachmaninoff at his Beverly Hills home. One night at a restaurant we met Stokowski and a few of his Los Angeles players. One of them began to talk about their national tour with the air of a missionary bringing culture to the hicks of the hinterland. Stokowski jumped on him, saying, "You don't know anything about this country. Do you think our work has been so useless all these years? Let me tell you, the backwoods of America are packed with good musicians, good orchestras, and very sophisticated audiences. Just try to give them less than your best programs and performances—you'll never forget it, nor will they. The smaller the city, the bigger the fiasco." Rachmaninoff smiled one of his rare smiles in agreement.

During the winter Stokowski had to audition for replacements of those in the orchestra who were being drafted. The war was fast making the term *youth* proportionately less applicable, and it was dropped from the title.

Toward the end of April the orchestra reassembled as the All-American Orchestra and started rehearsals for an eight-week tour of thirty cities, from Boston to Los Angeles and from Toronto to San Diego. Once again Stokowski faced the task of working with a group that introduced many new members. Again he succeeded in creating a first-class orchestra that could stand any comparison.

Stokowski's attitude throughout the tour was one of "benevolent paternalism," according to Mrs. Betty Stern, his secretary at the time. He appreciated the players' willingness to experiment. "I have many ideas," he said. "These young folk help me to develop them." They experimented with a one-headed drum, steel- and copper-strung violins, and a new, electronic keyboard instrument.

Glowing reviews followed the tour across the country. A representative one appeared in the *Omaha World Herald:* "There was an unflagging zest and vitality of youth in every measure of the program . . . an immaculately clean technique in formidable difficulties and unfailing response to every subtlety of direction."

Considering the pressures of travel and often less than perfect conditions, the quality of their performances was astounding. They slept on trains and played in gymnasiums and football fields, with no days off between concerts. The unifying power, of course, was Stokowski.

Not the least of his virtues was an unassuming sense of humor. In Toledo, they played in an open-air auditorium next to a zoo. In the middle of the Franck symphony, the peacocks made such a noise that Stokowski stopped, turned to the audience, and apologized for disturbing the peacocks.

Gwendolyn Koldofsky, the distinguished vocal accompanist, teacher, and coach, told me that she and her husband were in Toronto when the Stokowski group arrived. The concert was to open with Brahms's First Symphony. "For days," she said, "my husband kept saying how he anticipated the sound of those great opening chords from Stoki. But alas —when the first majestic chord was played, the huge audience sprang up noisily and drowned out the following phrases with the lusty singing of 'God Save the King,'" as was the Canadian practice before a concert. Stokowski was highly amused, explaining that he had carefully placed the anthem at the end of the program because the monumental opening of the symphony would have had less impact following the regal character of the anthem.

The tour came to an end on June 29, 1941, under a setting sun at the Pasadena Rose Bowl. The ninety thousand seats of the stadium were reduced to an effective segment accommodating fifteen thousand. Stokowski used his self-designed accustical reflector, which projected sound forward from the platform. "The unamplified orchestra tone of the well-publicized aggregation of new musicians," wrote Isabel Morse Jones of the *Los Angeles Times,* "was vibrant, rich, and capable of a wide range of color even outdoors in the huge stadium." The concert brought the remarkable orchestra to a brilliant climax, and unfortunately to an untimely conclusion.

Barely a month before, Stokowski, full of optimism, had announced that the third tour was to be more extensive than the previous two, encompassing the United States, South and

Central America, and Mexico. He also mentioned future tours of Europe and the Orient. All plans had to be abandoned as the United States became ever more deeply involved in World War II. Everything was sacrificed to military needs. The armed services monopolized all transportation, and virtually every young man was drafted. Columbia Records had to withdraw its financial support, and no other backers appeared. The All-American Orchestra was no more.

At least a testimonial to Stokowski's achievement and the quality of his orchestras remains through the recordings made at the conclusion of both tours. Outstanding among major works are Brahms's Second and Fourth Symphonies, Dvořák's *New World* Symphony, Schubert's *Unfinished* Symphony, Richard Strauss's *Tod und Verklärung*, Mussorgsky's *Pictures at an Exhibition* (orchestrated by Stokowski), Stravinsky's *Firebird* Suite, and several Bach-Stokowski transcriptions. "Firsts" included Henry Cowell's *Tales of Our Countryside*, "Guaracha" from Morton Gould's Latin-American Symphonette, and the Scherzo from William Grant Still's Afro-American Symphony. One sour item was Stokowski's only recording of Ravel's *Bolero,* an inexplicably static performance of just the sort of piece in which one expects Stokowski to be electrifying. No matter. All the other recordings are remarkable for the warmth and sensuousness of this newly fledged orchestra's sound, all but indistinguishable from the most mature and seasoned orchestras conducted by Stokowski.

It is hard to overestimate the far-reaching extent of Stokowski's achievement through the tours of this orchestra. The entire conception has been termed "a unique event in American culture and in the history of music." Many members of the orchestra began splendid careers emanating directly from their association with the supreme architect of orchestras. Such eminent principal players of major American orchestras as oboist Harold Gomberg, clarinetist Robert

McInnes, hornist Edward Murphy, concertmaster Paul Schure (who next held that position with the Los Angeles Philharmonic), flutist Albert Tipton, and bassoonist Manuel Zegler were all alumni of the All-American.

As Elizabeth Waldo of Los Angeles, a principal violinist on both tours, put it, "I observed with utmost benefit so many of Stokowski's approaches to music. They became a part of my permanent thinking and all my future activities." Inspired by the native Indian cultures encountered on tour, this dynamic violinist, composer, and conductor has evolved into a foremost interpreter and musical archaeologist of New World music, ancient and modern. Actually she was able to realize the goals of Stokowski's canceled third tour through numerous trips with her Pan-American Ensemble and Pre-Columbian Orchestra.

The fruitful careers of many American musicians attest to Stokowski's orchestra as an unparalleled force in the development and recognition of American talent. It was equally a force for inter-American amity.

11

No sooner had Stokowski bid his newest orchestra a reluctant farewell than he headed east on the Super Chief where we accidentally ran into each other. The Super Chief was more of a club than a train, with showers, manicurists, and telephones. Its members were travelers who would not, or could not, fly. Stokowski, of course, was a charter member. I was on board because I had been unable to get on a flight to Chicago, where I was due to play a recital. Our meeting provided a chance for catching up on each other's recent activities. Stokowski said that he was on his way to conduct a few concerts with the Philadelphia "bunch" and that he was also considering an invitation to co-conduct the NBC Orchestra with Toscanini on a long contract. He planned to accept on condition that he could also record a large number of important works with them.

At that point, NBC was ready to concede to anything that Stokowski demanded. Although the Maestro had not yet tendered his customary biannual resignation, NBC was taking no chances. It wanted a conductor who, if necessary, could fill Toscanini's shoes. Toscanini was seething with rage, having discovered that many of the men within the orchestra that NBC claimed it had "expressly created" for him were playing other programs under other conductors in recordings and commercial radio shows.

Even though Stokowski turned out to be not much less intractable than Toscanini, NBC had reason to pride itself on its foresight when the Italian maestro announced that he would not return that season. Stokowski could not pretend to be too downhearted at this news, since it offered him the coveted possibility of inheriting a prestigious New York orchestra under his sole command.

RCA also had cause for self-congratulation. Its ready assent to Stokowski's recording demand paid off handsomely. For the next few years, his symphonic discs outsold all others.

The recorded repertory was chosen from the concert programs that drew huge radio audiences for such plums as the American premiere of Prokofiev's cantata *Alexander Nevsky* and excerpts from the same composer's opera *The Love of Three Oranges.* Stokowski also recorded Rimsky-Korsakov's gaudy *Russian Easter* Overture, which emerged as a polished masterpiece under his unconstrained, yet sensitive, interpretation.

Stokowski got along personally far better with the NBC orchestra than he had with Toscanini's New York Philharmonic. The musicians adjusted to him and to his style—all of them, that is, except for concertmaster Mischa Mischakoff, who openly displayed his displeasure at Stokowski's free-wheeling alterations of scores. Later, it was rumored that Toscanini had complained to Gen. David Sarnoff, head of NBC, that Stokowski was "ruining" his orchestra by reseating the players and insisting upon "free bowing." Stokowski kept his temper under admirable control when he heard this. "Some conductors," said Stokowski with a quiet smile, "insult their players and call them peculiar Italian names but—that is not what makes them great."

When Stokowski accepted the NBC post, he was entirely aware of the hazards of co-conductorship with Toscanini. But he was equally aware that the association with a fine orchestra combined with the technological expertise of this

electronic empire provided an unusual opportunity. The
NBC empire was an ideal organization to further his acoustical proficiency and scientific ambitions. But now in addition
lurked the unexpected chance of becoming the guiding hand
of its orchestra. To make the most of the situation, Stokowski
wrote to Phil Kahgan in Los Angeles.

October 13, 1941

DEAR PHIL,

If you can spare the time, would you mind listening to
the NBC broadcasts . . . sending me little notes each
time . . . especially I would like to know whether there
are any *pp*'s you did not hear, any *ff*'s that did not sound
well. Is the balance, the clarity of separate instruments
good? If you can do this, you will help me very much in
trying to make the transmission ever better.

Always with friendship,
S

In response, Kahgan wrote and telephoned his reactions and
suggestions, which Stokowski instantly acknowledged with
gratitude, always explaining his method of rectifying what
was wrong in time for the next broadcast.

Unfortunately, the quality of Stokowski's broadcasts became quite irrelevant in the spring of 1942; Toscanini had
concluded that Europe was committing suicide and that conducting an excellent American orchestra at an unequaled
salary was worth certain annoyances. He needed little per-
suasion to assume his NBC post again.

This time, Stokowski did not walk out. He merely adjusted
his timetable and stayed on. However, when he heard that
Toscanini was to conduct the American premiere of Shostakovich's Seventh Symphony, which the composer dedicated

to Russian heroism when the Nazis laid siege to Leningrad, Stokowski became incensed. Months before, he had urged NBC to purchase the rights to a first American performance, which he would conduct. He wrote Toscanini explaining the situation and asking him to relinquish the premiere. Toscanini replied with a long letter explaining the feelings of "an old Italian conductor who fought against Fascism" and for whom the work and the performance had "a special meaning."

Stokowski, either misinterpreting Toscanini's letter or indulging in sarcasm, answered, "I am glad you are willing for me to make the first radio broadcast." Toscanini wrote back immediately saying that Stokowski had obviously misunderstood him, concluding with, "Try to understand me, my dear Stokowski. . . . Happily, you are much younger than me, and Shostakovich will not stop writing new symphonies. You will certainly have all the opportunities you like to perform them. Be sure you will never find me again in your way."

Stokowski made sure. Immediately he severed his association with NBC. He threw himself into other activities and completed a book on which he had been working for two years, *Music for Us All,* published in 1943.

With the war reaching horrendous proportions, Stokowski joined the fray with indefatigable energy. He conducted Red Cross and USO benefit concerts from Philadelphia to Pasadena, he led army bands from Fort Dix, New Jersey, to San Pedro, California. He made a brilliant transcription of the "Star-Spangled Banner," with which he opened every occasion. With Edward G. Robinson as master of ceremonies, he conducted an all-Russian program at the Hollywood Bowl, opening with the national anthems of the United States and the Soviet Union, "in tribute to the gallant Soviet soldiers who are fighting off the German invasion."

Responding to this event, superpatriots labeled Stokowski a "Red," and the American Legion and the D.A.R. declared him "un-American." He began receiving threats against his life and once again he "packed" the two automatic pistols he had carried when his daughters were threatened by kidnappers.

In 1944, Stokowski was invited by New York's Mayor Fiorello La Guardia to perform, conduct, and direct a New York City Symphony Orchestra. The idea emanated tangentially from a real estate foreclosure for back-taxes on Mecca Temple on Fifty-fifth Street, whereby the city assumed possession of the famous white elephant. A close friend and adviser of the mayor's, the musically gifted attorney Morton Baum, had suggested that the awkward structure was ideally suited as a center for music, drama, ballet, and opera. The building's labyrinth of rooms would provide adequate practice quarters, rehearsal spaces, and storerooms for scenery and costumes, while the two-thousand-seat auditorium could be used for all types of performances.

Baum then headed a distinguished committee that announced a policy of making the highest quality entertainment available at prices far below the usual scale and devoting a considerable proportion of the programs to the works of contemporary creators. This was right up Stokowski's alley, and he accepted the post immediately. The bizarre hall and its acoustical problems were no strangers to him as he had conducted both All-American orchestras there and had overcome some of its difficulties by the use of an acoustical shell and risers. He returned to New York, offered to serve without any financial compensation, and appointed Sylvan Levin his associate conductor. While Sylvan was handpicking the orchestra, the peripatetic Stokowski participated in a series of twenty-five symphonic concerts shortwaved by Armed Forces Radio to overseas troops. He shared the podium with Toscanini and William Steinberg.

Within a month, Stokowski launched the New York City Symphony on a series of concerts that won audiences and critical plaudits as he had won them with his Philadelphia Orchestra concerts, by playing exciting programs beautifully. In no time, he had stamped the Stokowski trademarks —tonal vibrancy and high technical finish—upon this new group. His imaginative programs introduced a wide repertory ranging from Bach's *Saint Matthew Passion* to fascinating premieres such as Paul Hindemith's Violin Concerto, with Robert Gross as soloist; Anis Fuleihan's Theremin Concerto, with Clara Rockmore as soloist; and Nathaniel Shilkret's Trombone Concerto, with soloist Tommy Dorsey. The season itself was a triumph and served to establish one of the city's most valuable institutions.

Stokowski himself could not have been more generous or cooperative. He brightened the Christmas season onstage by subsidizing a pageant, followed by a backstage wine-and-cheese supper for the personnel of the City Center, whose scanty resources were unequal to such festivities. He also launched a Veteran's Music Service at the City Center, designed to supply advice and assistance to returning servicemen. The visionary project was headed by Stokowski, Newbold Morris, the chairman of the board, and Claire Reis. The city center also sponsored a series of symphonic concerts conducted by Stokowski for hospitalized veterans in and around New York.

Stokowski somehow found the time to accept the invitation to become musical director at the Hollywood Bowl, signing a three-year contract, which was to start with the 1945 summer season. He was to be in charge of all recordings, radio, and motion picture plans. "Symphonies Under the Stars" was a spacious and spectacular concept. The Los Angeles Philharmonic constituted most of the orchestral personnel, again assembled by Phil Kahgan for his friend "Stoki." Glamorous soloists, guest conductors, a lighthearted public swarming with film celebrities, perfect weather, a moonlit shell, and agreeably comfortable programs made them festive occasions. Up to this time, they had lacked the leadership that could provide a constant standard of first-class programs and sounds. Four months in advance of Stokowski's expected arrival, he wrote to Phil Kahgan:

February 15, 1945

DEAR PHIL,

I am going to arrive in Hollywood the first possible moment. Tell everyone it will be May First, but personally I am hoping to make it about two weeks before then so that you and I can plan everything well ahead of time. The success of the concerts greatly depends on the quality of the orchestra. With only two rehearsals for each symphony program we must be sure to have an intelligent, quick, and willing group of players who are masters of their instruments. So please don't promise anyone anything until you and I have a good talk in your lovely wine cellar.

With love to you all,
S

As February yielded to March, it was evident that the glamorous debutante, Gloria Vanderbilt di Cicco, had become a steady attendant at Stokowski's City Center concerts and was often seen being driven home by the Maestro in his limousine. But few sniffed the fragrance of a romance until April 12, when the conductor, supposedly en route from New York to the Hollywood Bowl, stopped off at Reno, Nevada. This was one week before the Vanderbilt heiress had fully complied with the residency requirements for her divorce from the man whom she had married four years before. When Gloria met the Maestro's train and then drove him to a country estate in the Nevada section of Lake Tahoe, there remained but one question: When and where would they get married?

On April 21 they were married in Mexico. They spent their honeymoon night at the Hotel De Ansa in Calexico, a U.S. border town, where with superb naïveté Stokowski had reserved rooms in the name of Stanley "to assure privacy." Stokowski never seemed able to realize the immense gulf that would always remain between his public life and the private life he sincerely sought. Even the Garbo episode had not taught him this, and he was incensed over the explosion of publicity that this "quiet Mexican elopement" had set off.

For the third time, Stokowski found himself married to a dark-haired woman who was a figure in the social history of American wealth. The pretty bride, who harbored artistic ambitions, had just inherited an estate of almost $5 million on her twenty-first birthday. Although the bridegroom of sixty-three had trimmed his age to fifty-eight, newspapers still said that Gloria had married a man "old enough to be her grandfather." The newlyweds traveled in Mexico for several weeks and then headed for Stokowski's home in Beverly Hills, in good time for the summer concert series.

On July 10, Stokowski and the Hollywood Bowl Symphony Orchestra opened the twenty-fourth season of "Symphonies Under the Stars" before an audience of fourteen thousand. Gloria Vanderbilt Stokowska, as she called herself according to Polish protocol, sat in a front-row box in her new role as a patroness of musical art, with her guests Douglas Fairbanks, Joan Crawford, Franchot Tone, and Frank Sinatra.

Stokowski had always relished the glamorous aspects of Hollywood. Now that he was at the zenith, he had painstakingly designed the title page of the program, spelling out in his own handwriting "Stokowski, Music Director, Conducting the Hollywood Bowl Symphony," specifying the exact size, sequence, and design of each word, and sent it from New York to Phil Kahgan, to be precisely executed.

The Hollywood Bowl amphitheater gave full rein to Stokowski's announced plans for staged concert versions of *Aïda* and *Carmen* with real animals stalking the stage. He found himself battling the orchestra board to "sell" the appropriateness of *Parsifal*. They won: "No fun, no box office."

There were no battles to fight over the favorite repertory of the Bowl audience, which found Stokowski in perhaps his truest element. In the tone poems of Richard Strauss, the waltzes of Johann Strauss, the ballets of Stravinsky, the Hungarian Dances of Brahms, and Falla's *El Amor Brujo*, Stokowski wove magic spells, summoning his innate cinematic gifts to portray moods and characters in aural close-ups.

All of these works plus such large-scale war-horses as Brahms's First Symphony and Tchaikovsky's Sixth were duly recorded by RCA Victor. There is also a rare (for Stokowski) Haydn recording—the Serenade from the String Quartet in F, op. 3, no. 5, in Stokowski's orchestral transcription.

A significant record was scheduled but never materialized —the Chopin F-minor Piano Concerto with Artur Rubinstein as soloist. It did not come about according to Rubinstein, because of the decision of the orchestra board to reduce the number of Stokowski's rehearsals. The Maestro refused to comply, saying he would pay for all the extra time he required. Within ten minutes of rehearsal time, it became clear that the soloist and the conductor were at sixes and sevens. Despite their best efforts, they could not agree about anything—tempi, dynamics, balances. It was obvious to one and all that so far as this concerto was concerned, Rubinstein and Stokowski were Poles apart. Rubinstein later figured out that their disagreements had cost Stokowski so much "overtime rehearsal" that he retaliated by sabotaging the performance, making it unsuitable for recording.

Stokowski's overall reaction to the Bowl season is reflected in a letter of July 20, 1945, to Sylvan Levin, filled with his unusual enthusiasm, joy, and optimism:

We have formed an entirely new orchestra of one hundred players and it is superb. Everyone here is excited about it. They rehearse so quickly that I am able to do far more in one rehearsal than in two or three with a less expert and experienced orchestra. We have formed an entirely new chorus of one thousand voices, which next year we shall increase to two thousand. The concerts have been so popular this year that we are taking in about double the income of last year. This is very stimulating to everyone, so that we are formulating plans for next season on a much larger scale. In a word, we have already achieved here the ideals I had for City Center.

Two weeks before this letter was written, Stokowski had announced to the New York City Center board, his intention to resign if his demands were not fully met. He hinted at this in an outspoken letter to Sylvan written on July 6, the day of his resignation:

It seems to me that my idea of City Center and the conception of the committee is quite different. When I return, I am going to try hard to make the committee understand.

What Mayor La Guardia said to the directors was a great surprise to me, saying "sixty-five men make a good orchestra." This depends upon *what* is played and *where*. In City Center, sixty-five men could not possibly play *Heldenleben* or the Shostakovich Seventh Symphony because of the size and bad acoustics of the hall. For next winter I am asking for *nine extra strings* so that they will not be drowned out as they now are by woodwinds and brass.

Mayor La Guardia's idea that "music must pay for itself" shows that he is not thinking clearly. All art needs subvention of some kind. Education, hospitals, libraries, post-offices, and many other things do not pay for themselves and yet are a necessary part of civilized life. Instead of Mayor La Guardia saying disparaging things about me (though he didn't mention my name) he might have thanked me for giving a whole season of work without compensation and for giving up many engagements all over the world, which could have given me a large income as well as the pleasure of traveling. As people do not seem to understand my giving my services for idealistic reasons, I am not going to do it any more. People are going to pay me in future as Hollywood does. The only exception will be City Center, as I promised to give my services there next winter and I will keep my word.

He did indeed, but early in 1946, the twenty-seven-year-old Leonard Bernstein, following Stokowski's example, offered to assume the responsibilities of the meagerly supported group. He too gave his services gratis and for three years donated his great talent and tireless work to its continued artistic fulfillment. Finally, however, the combination of economic and political pressures forced him to quit. The orchestra itself passed into history, while the ballet and the opera companies went on to contribute to it.

Stokowski returned west to bask in the California sun and to stamp the musical scene with his personal brand. On veteran's night, Frank Sinatra was his soloist in a group of ballads centered around Jerome Kern's "Ol' Man River." Stokowski staged a concert version of *Fledermaus* with every film star in town as the party guests. He led a Gershwin-Rodgers-Berlin program as a benefit for the Hollywood canteen that entertained members of the armed forces, and he organized a charity concert for wounded veterans sponsored by the musicians' union. For this, Phil Kahgan rounded up 175 of southern California's top musicians—"the biggest symphony orchestra I ever conducted," as Stokowski put it. "It was a thrilling experience."

At the end of that second season, Stokowski evidently felt the need of more serious and substantial excitement, for he suddenly broke his contract and walked off in a huff. To the followers of his career, his exit was as unexceptional as it was hasty.

With Stokowski's abrupt departure from Hollywood, conflicting stories began circulating from coast to coast that made every version of the "real reason" entirely conjectural. Some said that despite Stokowski's unparalleled success, he derived very little artistic satisfaction from the quality of sounds that emanated from the orchestra, caused entirely by the insoluble acoustical problems of the Bowl. When I asked him about this, he answered, "It was sometimes very good, sometimes very bad. The wind or the birds or airplanes could ruin the most beautiful effects. There is no outdoor arena that isn't kinder to the eyes than to the ears."

Others said that Gloria very much missed the social world into which she was born. Still others said, "Not at all. She's a Bohemian at heart, and the movie colony was not the atmosphere for her to pursue her own artistic interests—painting, poetry, and the theater."

I am inclined to believe that cheerfully unaware of all this, Stokowski left quickly because of a letter from Arthur Judson stating that he had "an important proposal" to submit on behalf of the New York Philharmonic. He said that he would be glad to fly out and confer with him at the very first free moment. Stokowski replied by telephone, saying that the Stokowskis were leaving on the weekend to take up residence in New York, and Judson promptly invited Stokowski to luncheon at the Lotus Club. Judson was not surprised, he said later, when, before hanging up, Stokowski added gratuitously, "It will be a pleasure to see you again."

"If I hadn't thought he would be so interested," said the canny Judson, "I wouldn't have written him."

Judson had been alerted by intimates of Stokowski that the former lord and master of the Philadelphia Orchestra was just about fed up with the short-lived orchestras and seasonal engagements to which he had given so much of himself, his time, his strength, and (except for the Bowl and the NBC) even his services without remuneration. Now he was ready for a permanent and important post in the right place.

No persuasiveness was needed to convince Stokowski that the right place was sophisticated New York, where his talents could find their most effective scope. Through a combination of "fortunate circumstances," as Judson put it, the one major conductorship of a great American orchestra available in the foreseeable future was that of the New York Philharmonic, from which Artur Rodzinski was about to resign. Before anyone had surmised that Stokowski might be induced to leave California, Dimitri Mitropoulos had been approached and had accepted an invitation to replace Rodzinski. He had not been offered a contract. There was no question in Judson's mind that if Stokowski would share with Mitropoulos the remaining portion of the season after Rodzinski's resignation, the board would soon offer Stokowski the post permanently and just about whatever else he wanted.

Judson never mentioned the crucial plight of the Philharmonic. He did not have to. Everyone knew how this orchestra had been in trouble ever since Toscanini's resignation in 1936, and how Rodzinski had openly and vociferously condemned Judson's self-serving management as the primary cause. Around 1930, Judson had acquired a subtle stranglehold on the concert business through Columbia Artists Management. The organization's activities had many ramifications, but the one which affected the Philharmonic was Judson's firm control over the musical activities and destinies of many famous orchestras, conductors, and soloists, who performed according to his bidding or else. This meant not only where they played but also what.

The programs of the Philharmonic consequently had suffered, and the orchestra had long been stamped as a declining institution, one that played little part in New York's intellectual life. It compared unfavorably to the Boston Symphony and the Philadelphia Orchestra, which both commendably reflected their communities' cultural ideals, aesthetic pride, and moral responsibility. Moreover, in each of those cities and for many long years, one conductor alone had created and shaped an elegant ensemble with his powerful temperament and consummate artistic obligation.

The Philharmonic was "a horse of a different color." Too many nonentities, too many mediocrities, had ridden on its back. So had a few masters, but for too short a time. During the eight continuous years when Toscanini lashed the Philharmonic mercilessly into a precision instrument, the brilliant performances were lavished almost entirely upon the classic literature, the "standard fifty masterpieces."

Ever since Toscanini's departure, there had been little music-making that was inspiring or exciting. For a successor, he had suggested Wilhelm Furtwängler as principal conductor with Rodzinski to assist him. The shocking recommendation was ignored when news stories and photos revealed that the German conductor had made a "pro-Nazi" speech publicly, that he had conducted a concert at which Goebbels had spoken, and that he had accepted a decoration from Mussolini during an Italian tour. Toscanini had also suggested Fritz Busch, who said that he was honored but was thoroughly satisfied with his current and far less demanding post in Copenhagen.

Judson thereupon announced five conductors to share the next season, one of whom would be invited at the season's end to serve as principal conductor through the consensus of public and critical opinion. Georges Enesco, Carlos Chavez, Arthur Rodzinski, Igor Stravinsky, and John Barbirolli were named to appear. Three composer-conductors were chosen in order to refute the criticism of the Philharmonic as an anti-cultural organization that promoted virtuosity rather than the cause of music.

In mid-December, Judson made the startling announcement that John Barbirolli had been awarded a three-year contract. Not only was an appointment made in mid-season an unprecedented action in the orchestra's history, but it was made before all the appearances had taken place. The news put Toscanini into a paroxysm of indignation at not having been either consulted or notified. The offense enabled NBC to snatch him away from the Philharmonic, to whom he had previously promised guest appearances, and served to justify Toscanini's acceptance of NBC's offer.

Although Barbirolli's Philharmonic debut had made a fairly favorable impression, his premature appointment set the skeptical press and public solidly against him. The extent of Judson's dictatorial powers can be therefore estimated by Barbirolli's six-year tenure, during which the critics lambasted his programs and concerts, box-office receipts shrank, recordings and record sales declined, and the radio audience simply fell away. The orchestra became demoralized.

Judson then suggested to his rubber-stamp board that Rodzinski would be an excellent man to build orchestral discipline and confidence, despite his history of eccentricity and contract-breaking. Rodzinski was invited and seemed pleased to accept. Although there was an almost instantaneous improvement, he was literally starting from the bottom. It would have been impossible for anyone to ameliorate within one season the damage that had been accomplished over so long a period. He worked on with ever better results for almost three years.

The long association between Stokowski, Judson, and Rodzinski in Philadelphia had enabled them to get to know each other's habits and patterns, or so they thought. Although Judson was prepared for Rodzinski's unshackled independence, he had not anticipated that it would ever assume the proportion of a personal attack on him. But finally Rodzinski could no longer tolerate the situation and announced his intention of resigning, charging that Judson had shackled conductors and misused the orchestra as a window display to advertise his artists and had thereby usurped Rodzinski's artistic freedom and authority. When Judson and Stokowski met that fateful day, after their amicable cross-country phone call, he merely told Stokowski that he and Rodzinski were too far apart in their objectives, that it had become impossible to work together any longer, and that Rodzinski's resignation was imminent.

Stokowski took this in stride, for gossip had already apprised him of the facts. He recognized the validity of Rodzinski's accusations and also of Judson's pragmatic concern about the orchestra's shoddy image. He also knew, at first hand, the Philharmonic's notorious undependability and hostility. He well remembered the difficulty he had experienced with the orchestra and his 1930 resolution never again to conduct it. Nevertheless, he told himself, in seventeen years things could change. Moreover, even in its most neurotic days it was still capable under Furtwängler, Walter, and Toscanini of proving what a remarkable ensemble its superb personnel could achieve. Fervor and passion were missing, but with time, sufficient stimulus, and a guiding policy, there was no reason why they too could not be resuscitated. It was worth trying. Stokowski said he would accept the challenge.

When he began to rehearse the Philharmonic in early January of 1947, he was pleased and not too surprised to find an aggregation of players far more dignified and realistic than he had expected. Now, at least in the nonmusical sense, they "knew the score." With quiet determination, they got to work. This time, Stokowski's unsurpassed qualities came through clearly. His magnetism and watchfulness inspired the players' attention, stimulated their pride, and pointed the way to greatness.

Mitropoulos's first concerts with the Philharmonic had been meticulously covered by the city's leading critic, Virgil Thomson. In the *Herald Tribune,* he wrote a summation of the 1946 symphonic season:

The Mitropoulos concerts were wholly dependable technically. Musically they varied a good deal. Some of them were nervous and violent, others calm almost to the point of platitude. . . . He is a great workman, certainly. He is an interesting musician, certainly. The exact nature of his musical culture and personality remains, however, vague. He seems to be oversensitive, overweaning, overbrutal, overintelligent, underconfident, and wholly without ease. He is clearly a musician of class, nevertheless, and a coming man of some sort in the musical world.

Of Stokowski's first concert with the Philharmonic on January 3, 1947, Thomson wrote:

The return of Jacques Thibaud, violinist, to the American scene after a fifteen-year absence and some high-powered musical magic on the part of Leopold Stokowski, conductor, set apart as memorable last night's concert of the Philharmonic Symphony Orchestra in Carnegie Hall. The program itself, moreover, was one of no mean distinction, containing, in addition to Mozart's familiar Overture to *Don Giovanni,* Lalo's *Symphonie Espagnole,* two of Milhaud's *Saudades do Brazil,* and Hindemith's elegant First (and only) Symphony, not to speak of a transcription by Mr. Stokowski of a ravishing Victoria motet. . . . As for Mr. Stokowski's conducting, it was pure miracle from beginning to end. Often in the past, critics, the present one included, have protested at errors of taste on this conductor's part. Last night there was none. Everything was played with a wondrous beauty of sound, with the noblest proportions, with the utmost grandeur of expression. The perfection of tonal rendering for which Stokowski and his Philadelphia Orchestra were so long famous was revived last night with the Philharmonic men in a performance of Debussy's *Afternoon of a Faun* that for both beauty and poetry has been unmatched for many years, if ever, in my experience.

Stokowski's conquest of New York's orchestra, public, and press was remarkably comprehensive and continued for three years. He conducted them in over forty concerts the first season, over thirty in the second, and more than fifty in the third. In the meantime, Bruno Walter had been appointed musical adviser, but the Nazi holocaust that had claimed so many of his cherished friends and relatives had left him a crushed man. Moreover, his total lack of affinity for contemporary music eliminated him as a candidate for a permanent conductorship. For the final stretch, Charles Munch had joined Mitropoulos and Stokowski, but the Boston Symphony Orchestra's timely offer of its directorship made him drop out.

What was happening at the Philharmonic and why was no mystery to Stokowski. He knew that Judson's strong personality and ambitious nature had often worked against the orchestra and its conductors. Judson had acted as a dictator rather than a mediator able to reconcile the inevitable conflicts between a proud conductor and stiff-necked trustees. Stokowski, however, was not going to put up with any interference. At the Philharmonic, he took over without a further word to or from Judson and his board.

Halfway through the first season, the exacting Virgil Thomson wrote, "Today, the Philharmonic for the first time in this writer's memory is the equal of the Boston and the Philadelphia orchestras and possibly their superior." He was careful to acknowledge Rodzinski's preparatory benefactions.

Thomson, incidentally, had never found credible Judson's claim that Rodzinski left the Philharmonic because he had been offered a better job. "There is no better job," he wrote, and Stokowski was gradually coming to this conclusion.

No one could tell what was going on behind the scenes. For more than a year, everyone momentarily expected the permanent appointment of Stokowski by the Philharmonic officers and board. Finally, Stokowski decided to play what in 1916 had proven to be his trump card, the work that had won him world fame—Mahler's *Symphony of a Thousand.*

On April 6, 1950, Leopold Stokowski conducted the New York Philharmonic Orchestra in Mahler's Eighth Symphony in Carnegie Hall with the Schola Cantorum, Westminster Choir, and the Boy's Choir from Public School no. 12 in Manhattan as the assisting choruses. Soloists included Frances Yeend, Uta Graf, Camilla Williams, Martha Lipton, Louise Bernhardt, Eugene Conley, Carlos Alexander, and George London. Wrote Virgil Thomson in the *Herald Tribune:*

> Mahler's Eighth Symphony as directed last night by Leopold Stokowski in Carnegie Hall, was a glorious experience to one who had not heard it before. Its sculpture of vast tonal masses at the end of each of the two movements was handled by the conductor in so noble a manner that the sound achieved monumentality while remaining musical. The effect was unquestionably grand. . . . One is grateful to Mr. Stokowski and to his assembled forces for letting us hear it. Also for giving it to us with such great care for musical decorum. Such handsome loudness as took place in both perorations one does not encounter often in a lifetime.

The opinion was unanimous. But the charm did not work. A few weeks later, the august board of the New York Philharmonic, with Judson's full approval, announced the appointment of Dimitri Mitropoulos as its permanent conductor. The musical world was stunned. This was a prodigious mistake, a notable example of immeasurable stupidity and treachery. How come? No one will ever know.

Columbia Records also muffed an opportunity to catch Stokowski in a moment of exceptional glory by neglecting to record the Mahler. (Fortunately, a splendid "pirate" recording exists.) Columbia, however, did manage to capture one of Stokowski's greatest performances of this period—that of the American premiere of Vaughan Williams's wisest and most poetic symphony, the Sixth.

With the appointment of Mitropoulos, Stokowski took off for Paris, while the Philharmonic followed another downward path. The orchestra would have to wait another eight years before an enlightened new board would fire Judson and allow an invigorating breeze to blow into the Philharmonic bearing the young American Leonard Bernstein.

"Paris was beautiful beyond words," Stokowski said, "and there I was so pleased to meet some fascinating American artists I had never known." Evidently, he concealed his pleasure at meeting the noted American composer and author Ned Rorem, who has penetratingly revealed his feelings about Stokowski for this publication:

> Like everyone of my generation I was weaned on Stokowski. From *Saint Matthew* to *Sacre* "his" classics give off an opulence so contagious that we all were immured in the viewpoint—or earpoint—whether or not we approved. Being idolized by the vast unwashed and the idle rich, as well as by specific eccentrics (i.e., poor composers), Stokowski became, with the Garbo-*Fantasia*-Vanderbilt era, a legend. Legends, emerging as they do from myths, can never by definition be touched personally; and indeed, I never truly knew the man. But we did have a certain professional rapport which I now recall with mixed feelings.
>
> During the early 1950s we were introduced a couple of times in Paris. His cool social loftiness (in contrast to his conductorial fire) was intimidating. I had no idea that he remembered these meetings (maybe he didn't), much less that he knew my music, when a decade later he included my *Eagles* on his debut(!) concert with the Boston Symphony. I was impressed that he had not contacted me, that he had not (unlike most performers who deign to play American music) insisted on a premiere; rather, that he simply programmed this already published music as though it were a natural repertory item. His broadcast of *Eagles* (10 March 1964) was the most glamorous interpretation I ever heard. I admired Stokowski, as all composers must, for the attitude that the newness of new music is irrelevant to its worth: our music is music, not "modern music." . . . When I told him this a year later (at another of those strained backstage encounters), he greeted the praise with a glazed stare and didn't seem to know who I

was. . . . In April 1972, I sent to Leopold Stokowski a ninetieth birthday homage in the guise of a heartfelt and handwrought salute. He never acknowledged it.

In the early fifties, the game of musical chairs was being played in San Francisco where another conductorial legend had arisen. Since 1936, Pierre Monteux had elevated that beautiful city's orchestra to a stellar position. Following his resignation in 1951, there was an interim period of two seasons during which the orchestra sought an adequate replacement from, among others, Leinsdorf, Solti, Schippers, Stokowski, and Enrique Jorda, the eventual successor.

The orchestra's press representative, Eric Rahn, relates that he and manager Howard Skinner met Stokowski's transcontinental train at the Oakland terminal in November 1951, arriving in Skinner's commodious Lincoln. Although traveling by regular Pullman, Stokowski appeared with a mountain of luggage—two steamer trunks, garment bags, and briefcases—for which his hosts ware totally unprepared. Hastily, a taxicab was hired to supplement the overloaded Lincoln, and they proceeded as a caravan to Stokowski's hotel.

To Rahn's surprise, "Stokowski was not only unperturbed by all this," he said, "but in fact he obviously relished the celebrity role and savored the attention." During a dozen appearances within two successive seasons, Stokowski recorded two albums with the orchestra for RCA, only one of which was released, the stunning version of excerpts from Mussorgsky's *Boris Godunov* with Nicola Rossi-Lemeni, the San Francisco Opera Chorus, and a boy's chorus.

Musical scuttlebutt insisted that of all the guest conductors Stokowski was actually the San Francisco Symphony Orchestra's de facto conductor, that he had the post "in the bag." The reason he was not invited may possibly be explained by two incidents that Charles O'Connell enjoyed telling. When Stokowski rehearsed his own orchestration of Mussorgsky's

Pictures at an Exhibition, he faced a group that had been meticulously prepared by Monteux and had been taught to revere Ravel's ravishing instrumentation of that piece. "In the midst of the rehearsal," related O'Connell, "one of the second violinists busied himself practicing the Mendelssohn Violin Concerto, which his colleagues could hear but in the great orchestral tuttis Stokowski apparently could not." Finally, Stokowski noticed some disturbance and stopped the group, but the mischievous musician, not having his eye on the conductor, went on for a few bars. No one knew how Stokowski was going to take the situation. Stokowski rose to its humor and to everyone's surprise said suavely, "There, gentlemen, is the kind of enthusiasm I want."

During another rehearsal, this time of Schubert's *Unfinished* Symphony, Stokowski had inserted a gratuitous part for bass clarinet. "It so happens," wrote O'Connell, "that the player of this instrument was a quite temperamental gentleman as well as a composer, and when he saw Stokowski's addition to Schubert's score, he was possessed by fury." When he expressed his feelings resonantly, Manager Skinner saved the day by persuading him to sit through the symphony pretending to play, but sounding nothing. "The compromise was effected. Stokowski didn't notice," O'Connell concluded.

Really? Stokowski was merely being politic, for he knew that this orchestra was strongly represented on the administrative board. When the time came for final decisions, few musicians supported his nomination. His uncommon restraint, however, indicated to many that he would have welcomed the post, at least for a while.

Instead, the early fifties saw him frequently in the United States and Europe as guest conductor. Between his first and second visits to San Francisco, he appeared in England for the first time in forty years at the 1951–52 Festival of Britain.

In 1952, Stokowski was given the Alice Ditson Award for his "adventurousness" following a concert at Columbia University that climaxed a festival of American music. Later that season, under the joint auspices of the American Composers's Alliance and of Broadcast Music, Incorporated, he presented two concerts at the Museum of Modern Art. In a preliminary speech Stokowski sounded another of his prophetic phrases: "The composer usually has to wait for somebody else to play his music. Some day, like the painter, he may be able to work directly on the materials of sound, on the [tape] recorder for example."

For the next two years he traveled through North and South America on various guest-conducting tours. In 1953, Stokowski conducted six Sunday radio concerts entitled "Twentieth-Century Concert Hall" under the dual sponsorship of the American Composers's Alliance and CBS. The exceptionally imaginative programs included works by Heitor Villa-Lobos, Ralph Vaughan Williams, Joaquin Turina, Ben Weber, William Grant Still, and Silvestre Revueltas.

In 1954, he had a particularly enjoyable experience in Cleveland, crowned with success and pleasure when George Szell invited him to conduct the superlative orchestra that Stokowski termed "in a class by itself." A month before his arrival, he had been invited by Professor Fred Rosenberg of the Cleveland Institute to conduct his Youth Orchestra of musicians who were seven to fifteen years of age. The courtesy and precision of Stokowski's correspondence in preparation for his two unremunerated rehearsals with the youngsters were no less than if he had been accepting the highest paid dates with a celebrated orchestra.

But there were conditions: absolutely no publicity, no photographs, and no visitors. Stokowski appeared exactly on time. After rehearsal, he asked each player, "How old are you? What do you plan to do in music?" Suddenly, a man appeared pointing a camera. He moved up to get a close shot of the famous profile. A flash went off. There was a dramatic silence as Stokowski turned and focused an icy stare on the offender, saying, "Bring me that camera!" Professor Rosen-

berg then recognized the hapless photographer as one of
Cleveland's most prominent citizens, who sheepishly and
promptly obeyed Stokowski's demand. With a furious gesture, the Maestro ripped out the film, held it high for a
moment, and then returned the camera in regal silence.

The same year he visited Florida as guest conductor of the
Miami Symphony Orchestra. A promotional broadcast was
arranged on which Stokowski would be interviewed personally by John Prosser, the manager and executive vice-president of station WKAT, before the performance. Stokowski
stood alongside Prosser, who began to read his script and
stated that Stokowski was born in 1882.

At this moment, listeners heard an angry shout: "No. No.
No. No. No. That isn't true. I was born in 1887."

Prosser chose to disregard this, continuing, "He was born
of a Polish father and an Irish mother." Another shriek rent
the airwaves, and the same interrupting voice screamed, "My
mother was not Irish. This is terrible. Where did you get that
stuff?"

This time, Stokowski, determined at all costs to preserve
his mythic origins, seized the first page of the script off the
announcer's stand and attempted to pull Prosser away from
the microphone. Shaking himself loose, Prosser commanded, "Cut the broadcast." The red carpet had been
pulled out from under Stokowski's feet.

In reporting this pitiful scrimmage, the *Miami Herald*
wrote, "The estranged husband of heiress Gloria Vanderbilt,
an aspiring actress who readily admits to being 30, then
strode onto the concert stage and gave a performance that
the critics found 'electrifying.' " Music was always his eternal
solvent—his only one, especially at this time in his life when
he was subtracting the years and doubly conscious of them
because of the disparity in age between himself and his wife.

When the white-maned maestro married the beautiful
young princess of one of America's royal families, many people spoke of the numerous traits they shared that assured

their compatibility—charisma, mystery, perfectionism, a detestation of parties, and a keen awareness of the value of time and of disciplined work. Halfway through the decade of their marriage, everyone wondered what impish destiny, what demonic genius could have contrived such a mismatch. After ten years and two children, Gloria sued for divorce on the ground of "incompatibility of character."

In the beginning the whirlwind courtship and the elopement with a girl younger than Stokowski's own first daughter pointed to a passionate romance, and Gloria in various interviews did express herself as being "madly in love." And why not? This "poor little rich girl" who had all the accoutrements of wealth and social position had endured a miserable and lonely childhood. She also harbored undeveloped artistic talents and unfulfilled ambitions that set her apart from her luxurious, but philistine, milieu. Stokowski represented the world of culture and art. Theoretically, they had the makings of a deeply rewarding relationship, for Gloria was gifted and sensitive and lovely, with a soft, sad smile. But it does in fact take two to tango, a dance Stokowski never learned. Each time he sat it out. As one colleague put it, "Stoki's marriages weren't marriages—they were mergers."

For a while, their lives together appeared to be pleasant and tranquil as Gloria busied herself making a stunning country home on her Connecticut estate, where they lived in relative isolation. Gloria again began to work on the hobbies that she took very seriously: painting, sculpting, and writing poetry. Inasmuch as her husband was often absent filling his engagements, she next acquired and decorated a magnificent twelve-room apartment on Gracie Square in New York and devised a studio for herself on another floor. She also cooked, shopped, and saw friends.

In 1950, Gloria gave birth to a boy, named Leopold Stanislanovicz. The Russian ending to the Polish name was no more authentic than Stokowski's accent. The next year, a second son arrived, whom they named Christopher. Gloria smothered the children with love. In her court trials she had said, "Children can be so lonely. I wanted to grow up and marry and have a lot of children and love them so much that they'd never be lonely or unhappy." Perhaps that was too unrealistic a hope, but she obviously did her best with Stan and Chris and the two sons she had with her third husband, Sidney Lumet, a dynamic film and television director who was exactly Gloria's age.

Stokowski gloried in his two sons. Throughout the rest of his life, he remained unusually devoted and attentive to both of them. They reciprocated, and fortunately it did not conflict with their deep and constant love for their mother.

By 1952, the few people with whom both Stokowskis had some semblance of a social relationship noticed that Gloria was becoming more and more depressed. She complained that her paintings were emerging "dark and tormented." She suffered dizzy spells. Always, she had a charmingly hesitant speech. Now, she began to stutter. When the fainting spells increased, her doctors recommended psychiatric therapy.

Gradually, she began to acquire new insights, to gain confidence, and to assert her creativity and independence. Stokowski had particularly admired her long dark hair, which she wore in braids down to her forearms. In a healthy sign of rebellion, she cut it short. Stokowski fumed with rage. Guests related that Stokowski did everything possible to embarrass her by being rude to her friends. The rift kept widening. Their home life became a domestic hell. When she announced her intention of suing for divorce, Stokowski threatened, "If Gloria leaves me, there will be a custody fight that will make the court battle her mother and aunt waged look like a picnic." The marriage was doomed, but he would not face it.

An article in *Look* magazine in 1956 described Gloria's relationship to Stokowski as being "like that of an Arab wife: obedient, almost slavish, doing everything for her husband and her children and nothing for herself." That was now all over and done with. She moved out of their apartment with the boys, saying, "Leopold is a genius and dedicated to his work. For the past three years I've lived practically alone— Leopold was often gone on concert tours for as long as seven months at a time. I was left the choice of going out without him or remaining a recluse. I want to start a new life for myself and my children. There is no bitterness between us."

One would have to question that final statement. My offer to interview her for this book was declined in a brief note from her secretary, stating that she was unavailable for comment. Nevertheless, one cannot ignore the fact that regardless of their domestic blisters, Gloria was the mother of the children he most loved. "Stoki's superdevotion to the boys may partially be accounted for," Evangeline told me, "because he might have felt that he had not established a really close relationship with his three girls." And for a man so concerned with his public image, the boys were also, one would have to surmise, yet another proof of his potency and his power.

12

ALTHOUGH STOKOWSKI rented an attractive New York apartment immediately after the divorce, he felt like a man without a home, for Stan and Chris went to live with their mother. Almost every other night he would have the boys at his place for supper, and on the other evenings he would sit at Gloria's table while they had their dinner. When Gloria put an end to that, Stokowski became a lonely man. Years later, in the muckraking custody suit that he initiated, Gloria denounced him "for hovering over the boys like an overanxious, harassing and harassed great-grandmother, creating neurotic explosions." The hurt of the sudden separation was great. It made him more conscious of his other need—a podium of his own.

It so happened that the orchestra of Houston, Texas, was looking for a prominent permanent conductor. Stokowski was familiar with this orchestra, having guest conducted it in 1951 and again in 1953. He knew its founder, the legendary Miss Ima Hogg, and its exceptionally qualified manager, Tom M. Johnson. He had also learned something of the fascinating history of the city and its orchestra, which has been documented by Hubert Roussel, the music and drama critic first for the *Houston Press* and later for the *Houston Post*, in his informative book *The Houston Symphony Orchestra, 1913–1971*.

214

Hardly more than a year after its founding in 1836, Houston had a musical theater going full swing before the town had either a church or a jail. Obviously, a community that Roussel described as "little more than an extraordinary abundancy of magnolias and snakes" and that immediately had to provide entertainment of this sort must have boasted a sizable and sophisticated group of native settlers, including a generous representation of well-educated Europeans.

The town expanded dramatically in every direction. In this century, its physical appearance became a miracle of modernity and the population grew to be the sixth largest in the country. A city of this magnificence, yet full of old world charm, should certainly have enough music-lovers to support a local orchestra. Who would assume it and when?

The star performer in this drama was the daughter of James Stephen Hogg, a young district attorney soon to be the first native governor of Texas. In the summer of 1882, the year of Stokowski's birth, a daughter was born to the Hoggs who they named Ima, after the heroine of a novel by James Hogg's admired oldest brother, Thomas. Ima's love for music, her devotion to Houston, and her constancy to standards and purpose were greatly responsible for the formation of a symphony orchestra in 1913. It took twenty years of intense effort before the ensemble emerged from the experimental stages to a semiprofessional state.

The orchestra came of age in 1936, when Serge Koussevitzky highly recommended an exceptionally gifted and cultured young conductor, Ernst Heinrich Hoffmann. A modest leader possessing solid musicianship, the ability to develop balance, tonal quality, and precise ensemble, Hoffmann attracted to the opening concert an audience of thirty-seven hundred, which, writes Roussel, "found reasons for greeting the new conductor with more than merely courteous interest." He remained in charge for eleven years, the longest tenure that any conductor has ever held in that post.

Hoffmann's last season was shared with two guest conductors, Carlos Chavez, a model of Mexican suavity, and Efrem Kurtz, a forty-year-old Russian conductor who had come to America via the Ballet Russe de Monte Carlo and who was eventually awarded a three-year contract. Kurtz became popular, and not only in Houston. Under a contract with Columbia, he went north to record with the New York Philharmonic, which spurred resentment in Texas, and provoked the board to take on guest conductors for the next seasons. One of them was Leopold Stokowski.

In 1953, Kurtz was dismissed with a year's grace to effect other plans. The next season concentrated upon guest conductors, mainly those who might be available for a continuing association. Those invited were Hugo Rignold, Erich Leinsdorf, Ernest Ansermet, Maurice Abravanel, Ferenc Fricsay, and Milton Katins, but none stayed on.

Finally, President Ima Hogg took off for New York to do a bit of sleuthing. After a fruitless week, she was about to return when a sudden inspiration seized her. She called up Sir Thomas Beecham's manager, Andrew Schulhof, who also managed Stokowski.

"What's Stokowski doing these days," she asked.

"Not too much," Schulhof answered. "He's very hard to handle and seems terribly depressed."

"I'm interested."

Stokowski was then guest-conducting the Detroit Orchestra. Schulhof called him, and within a few days Stokowski had signed a three-year contract to become principal conductor of the Houston Symphony at the start of the 1955–56 season. He was to conduct at least ten of the twenty subscription concerts each season and would act as the orchestra's director with full powers.

When the 73-year-old Stokowski came down one sweltering August day to look things over in advance, the board wondered if they had made a serious error. The inharmonious clash of his attire, his discordant pronunciation of Houston as "Hooston," and his insistence upon meeting "a real Texas cowboy," an image that the sophisticates had made every effort to obliterate, all perplexed the Houstonians. The resourceful welcoming committee handled his last request by taking him to an amusement park where he met a deputy sheriff at a pony ride and was duly photographed while somberly accepting the badge of an enrolled member of the sheriff's force. He was absurdly vain about it and displayed it on every possible occasion, and the next year, when he came back, he called the sheriff up to "report for duty."

Administratively, he began to readjust himself to undertake the responsibilities of an overall music director, a role he had not played since 1936. He consulted with the orchestra's officers and board members, to whom he was courteous but remote. "Do you want the Houston Symphony to be good, very good, or equal to any in this world?" he inquired of the board, artfully preparing the way for the usual Stokowski blitzkrieg that would assure him everything he wanted exactly the way he wanted it. He examined the concert hall meticulously and critically, noting every acoustical weakness. Stokowski returned to New York, stayed six weeks, and arrived back in October without a moment to spare in preparation for the 1955–56 season. It was a hint to the observant that Houston did not loom in his mind as another Philadelphia.

Nevertheless the Stokowski concerts duplicated the glamour and excitement that characterized previous opening seasons in Cincinnati, Philadelphia, New York, and Los Angeles. His celebrity immediately produced an unexpected dividend when a portion of the dress rehearsal for the inaugural concert was nationally telecast on NBC's program "Wide, Wide World." It was the orchestra's debut on network television and featured the premiere performance of Alan Hovhaness's *Mysterious Mountain,* commissioned specifically for the Houston opening.

On opening night, the audience heard their orchestra play with the inner warmth, richness, and depth of sound that had brought the Philadelphia Orchestra to the summit of beauty and perfection. The program included Wagner's *Meistersinger* Prelude, Brahms's First Symphony, Ravel's Second Suite from *Daphnis et Chloé,* and the Hovhaness composition, for which the composer was present. The program was an architectural model of Stokowskian proportion.

There had been considerable apprehension on the orchestra's part that Stokowski would fire personnel ruthlessly. Instead, he merely added two splendid artists, Robert Slaughter as first violist and Margaret Auë as first cellist. As usual, he altered the disposition of players according to the needs of the Music Hall. His objectives remained the same: to obtain large amounts of volume without distortion and to allow solo instruments to be heard clearly and with instantly recognizable individuality. Stokowski turned his attention to the hall itself—its timbre, its transparency, its congeniality to any volume of sound the conductor demands. Ima Hogg came to every one of his rehearsals and became fascinated with his acoustical experiments. During the second season she presented a Christmas gift to the orchestra, a new shell for the Music Hall's stage with a Stokowski sound-reflector. Stokowski reciprocated with a gift of four "acoustical panels" of dubious sonic value.

As the 1956–57 season developed, it was obvious that Stokowski had the orchestra working at the peak of its form. Roussel wrote, "The noble sonorities he repeatedly coaxed from the instruments were examples of the genius of his talent." One explanation for the supersound was a formidable instrument that Stokowski devised, an electronic two-octave cello with a fingerboard that supported his double basses. With the volume up, its bass-range dynamics could shake the rafters, but Stokowski's sensitivity and subtlety kept it undetectable except as a wondrous supplementary effect.

Throughout his career, Stokowski had so few musical "accidents" that when one did occur, the gossips spread it to the far corners, but they rarely noted that when Stokowski made a blooper, he rarely palmed it off and usually took the blame. For an all-Russian concert in Houston, his soloist in Prokofiev's G-minor Violin Concerto was the American, Fredell Lack, an artist to her fingertips, who had made it in the biggest towns, married a Houston physician, and became an honored resident. As the generally superb performance was drawing to its close, the tricky rhythmic changes on the last pages of the work caused a mix-up and the orchestra finished first. Stokowski waited for his soloist, then calmly turned the pages of the score back to the coda and indicated that it was to be repeated, whereupon everyone finished on time to great applause for Miss Lack's beautiful performance until disaster struck, for her presence of mind thereafter, and for Stokowski's tacit and gallant admission that it was his fault. Nevertheless, Stokowski stalked off the platform in a fury, never uttering one word of explanation, apology, or good-humored banter to his soloist. An incalculable man.

The only predictable aspect of Stokowski was to be found in his programs: Almost every one offered a Houston premiere and the expectation that, whenever possible, the composer would appear in person. During Stokowski's tenure, novelties included Henry Cowell's Sixth Symphony; Howard Hanson's G-major Piano Concerto, with Rudolf Firkusny as soloist; Shostakovich's Tenth and Eleventh Symphonies; Wallingford Riegger's *Dance Rhythms;* Peter Mennin's Sixth Symphony; Charles Ives's *The Unanswered Question;* Khachaturian's *Festive Poem;* Michael Tippett's dance suite from his opera *The Midsummer Marriage;* Thomas de Hartman's dances from his opera *Esther;* Fikret Amirov's *Azerbaijan Mugam;* and Natasha Bender's *Soliloquy* for oboe and orchestra. Utilizing the Houston Chorale, Stokowski introduced Carl Orff's *Carmina Burana* with sensational effect; on a later occasion another Orff concoction, *The Triumph of Aphrodite,* which turned out to be a ponderous fiasco; and Sibelius's *Hymn to the Earth,* in tribute to the composer's ninetieth birthday. Stokowski's representation of contemporary styles also included such established modern classics as the works of Ravel and Vaughan Williams. There were, of course, the traditional masterpieces, including concertos with excellent soloists.

During Stokowski's period, Ima Hogg informed the society of her wish to retire from the presidency, and she was replaced by Gen. Maurice Hirsch, a distinguished attorney and passionate music-lover whose mother had been a member of the original board of directors. General Hirsch's board decided to take stock of Stokowski's reign to date, admirably summed up by Roussel: "The truth was that Stokowski had found in Houston an already excellent orchestra; in the sense of actual construction there was not much left to be done. There was no doubt that Stokowski's effect, in that special regard, had been felt. To the players, however, he often seemed coldly remote, a self-centered and unapproachable figure. They felt they were much taken for granted. At rehearsals the master had an air of imperial gravity, but if he was irked, could be melodramatic in his tantrums."

Stokowski had been given carte blanche concerning his programming policy and musical philosophy, and the audiences had been extraordinarily open-minded, even when subjected to such torturous experiences as Ernst Křenek's Cello Concerto or Olivier Messiaen's *Réveil des Oiseaux.* But by the time the three-year contract expired at the end of the 1957–58 season, it was evident that a certain disenchantment had set in.

The subscribers had begun to feel that Stokowski had exceeded the limit of reasonable experimentalism. They began to stay away, to complain to the management, and to threaten the discontinuance of their subscriptions. When the orchestra realized that their conductor was no longer attracting sold-out houses, it became distracted and nervous. There was only one way out. Stokowski was asked to cease overplaying the music that had alienated the subscribers and was merely offered a season-to-season contract.

He accepted, but from that moment his relation to the orchestra and the board was more cursory and frigid than ever. That winter, he spent less than a month in Houston, performing four all-Brahms programs, then skipping out of town not to reappear until mid-March. Next, he announced a performance of Schoenberg's *Gurrelieder,* scored for three choirs, and he requested the Houston Chorale, the State University Chorus, and an outstanding black chorus. The university chorus balked at singing with a black chorus, and was supported by the orchestra board. Stokowski walked out and announced his intention to leave "an environment so full of prejudice."

Whether or not the racial incident was the primary reason for Stokowski's sudden decision, his sincerity on this issue is beyond question, as the following, written to William Grant Still in 1937, attests: "I hope to play your Second Symphony in concert soon. Do you have a title that would make the public realize that while you are in every way an American, you are of African origin? . . . It would be good for the public to realize how great is your achievement." Still subtitled this symphony *Song of a New Race.* Stokowski conducted it and many of his other works. It was difficult enough in those days to introduce black artists without patronization, but urging Still to assert his blackness with pride is a reliable affirmation of Stokowski's freedom from bigotry.

When Stokowski took an extended leave of absence in 1960, Tom Johnson secured a pair of coveted dates for the alluring Sir John Barbirolli, who was on temporary absence from the celebrated Hallé Orchestra. When John and Evelyn Barbirolli arrived in Houston, everyone fell in love with them. They were warm, open-hearted, and unaffected people and proved irresistible to concert audiences.

A superbly chosen and performed program captivated the entire town. In the *Chronicle,* Ann Holmes said, "The thrill came back into Symphony Hall last night." And T.V. Thompson in the *Press* called the evening "a lesson in pure beauty." Hubert Roussel stated in the *Post* that "Sir John had imparted a magnificent lesson to the orchestra at a very desirable time." Inevitably, everyone concerned began to explore the possibility of enticing or bribing or snatching Barbirolli away from Manchester to Houston.

Stokowski was bound to hear of it. And so, five years after appearing in hospitable Houston and being received with open arms by a city ready to adopt him as the father of its musical family, he announced that the 1960–61 season would be his last. Houston had never become Stokowski's home, or even second home, and none of the aristocracy of the orchestral court ever became "his people." But he did have a coterie, and as usual kept them to himself and at his service.

On Stokowski's very first visit, when he befriended Kenneth Trammell, the stage manager of the Music Hall, he asked, "Kenniss, what kind of whiskey do you like, Irish or Scotch?" When "Kenneth" replied, "Scotch," Stokowski said, "You can't be all bad." That was the tone and mood of the relationship that sprang up between "Kenniss," his associate, Hymie, and the orchestra handyman, Willie. They drove Stokowski to and from rehearsals whenever Tom Johnson did not and took him in their cars for sightseeing trips and to their homes for dinner.

"And always," said Kenneth, "his favorite topic was Stan and Chris, and Chris and Stan. Once, when one of my stagehands had his little boy with him, Stokowski noticed the boy's boots. He stooped down, examined them carefully, and said, 'I've got to get my sons some of those for Christmas.' After concerts, Maestro would call the stagehand and his son to the dressing room and talk to them at considerable length. He adored children. After his fall session, just before returning to New York for the holidays, he would give a party in the lobby of the theater on a Saturday afternoon for the children of the orchestra members. During the afternoon the adults would stand around and talk to one another. He would mingle with nobody but the children."

Kenneth recalled that on the night of Stokowski's last concert in Houston, the Maestro walked into the theater, went directly backstage, and said, "Kenniss, tonight after the concert I want to see you and Hymie in my dressing room." After the concert, they started for the dressing room, and "there stood a dozen or so society people waiting. I couldn't barge in there with all those important people waiting," Kenneth said, "so we left to join the others. Within two minutes the business manager came back and said, 'Kenneth and Hymie, the Maestro wants to see you right now.' So we went in, wading through the throngs of people who had gathered in front of his door. He was alone, greeted us warmly, pulled out a huge flask from his overcoat pocket and poured drinks for the three of us. We sat there, talking about everything, and he wouldn't let us go for almost half an hour. Then we got up and walked past all those people still standing there. I told Hymie this was his goodbye and his way of thanking us for whatever we have done. And let me tell you that I was stage manager for seventeen years and the relationship with Stokowski was the highlight of this time."

William Lee Pryor, the editor of the University of Houston's *Forum,* told me, "Stoki telephoned me shortly after he got home. 'I've just written a letter to all three Houston papers,' he said, 'and I'm sending you a carbon copy. Please report to me how much they print and how accurately.' Not one of them published a word." They had obviously lost all interest in their former shining light. Financially, as well as artistically, his concerts had grown less and less successful. At the end of the former season, the inevitable deficit had been grudgingly assumed, but his tide had run out. This man had sailed through life winning almost every battle. Houston was not among his victories. And yet, it was not a failure. Hubert Roussel said in summation of Stokowski's reign over the Houston Symphony, "Stokowski's term meant much to the orchestra. . . . It had learned to live at the top of the mountain, and having become fully accustomed to that rarified air, was left a more established and confident body."

Stokowski had many other trials and triumphs throughout those years. One of the trials came in 1956 when he introduced Carl Orff's *Midsummer Night's Dream* at the Empire State Music Festival in Ellenville, New York. In a cast that included Stokowski's old Hollywood friend Basil Rathbone was Red Buttons, who ran afoul of the Maestro's temper by engaging in some good-natured rehearsal horseplay. Buttons's out-of-character puckishness drove the angry Stokowski from the podium. The conductor was cajoled into returning, but even he could not make the production a success.

Among the triumphs was a 1958 visit to the Soviet Union, where Stokowski conducted the splendid Soviet Radio Orchestra, playing the Shostakovich Eleventh Symphony with the composer on hand to embrace him. On this trip he also made a superb recording of Prokofiev's Fifth Symphony, released two years later. On his return, he conducted a top caliber pickup orchestra in the American premiere of the Ninth Symphony of his late friend Ralph Vaughan Williams.

In 1959, Fritz Reiner had a heart attack and Chicago turned to Stokowski, who was very glad to conduct a marvelous orchestra and to use it as an excuse to get to Houston as late as possible. In the Windy City, he performed the Beethoven *Eroica* and Kodaly's *Harry Janos* Suite "unsurpassed by any other performance I ever heard,," writes Herbert Ruhm of Vienna, "or by anything on records before or since. I had not dreamt music could be made to sound this way."

His Chicago triumph preceded his first regular engagement in an opera house. The New York City Center Opera

Company asked him to conduct a double bill of Orff's *Carmina Burana* and Stravinsky's *Oedipus Rex.* Actually, they were his choices. He was in the mood to do something spectacular now, when his Houston days were nearing an end and his personal life was in such turmoil. He was still in the throws of a bitter, mudslinging case for the custody of his sons. General Hirsch and Tom Johnson had appeared in New York as character witnesses for him, but it was impossible to counteract his ex-wife's humiliating accusations against him and his unsavory associates whom she named. The custody of the boys was awarded to Gloria Vanderbilt Stokowski Lumet in 1959, and of necessity, Stokowski turned all his energies to the City Center Opera.

Stokowski knew exactly what to perform. His choices were inspired. It would be hard to find two works by two modern composers that contain more cunning similarities and intriguing contrasts. Both are products of the tumultuous years between the two world wars. Both are based on old texts. Both seek contemporary meaning, even future forms, in ancient issues and musical art. Contrastingly, *Oedipus* is a granitic, ecclesiastic tragedy, whereas *Carmina* is a rapturously lusty piece of neoprimitivism. Neither of these works are operas: they are closer to dramatic oratorios, with most of the drama in wonderfully effective music, which Stokowski exploited thoroughly. Howard Taubman in *The New York Times* wrote, "For most of his long career in America, Mr. Stokowski had devoted himself to symphonic music. As a musician and public figure, his instincts have always been dramatic. His work with this double bill showed how much at home he could be in the opera house. For he has a magnetism as a conductor, as well as a drive and a sense of pace."

The next year, Stokowski's double bill offered a curious mingling of Monteverdi's *Orfeo* and Luigi Dallapiccola's *Il Prigioniero.* It was a curious combination that aroused curious critical reactions. Because Stokowski chose to use a mixture of old and new instruments for the seventeenth-century work and not to "reorchestrate" it, the Monteverdi emerged in its naked urtext, musically harmless and tasteful, but stylistically bridled and without harmonic tension. The modern piece was theatrically very effective, but not much more than reasonably communicative musically. A puzzled press and public treated the event respectfully and cautiously. Operatically, Stokowski was gaining experience and biding his time.

In the interim, Stokowski received an invitation from the Philadelphia Orchestra to conduct a set of concerts early in February of 1960. He accepted without hesitation. For nineteen years he had not wanted to set foot in Philadelphia, so poignant was his bitterness. It was said that in his cross-country journeys he would lower the window blinds as the train sped through his former home town. His reappearance in Philadelphia after so long an absence from the orchestra he had created was an impressive and moving occasion. The capacity house had been sold out the morning following the announcement of his program, which comprised compositions long associated with his career: Mozart's *Marriage of Figaro* Overture, Falla's *El Amor Brujo,* Shostakovich's Fifth Symphony, and Respighi's *Pines of Rome.*

Technically, his virtuosity was intact. Musically, he demonstrated eloquently what the years can bring to a musician who places his thoughts and energies at the service of his art. Thereafter, Stokowski appeared almost every year in Philadelphia until he left America permanently.

His reassociation with the London Symphony Orchestra also began in 1960, when the orchestra was at a very low ebb and would play for any conductor who had the money to hire it. A forceful young newcomer, Ernest Fleischmann, had just come upon the scene as general manager and was busy initiating and implementing new policies.

"Although Stokowski did express interest in the LSO invitation," said Fleischmann, "it was very difficult to get his acceptance. But the LSO persisted, and I found myself on a June morning awaiting his arrival at the Victoria Station in

London. I didn't know him at all, and I'd never heard him except on disc.

"When he arrived, we left immediately to meet with the orchestra. They got along famously from the start. Through the years, the ones who became most devoted to him were some of the greatest players and most skeptical members of the group, like Neville Marriner and Barry Tuckwell.

"After lunch, I took Stoki and his boys to his abode. Lord knows how he found it—it was one of those dingy little French hotels with a rattling openwork elevator. The hotel was over a smelly, mama-papa type restaurant. Stoki was evidently being frugal."

When I asked Fleischmann about the concerts, he chuckled and then said, "At rehearsals he would gloss over one detail after another which any other conductor would have slaved over until he got it right. Not Stoki. He'd just point at a fiddler in the seventh stand and say, 'You sir. You do not put bow on string. Put bow on string.' Everybody looked at everybody else, not knowing how to figure this out. He seemed to be saving everyone's energy, including his own. Then we'd get to the Royal Festival Hall, and suddenly Stoki would step up and the magic appeared. Every concert was an event. You know that hall . . . that dry sound it has despite the splendid acoustics? Well, when Stoki conducted the very first concert with the LSO, every member of the orchestra and of the audience, every newspaper critic, said that they had never heard such a sonority in that hall from any other orchestra or conductor. The same thing happened at that famous white elephant, the Royal Albert Hall. In that hall, Stoki conducted a Mahler Second that I've never heard equaled in my entire concert experience.

"For a while the arrangement worked splendidly. While I was with the LSO, he was reasonably faithful to this orchestra. But as the years went on, Stokowski was easily talked into conducting and recording other orchestras. The LSO thought they deserved his loyalty, as they were responsible for his second blossoming after Philadelphia. It was, in a way, a matter of honor, and therefore disappointing. Regardless, working with him was an experience.

"In Stoki they had a kindred spirit who was not only fascinated by experimentation, but by the whole new technology that surrounded the tonal world. How much he gloried in it, how much he himself fathered that which lifted the orchestra world to undreamt-of opulence!"

Following Stokowski's reunion with the LSO, he returned to New York. Throughout these years and until his final return to England in 1972, Stokowski lived in a spacious penthouse on upper Fifth Avenue with a stunning view of Central Park. Luxuriant yet utilitarian, piled with treasures and junk, it was a revealing reflection of the musician and man, full of curious mixtures of old and new, oriental and occidental, splashes of riotous color and moods of tranquillity.

The large living room was dominated by a magnificent Florentine carved wood fireplace opposite a numberless, one-handed clock, which virtually only he could read. The rest of the nonperiod furniture comprised couches, tables, chairs picked up all over the globe, complemented by accessories carefully placed to engage the eye—objets d'art that ranged from handsome glass and porcelain to exotic brasses and statuary. For his professional needs, Stokowski had three studio rooms crammed full of musical scores and books housed in metal cases, recordings, electronic equipment, musical instruments, diplomas, awards, decorations. In addition to his own quarters there was a guest room, a maid's room, and a room for each of his sons.

With Chris and Stan, Stokowski was a fun-loving father. He adored having the boys around so that he could join them in reading their books or in playing their games. Indeed, it was a father-son roughhouse that ended in the disaster of Stokowski's broken hip some six weeks before he was to appear at the Met.

He had been called in to replace Dimitri Mitropoulos, who had been scheduled to conduct eight performances of Puccini's *Turandot* before he became ill and was unable to appear. Stokowski was invited to take on the project, starting early in the spring.

One morning, he and his sons were playing football in the long hall of Stokowski's apartment when he slipped and fell on the highly polished floor. He managed to drag himself to his bed, refusing to admit that the injury was serious until a doctor diagnosed a broken hip and called for an ambulance.

The physician had been summoned by Natasha Bender, who, with her friend Faye Chabrow and unhampered by intrusive wives, had resumed a selfless devotion to Stokowski as unofficial majordomo of his household. These were the same two women who had "discovered" him in Philadelphia and had been with him, off and on, through the years.

The day before the accident, Stokowski had been recording an all-Wagner album for RCA, and he and Stewart Warkow were scheduled to hear the playbacks the next day. Warkow, assistant manager of the Symphony of the Air, who had met the conductor when the Maestro was performing at NBC, was by this time a close personal associate. He was naturally surprised to hear from Natasha early that morning.

"Stoki's had an accident," she told him. "I phoned the doctor, and now we're waiting for an ambulance. I'll get back to you later."

Filled with anxiety and impatience, Warkow grabbed a cab and got to Stokowski's apartment to find him in total agony, his face contorted with pain, trying to do push-ups in bed so as to prevent his muscles from going into spasm.

Stokowski was operated on the next day at the Hospital for Special Surgery. The day after that, Stewart, who had been staying at the house, took Stan and Chris to visit their father. "Stoki was heavily sedated," he said, "and when he saw us, tears streamed down his face. I had never before seen Stoki cry, and it broke me in two. He kissed the boys' hands as though to absolve them from blame. He pressed them to his side, the side that didn't have the new steel joint that would eventually enable him to function."

A few days later, Stokowski called Stewart asking him to bring the score of *Turandot,* which he worked on every day of the five weeks spent at the hospital. Sophia Jacobs tells of going to see him, bringing a gift of two baby pillows. "There he lay, drugged and in pain, while the whole bed was covered with marked-up orchestral parts. 'This score,' he said, 'is full of contradictions, and this balance here is not Puccini!' Later I was told that a comparison with another score proved him to be right. What astounded me was his ability to forget his physical condition in his enthusiasm for *Turandot.*"

Finally, Stokowski was allowed to leave the hospital. With Stewart's constant help and on crutches, he began rehearsals. Needless to say, Stokowski involved himself with every aspect of the performance, right to the sets, lighting, and costumes. This was no way to enlist the goodwill or support of Rudolf Bing. Despite the prestigious circumstances of the engagement, it was fraught from the very first moment with misfortune, dissension, and bitterness.

"Stoki worked under enormous difficulties," said Stewart, "not only physical. He didn't have the opera background or routine of a Leinsdorf or a Szell. He also hated the whole mechanism of the prompter, saying that he destroyed his direct communication with his singers."

Apropos, Erich Leinsdorf in *Cadenza* wrote, "Opera demands a large and clear manner of giving the time, while anything vaguely resembling conducting will do for a symphony orchestra. Among the symphony lions who ventured into the opera pit was Stokowski, who insisted on his style of batonless, beautiful air-molding. The first verdict of the Metropolitan Opera's insiders was that the chorus sang on Chicago time while the orchestra kept Eastern Standard."

On the night of the first performance, Stokowski entered the pit on crutches. What transpired thereafter was a performance that a few critics praised for "unprecedented orchestral and choral sonorities" but was torn to shreds on all other counts. Most stringently criticized was Stokowski's neglect in not giving cues to the vocal soloists, whose survival was credited entirely to the prompters.

However, at the end of the opera, there was a triumphant ovation for Stokowski when he took a solo bow, lifting both crutches straight in the air like victorious flags. But everybody was quickly sobered by the reviews—everybody, that is, but Stokowski, who was full of plans to conduct the operas of Wagner and Strauss and Prokofiev's *War and Peace*. Bing threw a cold towel on that by wryly suggesting Gluck's *Alceste* and one or two other works equally unsuited to Stokowski's disposition. Nevertheless, Stokowski fulfilled his contract to the letter, not missing one rehearsal or performance throughout the season.

The next year, Stokowski came back to conduct *Turandot* again, and this time the press really took him apart. They drove him to tactics he had not used since the Cincinnati conflict: He complained publicly about the Metropolitan and the lack of rehearsal time to *The New York Times*.

This gave Bing the chance he was looking for, to point out in rebuttal that Stokowski had not conducted a premiere but a revival from the previous season, which had been allotted at least as much rehearsal as any other opera produced at the opera house. He more than implied that the entire fault lay with Stokowski.

Stokowski's rejoinder appeared in the *Opera News* of February 24, 1962. The sarcastic innuendos rang out all too clearly: The conditions under which one must work in opera inevitably result in a loss of quality, said the conductor. He then bowed out, never to direct another Met opera.

Stokowski got revenge in his own fashion, with his special gift for saying the right thing at exactly the wrong time. On the surface he and Bing remained cordial in a frigid sort of way. One day they were talking about the new opera house in

Lincoln Center which, said Stokowski, opened such fantastic opportunities to the Met. "For example," he said, "why not have an adjustable proscenium to fold out for large-scale Handelian operas and be able to scale down for Mozart's *Figaro* and *Cosí Fan Tutte?*" Bing answered somewhat patronizingly, "My dear Maestro, don't you know that for the next thirty years, the repertoire is going to be Italian opera?" After a moment of silent thoughtfulness, Stokowski answered with the directness of a child: "Dr. Bing, do you mean you're only building an opera house for thirty years?"

A year later, at the famous gala marking the closing of the old Met, Stokowski, after conducting, interrupted the applause with an impassioned plea to all those in attendance to "save this beautiful old house!" Nothing could have been more distressing to the Metropolitan officials, to whom demolition of that beautiful old house spelled certainty and security for the new. But Stokowski would have his little joke, and it added enough fuel to the "Save the Met" conflagration to delay the wrecker's ball for quite a few months.

13

FOLLOWING HIS OPERATIC DEBACLE at the Met, Stokowski indulged in some unflinching self-analysis. Since Philadelphia, he had found no home base where he could live and work contentedly. Professionally and personally, he had been a nomad. The All-American Youth Orchestra, with those beautiful young talents, had been a romantic dream that had quickly faded. His coconductorships with Toscanini and later with Mitropoulos were finally frustrating, as were the ungratifying ventures with the Hollywood Bowl and Houston orchestras. Sometimes he wondered whether he ever should have left Philadelphia.

Early in 1962, a man named Gregory Roberts approached Stokowski's manager with an interesting proposition for a new symphony orchestra. He purported to have the backing of several wealthy individuals and had been well spoken of by some artists. Stokowski caught fire. Never had he been more eager or ready to build an orchestra of his own—and in New York! This would also provide an exciting chance to give opportunities to young people: It would be a sort of successor to the All-American Youth Orchestra. With Roberts as backer and executive director and Stewart Warkow as manager, plans were drawn up, the first season sketched, programs made, six concerts prepared, Carnegie Hall en-

233

gaged, auditions held, publicity pictures taken, and a press conference called.

With everything all set for his latest dream to come to fruition, Stokowski sailed for Europe to meet his summer commitments. Gregory Roberts's summer responsibilities involved keeping things shipshape in New York, a task he accomplished at considerable expense. Gradually, both the orchestra's reserves and New York grew too small for Mr. Roberts, who reportedly jumped ship and disappeared. Stokowski, alerted by his friends, hastened home to face two alternatives: cancel the season or meet the deficit himself. He decided on the latter and put up $60,000.

The first concert went off fairly well; the second was a phenomenal success and the critical raves were enough to start the ball rolling. New sponsors appeared, the foremost being Samuel Rubin, president of Fabergé. Impressed by Stokowski's precise presentation of a five-year plan, Rubin accelerated the creation of a small, but effective, symphonic organization—one that would go beyond an ordinary series of concerts—to further the education of young people by working with the New York Board of Education. The plan was to make concerts available to schoolchildren without charge and to create international goodwill through close association with the United Nations. The colorful opening concert of every season—complete with the diplomats, flags, and fashions of all nations—was dedicated to the United Nations, which was invited to consider the American Symphony Orchestra its orchestra.

Rubin's wife, Cyma, gave her all to many orchestra projects, starting with an art show as a benefit to raise money for a series of eight concerts that twenty-two thousand elementary school children attended free. Stokowski, meanwhile, was hatching a five-year plan to include tours of South America and Europe. The handsomest gift was a grant of $1.5 million from the Ford Foundation. The American Symphony became Stokowski's entire concern, though he still accepted brief guest-conductorships in the States and abroad.

Although the orchestra continued to pick up support, Stokowski donated large cash contributions annually to reduce the inevitable deficits and conducted without fee until the day he left in 1972.

He spent almost every weekday afternoon auditioning young musicians—at least twenty-five each week. He listened to anyone who had sufficient working experience or had studied seriously enough to merit a hearing. If the talent was exceptional, it got hired. Stokowski was invariably polite, even to poor players. Never discouraging, he took copious notes at each audition, which he entered together with a rating of over two thousand performers in a huge notebook kept for the purpose of finding instantaneous replacements.

His concertmaster was Murray Adler, an excellent musician who at first was not interested in the position. However, when Stewart Warkow pressed him, he agreed to play for Stokowski, as long as the Maestro did not consider it an audition.

"You can do anything you want to," Stokowski said to the young man after he had finished playing, "but you must look for every chance to perform. That's the important thing."

"Do you know where I'm playing now?" asked Adler. "At the nightclub Copacabana for a hot singer."

"Don't feel so sorry for yourself," Stokowski replied. "Brahms played in a Vienna brothel to make a living!"

Adler was impressed, and not long thereafter he became concertmaster. "The man hypnotized me," he recalled. "I rearranged my whole life to take a job that would enable me to associate with him."

Long the champion of women in orchestras, Stokowski had hired twenty for the All-American, an unprecedented number in 1940. In the American Symphony, there were forty-two the first season and even more in subsequent years. During the second season he appointed a female assistant conductor, Judith Somogi, who was launched on an excellent career of many appearances, from the New York Philharmonic to the Los Angeles Symphony. When Adler resigned as concertmaster of the American Symphony, he was replaced by Mary Freeman Blankstein, who served during the last four years that Stokowski was its director. All minority groups were also represented, with an exceptional number of talented and skilled Orientals. Though many of them were not yet union members, generous allowances were made by Local 802.

A significant aspect of Stokowski's work with the American Symphony was his ability as the most imaginative and expert program-maker of all conductors. He always provided an extraordinary blend of music, with a dramatic sense of both unity and variety that would attract and hold many different audiences. Within three years of its inception, the American Symphony was giving four kinds of programs, the regular concert fare for adults, the regular youth concerts for teenagers, another series for subteens, and still another series for children of five, six, and seven—"and all at lower prices, so that the youthful audiences will later become music-lovers who attend adult concerts," Stokowski explained.

In these numerous and unusual concerts, he introduced several young associate conductors, including David Katz, José Serebrier, and Joseph Eger, who made solid cultural contributions to New York's musical life. One typically varied program for the teen-agers featured Bizet's sparkling Symphony in C, Lucien Cailliet's gay Variations on *Pop! Goes the Weasel,* Vaughan Williams's Fantasia on "Greensleeves," Natalie Bender's *Children's Suite,* Leopold Mozart's *Musical Sleigh Ride,* Aaron Copland's setting of "I Bought Me a Cat," Johann Strauss's *Tritsch-Tratsch Polka,* and the "Dream of a Witches' Sabbath" from Berlioz's *Symphonie Fantastique.*

Stokowski made history in the 1965–66 season when he conducted the American Symphony Orchestra in the world premiere of Charles Ives's Symphony no. 4 at Carnegie Hall.

He stationed one of his associates, David Katz, at stage rear to lead a choral group from the Schola Cantorum and kept another, José Serebrier, nearby to assist with the rhythmic complexities of the second and fourth movements. At the conclusion of a stupendous performance, the capacity audience burst into deafening and enthusiastic shouts. The excitement was partly due to the music and partly due to the 83-year-old Maestro at the height of his powers.

Stokowski that night and again in 1970 revealed a challenging masterpiece that abounds in an individuality ranging from dissonant devices anticipating Stravinsky and Schoenberg to hymnal tranquillity. Stokowski had been planning to present this work for fully a decade, ever since isolated pages began to show up in Ives's copious files.

In the excellent recording the orchestra made, one senses music of far more than topical interest. The same was true of the orchestra itself, to which Stokowski brought an extraordinary degree of professionalism and expressivity.

During his New York–based period, Stokowski usually dined at home and spent the evening poring over scores, old and new, preparing for future concerts and recording sessions. Sometimes, he visited friends and occasionally attended a concert, the theater, or a ballet. Weekend afternoons were often spent at picture galleries and museums.

On rehearsal days, Stokowski was scheduled to work with the orchestra from 10 A.M. to 12:30. Invariably, he was on stage considerably earlier to count the heads of those who heeded his "suggestion" to warm up beforehand. He conducted about twenty-five concerts a season with the American Symphony, requiring no less than four rehearsals per program.

On concert days, he held neither rehearsals nor auditions, saving his energy for the performance. Following the concert, if some apropos social event had been planned, he would usually attend.

In 1967 when he had just returned from guest conducting

in Budapest and Bucharest, I told Stokowski I wanted to do an article on the American Symphony. "Fine," he said, "but before you come up to the house for a talk, do come to some rehearsals and the concert, perhaps the first one."

Knowing Stokowski's musical habits, I arrived at 9:20. The stage of Carnegie Hall was empty except of course, for one musician—Leopold Stokowski, who sat on a high stool bent over the scores that lay on the conductor's stand. There was a spotlight on the golden-white head, and he was dressed in a dark, silk tunic with the collar open. The man was wrapped in complete concentration, interrupted by an occasional handshake or nod or spoken word of greeting as the players began to arrive. Every few minutes someone would come up to ask a question. Stokowski would open one of the scores, study it for a few seconds, and then answer. At other moments he would call out to a player to come over, show him a spot in a score, and give some directions.

At 9:55, Stokowski closed the scores in front of him, said, "Good morning," and waited for absolute silence. Then, he signaled to the oboist to give the orchestra the A to tune by and at the dot of 10:00 Stokowski said, "Canto," by Peter Mennin—the first number of a typically Stokowskian program consisting of a preludial composition by a contemporary American; the Brahms Violin Concerto, featuring the American violinist Joseph Silverstein; and one of the most brilliant of symphonies, Prokofiev's Fifth, for a sensational climax.

This was a "first-reading" rehearsal of everything but the familiar Brahms music. Stokowski says, "This is a slow four—just watch me closely." He beat one measure in silence to indicate the tempo and then cued them in. The music went splendidly. In two or three places, Stokowski said, "Let's try that once again," and at the end, "I want this to die away very gradually until nothing remains." The effect was so perfectly executed, as Stokowski's hands parted at snail's pace, that one could not be sure when the sound had actually disappeared.

When the musicians had closed their scores, he said, "On my recent trip, I noticed some prejudices that interested me. The Europeans think that the age of an orchestra is the significant thing and that a five-year-old orchestra like ours needs many more years to develop. Well, I know orchestras that are a hundred years old, and ever since I've been hearing them they play worse every year." When the laughter subsided, he added, "They also think that a youthful orchestra can't play with enough passion and expression. I told them that I think the young people of today are not only emotionally vital but mature more fully and quickly than their elders did." An appreciative murmur went up. He went on, "They also think, as Voltaire did, that women are only good in the kitchen, the salon, and in one other room I shall not mention. I told them they're dead wrong and I feel sorry for them that they didn't realize what wonderful musicians, what wonderful instrumentalists women have become in our century." Applause.

Then he said, "Brahms." The concerto was rehearsed without the soloist and the orchestral sections were worked on with an occasional comment from Stokowski. Without interrupting the sounds themselves, he would call out, "More crescendo, please" and "That's not quite together" and "Too loud, much too loud." Only at the end of the slow movement did he repeat anything: He made them play the last chord over and over again, saying each time, "Not in tune" or "Not well balanced."

At 11:00 sharp came intermission—for everyone but Stokowski, who stayed on stage to answer questions. When someone expressed surprise that Stokowski did not seem to stop for details or to correct errors in a composition that was new to the orchestra, he said, "That's a waste of valuable time unless something very basic is wrong. The musicians know—

most of them anyway—when they make mistakes. Why stop them? I just look at them, and our eyes usually meet. Most errors are corrected by the second rehearsal. That's when we start to work on interpretation and subtleties. And when the composers happen to be around and want to come, we always welcome them."

Two days later I attended the final rehearsal for the pair of concerts that Stokowski was about to present in Carnegie Hall. Again he arrived very early. There were also present dozens of youngsters who sat in the auditorium, schoolchildren whose teachers had written in requesting admission. They behaved beautifully, responding warmly and appreciatively to every moment of a work session that was full of highly technical matters which one would have thought way over their heads. Evidently, they sensed the tense attitude on stage and understood that a lot was at stake, that there was not a second to lose, and that Stokowski meant business.

He showed it by driving the players much more than at the previous rehearsals, pushing them to their highest standards. Once, when the speed of a particular passage was clearly beyond their capacities, he stopped them and, without looking at anyone in particular, said, "I will not tolerate carelessness. One careless player, like one bad apple, can ruin everything. Again."

At intermission, Stokowski shook hands energetically with a group of about a dozen black tots ranging in age from about three to seven who were budding violinists from the St. James School of the Arts in Harlem and pupils of one of the orchestra's first violin players. His guests stood around him in a semicircle, gaping in awe and admiration. Then Stokowski said, "I'm very happy to meet you. I congratulate you and wish you the best. You are doing something important because the world is very short of good string players. When you think you're ready, just let me know. I want to hear all of you, and maybe you'll be sitting right here, very soon."

When I returned home, I typed out some of the remarks I had jotted down during the rehearsals. Stokowski's tyranny over his orchestra has been noted by those who have managed to hear a rehearsal. One of his major weapons was sarcasm, which he used with devastating effect. "Will the strings play together? And will the virtuosi of the orchestra [as he referred to the first violins] kindly condescend to join them?" The threat of dismissal was also used by Stokowski with maximum efficiency. He once became infuriated over the inability of the orchestra to negotiate a sticky passage. He took out his pocket watch. "I'll give you ten minutes to learn this. After that I may call on any one of you, and if you can't play it, you can start looking for another job."

"Sorry," said Stokowski at another rehearsal. "Am I too fast for you? My fault. Sometimes I forget that I'm not in Philadelphia." At the next downbeat, every player was as set as an Olympic runner at the starting line.

The next night was the concert. A large, loyal audience welcomed Stokowski back, and he responded handsomely. The modern work, despite a fine performance, merely elicited a mildly approving reaction, and Stokowski's unerring sense of showmanship dissuaded him from calling upon the composer.

In the concerto, the violinist won a cordial response not only from the audience and orchestra but also from Stokowski, who exchanged a warm handshake with his soloist.

Then, following intermission, Stokowski had his inning. He stepped up to the plate and with his bare hands hit a grand slam homer, with Prokofiev's Fifth Symphony. The audience yelled its wholehearted enthusiasm, and in response he made the orchestra rise and share every ovation. Although he took only one bow alone, the final triumph was Stokowski's.

The decade 1962–72 was perhaps among the most active, enterprising, and triumphant of Stokowski's career. For him, youth was a state of mind, not a period of life. At eighty, the lure of adventure and the joy of living were as strong as they had been when he was eighteen.

Of course," he would say, "it is not alone physical vitality that enables me to conduct but spiritual energy that the composers communicate through their music. Beethoven and Brahms and Berlioz are present to help me, to inspire me to make their music come alive."

And it came alive constantly in the concerts of the orchestra to which he had given birth that year and in the dozens of others that he conducted in scores of cities in the United States and in Europe until he was ninety-five.

The exhausting schedule that he accepted was only matched by the demanding programs he devised, almost all of which included a "first" of some sort.

With his own ensemble, he produced such varied works as Mahler's *Resurrection* Symphony, Berlioz's *L'Enfance du Christ,* William Dawson's Negro Folk Symphony, Joseph Canteloube's *Songs of the Auvergne,* and not only Ives's fiendish Fourth Symphony but also his *Robert Browning* Overture.

One of the sources of deepest satisfaction in these years was Stokowski's renewed association with Philadelphia. His return visits to the superb orchestra he had built were marked by some of the greatest triumphs of his career. How those artists played for him! And how every audience leapt to its feet to cheer this legendary figure before he had led one note of music. At the 1967 concert given to benefit the striking orchestra, when the 85-year-old conductor led the ensemble before nine thousand people in Convention Hall, there was an unprecedented emotional scene with shouts and tears and Stokowski begging support for "this great orchestra which has a great past and an even greater future." Stokowski derived enormous satisfaction from learning that the Philadelphia Orchestra's board of directors was outraged over the public demonstration of where his sympathies and loyalties lay in this embarrassing labor dispute.

Stokowski also toured in ten concerts with the Boston Symphony Orchestra, introducing for the "first time at these concerts" the Prelude and Quadruple Fugue by Hovhaness and *Eagles* by Rorem. Despite his hectic tours, Stokowski was diligent about writing personal letters of appreciation. After conducting a weekend series of subscription concerts with the St. Louis Orchestra, he wrote the concertmaster, Melvin Ritter, "I feel I must write to thank you for your splendid playing, both as violin soloist and concertmaster. . . . Your command of tone is very unusual . . . it floats up above the whole orchestra because of its power and beauty." This was characteristic of dozens of gracious letters received by appreciative musicians who had previously heard only of his impersonal austerity and disdain toward orchestra players.

Through his long life, he had courted this unsavory reputation. But now his sensitive nature was taking on more mellow and genial colors. More and more musicians who came out of musical respect remained to love the man.

The transformation also affected his personal life. When his daughters Lyuba and Sadja gave birth to babies, one a boy and the other a girl, Stokowski wrote Evangeline and each of the girls very affectionate letters indicating how pleased and proud he was and how much he hoped that "the children will grow up to be very close."

In 1966, Evangeline, who was then the Princess Zalstem Zalessky, invited Stokowski to celebrate their common birthday (both were born on April 18) at a supper party in her sumptuous art-filled New York home. "With a prior announcement that the acoustics were terrible," Evangeline told me, "Stoki led 'Happy Birthday' as though it were Tchaikovsky's *1812* Overture. He was in the happiest mood I'd seen him in quite a time."

The perennial youth had mellowed sufficiently to acknowledge his real date of birth. He even permitted his ninetieth year to be celebrated as a benefit for his ten-year-old child, the American Symphony. Staged at the Grand Ballroom of New York's Hotel Plaza, it promised to be a festive occasion. On hand to toast the famous nonagenarian were Evangeline, his children and grandchildren, four hundred of his "'most intimate" friends and associates, and the brass section of his orchestra to play fanfares. There were a few brief speeches and a birthday cake. How could it fail?

"The only thing he could think of all evening," said Joe Sharfsin, his lawyer, "was the overwhelming fact that he was indeed ninety and still alive and that so many people were astonished at the phenomenon. They kept telling him how amazing it was for a man of his age to be so vigorous. Well, immediately after the event, he couldn't wait to get the hell out."

I visited Stokowski one evening before Christmas of 1966, and he was very far from happy. He appeared reflective and lonely as he walked me very slowly toward the rickety little desk near the large window that overlooked Central Park. Night after night he sat in that large room at that tiny desk, with one glaring fluorescent light that lit up his tired face, and a pocket metronome in his hand. That is where the preparation took place. In that austere setting Stokowski found his greatest joy and peace.

I had come to see him because I was writing an article for a national magazine on significant recordings of the year. He asked if I had heard his disc of Beethoven's Piano Concerto no. 5 with Glenn Gould and the American Symphony. I said I had. He fixed me with that Stokowski eye and said, "And you hate it."

"Not quite," I replied, "but I do find it somewhat distressing and inexplicable coming from you and Gould."

He then went into a long explanation of the Manhattan Center's miserable acoustics, of the long time spent in overcoming the difficulties of placing the piano so that the conductor could see and hear his orchestra as well as the soloist and the keyboard so as to synchronize the entire performance.

I finally said, "It seems obvious that everyone was doing everything except rehearsing enough to get the soloist, the conductor, and the orchestra into musical alliance."

"Correct," he said. "Are you writing about it?"

"No," I said. "That's my Christmas present to you."

As Stokowski approached ninety, the musical world prepared to honor the now historic figure whose concerts continued to be exciting occasions. The Academy of Arts and Letters had made him an honorary member, and the National Endowment for the Arts awarded his orchestra a $50,000 grant. London Records and RCA were issuing commemorative albums, and radio stations were planning programs in observance of his innovative recordings, his continuing interest in everything new, and his phenomenal ability to inspire composers and collaborators and to captivate audiences. These alone merited signal recognition from the world he had so handsomely enriched.

Great preparations were under way by the Philadelphia Orchestra Association a long time in advance to stage a Pension Fund concert on October 11, 1972, sixty years to the day of Stokowski's initial concert with the orchestra. The gala event was to feature the original program conducted by the original conductor. Without a word to the general public, a circular sent out only to the subscribers resulted in a complete sellout by return mail. But then Stokowski had to notify the orchestra that unfortunately a bad accident prevented him from traveling. Many efforts were made to elicit a future date for the occasion, but that too, it was said, would interfere with Stokowski's recovery. With heavy-hearted reluctance and regret, the event was canceled and refunds made to the disappointed ticket holders.

When Stokowski terminated his affiliation with the American Symphony in 1972, the players reorganized themselves as a self-governing group, the only such major ensemble in the United States. In doing so, they received the Maestro's blessing, and he theirs. They had built themselves a home, and now he was returning to his—England.

14

THE RETURN OF THE NATIVE was greeted by the entire musical world of London with characteristic British admiration for courage and venerability. Toward personal friends, Stokowski was affable but circumscribed. He was solicitously cared for by Natasha Bender, who watched his every move; by Marty Wargo, his business manager; and by Jack Baumgarten, who handled the artistic details of Stokowski's professional activities.

In answer to the charges by many admittedly valued associates of Stokowski that Natasha had "destoyed" their relationship by being "overprotective," Baumgarten said, "That is not entirely true. Often a letter or a telephone call would come from someone Stokowski didn't want to see. Some of it was also sheer vanity. He was a beautiful young man, and he didn't want some people to see him grow older and more infirm. He would then say about a letter, 'Throw it away' or 'I'll take care of it later.' He let Natasha do as she pleased just so long as she didn't conflict with his desires. If she did, he showed his annoyance visibly."

Among Stokowski's closest friends was then-Prime Minister Edward Heath, a distinguished politician and an excellent amateur organist and conductor. They had a joyful reunion shortly after Stokowski's arrival at a luncheon in the home of Jack Lyons, a music-loving philanthropist and trustee of the London Symphony Orchestra. The topic of conversation was Stokowski's approaching gala concert at the Royal Festival Hall, where he would be conducting the LSO in the identical program he had played with this orchestra sixty years before. Heath told Stokowski that the hall had been instantly sold out and urged him to give a second concert at the Royal Albert Hall for the multitudes who had been turned away. Stokowski volunteered a repeat performance as soon as the mammoth hall was available.

The reappearance of Stokowski in London duplicated his return to Philadelphia, an event that tightened the throats and filled the eyes of all present. When the Maestro stepped upon the stage, the huge audience rose at once, cheering and applauding. And to a greater degree than ever before, this musician was unanimously judged to have given a masterly demonstration of an almost lost tradition of conducting.

In search of his happy childhood in London, he tried to find that little house with the garden in the back and the apple tree on whose branches he had sat so long ago, munching the luscious fruit. "I can't find that tree anymore," he said. "Perhaps someone cut it down." It had, in fact, been demolished by bombs during the war and replaced by a row of four-story dwellings, one exactly like another. So he set his sights beyond London and found a house some seventy miles south in Nether Wallop, an eleventh-century village with a population of 860 (it never rose above 960).

To get some idea of the environment in which Stokowski lived out his final years, I set out by train for Grately, five miles from Nether Wallop, which had no railroad station. Unable to find a taxi or bus, I was given a lift to Nether Wallop by a hospitable native, Ed Yates, who gave me a guided tour of the enchanting countryside—velvet meadows, willow trees, waterfalls along numerous crystal brooks. Driving into the picture-postcard village, we went directly to its focal point, the 900-year-old St. Andrew's Church, whose pastor, Reverend Mervyn Pitt, had appointed Stokowski honorary organist and choirmaster. When Yates had to leave, I was taken in tow by Jack Moulland, who had rebuilt Stokowski's house and had on occasion gone with about thirty townspeople to London to hear the Maestro, on buses hired by Stokowski, and to sit in choice, complimentary seats.

By the time we reached Stokowski's house, it had become quite apparent why the aging conductor had chosen to live in Nether Wallop: it was as far as one could get from the brash, tough, metallic, and materialistic din of the cities he had called home. Swinging Cincinnati, snobbish Philadelphia, neon-lit Houston, and bustling New York may once have offered something, but nothing like the unruffled serenity of this corner of the English countryside.

"Place Farm House" was the name of Stokowski's home, a two-story structure of red brick painted white that dated mainly from the sixteenth century, though some of it was older. It had six bedrooms, three baths, a large living room, dining room, and kitchen and had been remodeled to accommodate the Maestro's piano, gramophone, records, musical scores, and books. At the back of the one acre of property ran Wallop Brook, with a gurgling little waterfall. There was also, fittingly, an apple orchard. I could not imagine anyplace more suitable for the indomitable Stokowski than this peaceful retreat within an hour of London's concert halls and recording studios.

The general consensus during the early 1970s in London was that Stokowski the conductor had not been touched by the years. No matter where he appeared, in the Albert Hall or the Royal Festival Hall, with the London Symphony Orchestra, the London Philharmonic, or the New Philharmonia Orchestra, he excited a rapturous reception from the usually conservative British public that packed every one of his concerts. As always, his programs aroused anticipation and excitement. He was still the pioneer, rendering service to the contemporary composer. At age ninety-one, he studied and conducted a broadcast performance over the BBC of Havergal Brian's Twenty-eighth Symphony, which had been completed in 1967, when the British composer was also ninety-one. The sheer uniqueness and concept of the feat was electrifying. Stokowski also conducted his first British performance of Elgar's *Enigma* Variations, which was declared "the finest ever heard" by several critics.

Of course, these performances did not fail to produce some Stokowskiana. Stokowski's televised sixtieth-anniversary concert with the LSO was followed by a huge public dinner. The evening's soloist was the violinist Silvia Marcovici, a pupil and protégée of Henryk Szeryng, who told me that Stokowski raised a stentorian objection when he got to his table and discovered that his enticing soloist had been seated at another. After some speedy sleight of hand and diplomatic apologies, Silvia was placed at the head table opposite the Maestro. However, conversation was utterly impossible over the hubbub of a hundred throats loosened by gaiety and alcohol. With a tantalizing wink, Stokowski wrote something on a concert program and passed it over to his twenty-year-old colleague. He had drawn a large question mark—that was all. Rising to the occasion, the gifted young woman replied with an equally cryptic symbol—an exclamation point!

Stokowski's feverish activities necessitated considerable rest and change of personal climate. He bought a home in Vence, the artistic town in southern France where Henri Matisse had decorated the church's chapel and painted its delicate stained-glass windows and where Marc Chagall also made his home. When time did not permit a retreat to Vence or to Nether Wallop, Stokowski relaxed in his London pied-à-terre at the Stafford Hotel in St. James. It was only a twenty-minute drive to the West Ham Central Mission Church, a huge, reverberant hall where he first recorded with the National Philharmonic Orchestra, a distinguished ensemble of the best players in London. Sidney Sax, the founder and leader of that virtuoso group, recalled that on the first day of recording, the ever-coquettish Stokowski had walked in, looked around, and then asked, "Have you no ladies in your orchestra?" Sax replied, "Yes, our harpist. She's back there." Stokowski shook his head and said, "Not enough, and too far back."

Stokowski came to know some of his grandchildren during these years. Sonya's son Jan told me that he flew over in the summer of 1976 when Natasha was back in the States undergoing eye surgery and Sadja had taken over as housekeeper and companion. One day, Jan attended a recording session at the West Ham church. Jan told me, "The minute he stepped on the podium, the years just vanished. Almost instantly he looked vigorous and enthusiastic. I was amazed how fast everything went. It's a fabulous orchestra! They warmed up in about ten minutes, practicing a few bars from Bizet's *Carmen* and then from *L'Arlésienne*. 'All right,' grandfather called out, 'we're all set to go.' An engineer said, 'Sorry, sir. We have a problem that'll take about fifteen minutes to clear up.' Stokowski answered, 'That's tough. If you want to record this, it'll have to be right now,' and he gave the downbeat. 'No, no, stop,' the engineer pleaded. Grandfather said, 'You heard what I said. Keep quiet, we're starting again. You'll get it now or you won't get it.' Paul Myers, the producer, stepped in. 'You heard the Maestro,' he said quietly. 'This is a take.' Grandfather would stop to redo a section that didn't satisfy him. But time and again he would go straight through. The only thing they worked over several times is the part in *L'Arlésienne* where he has the trumpet start his solo facing the wall and, as it continues, gradually swing toward the mike. A terrific effect!" So it is, at the very least.

Although the British musical world could not find ways enough to demonstrate its appreciation of Stokowski, 1972–77 found him conducting fewer concerts and more recordings. His sixty-year recording career was the longest of any artist in the history of recording. His lifelong insistence on nonexclusive record contracts contributed to a bustling professional life, difficult for his new business manager and his musical assistant and extremely demanding upon himself.

After the entire sixtieth-anniversary concert had been documented live by Decca (London Records in the United States), Stokowski took off for a Prague debut with the Czech Philharmonic. His two SRO concerts in Dvořák Hall at the House of Artists, where the orchestra's recordings are made, yielded live recordings of Stokowski's interpretations of six Bach transcriptions, Scriabin's *Poem of Ecstasy,* and—the first appearance of an Elgar work in Stokowski's enormous catalogue—the *Enigma* Variations, which had been a specialty of his for over sixty years.

For British Decca, British RCA, Pye, and Desmar, he added significantly to his recorded legacy with works by Mahler, Vaughan Williams, Beethoven, Brahms, Tchaikovsky, Dvorak, Rachmaninoff, Berlioz, and Wagner. In 1974, he finally signed an exclusive contract with CBS (Columbia), although an escape clause left him at liberty to record for anyone any composition CBS declined to record. All of his albums for Columbia were produced by Paul Myers, vice-president and director of artists and repertory, and his associate, Roy Emerson, two of the most capable men in the recording industry. Their professional and personal association with Stokowski and his tiny coterie was exceptionally close and reveals an obviously affectionate, yet objective, observation of the musician and the man during his last years.

The orchestra that Stokowski conducted for his Columbia recordings, the National Philharmonic, comprised the finest players of London's five symphonic orchestras, whose first violin section included five concertmasters.

"It is impossible to describe," said Paul Myers, "the kind of respect that Stokowski commanded from this remarkable group. After they had tuned up under concertmaster Sidney Sax's direction, the double door would open and the nattily dressed Maestro would enter the rehearsal room. As the bent, frail figure slowly approached the podium, his right hand on Jack Baumgarten's left shoulder and his left firmly gripping a thick stick, the orchestra stood in silence for him until he had cautiously settled into his tall chair. Jack stood slightly behind Stoki to his right, ready to turn a page or to convey a message to or from the control room. Natasha hovered about in the background, making sure that Stoki had everything he needed, even orange juice in case he wanted a drink. When he came out, he was a very old man, at times apparently lost, not quite knowing where he was or why. But the moment he was on the podium, fifty years dropped away from him."

How much time Stokowski would allocate for rehearsal no one knew. Sometimes, it was a normal run-through with few or no stops. At other times, he would start a rehearsal that would almost instantly turn into a full dress performance of a complete work or movement of a symphony, sometimes followed by the next and the next to produce an unblemished "take." The orchestra and recording staff were always prepared for this, ready to capture his most inspired moments.

Rumors circulated that Stokowski had barely conducted and that this finest of all recording orchestras carried him through, but Myers denied the allegations. "Not a word of truth in it," Paul retorted angrily, "he conducted every note and knew exactly what he wanted. Just listen to the freedom of the Bizet recording, for example. There's no way to get such a flexible rubato with such flawless ensemble without conducting every note of every liberty, and only an absolute master in absolute control can achieve it. I won't deny that sometimes Stoki did lose his bearings, but never when he was actually conducting. One day he turned to me after we had had a particularly long session followed by a lengthy playback conference. He was fine until we were through. Then suddenly he became the very old man again and asked me,

'Where are we?' 'In the recording studios,' I answered. 'But in what city?' he asked. 'London.' Then he asked, 'Oh, is Oxford still there?' "

These lapses notwithstanding, he had wonderful ears to the last and such extraordinary eyesight that he never had to use glasses. Some say he abused these gifts by occasionally putting orchestras and soloists through needless difficulties. When I asked Paul Myers if the problem had arisen, he said, "This never occurred with the National, and to a man that orchestra adored him—I would even say, worshiped him." The uncharitable have ascribed this to the fact that Stokowski had not recorded one work with this orchestra that they had not performed a great many times together, which is contrary to the facts.

Stokowski was a notoriously unyielding person, but he appears to have grown less intractable with the years and finally to have acquired the ultimate wisdom of being able to laugh at himself. He was interviewed on a BBC television show by Henry Pleasants, who as a Curtis vocal student and as the music critic of the *Philadelphia Bulletin* from 1930 to 1938 virtually had grown up with Stokowski. In the course of the program, Pleasants teased Stokowski gently but pointedly about his mercurial accent, getting him to admit that some of its thickness emanated from the pleasure he got from a bit of leg-pulling and game-playing. Paul Myers told me that though a number of people were disturbed by this bantering, Stokowski himself enjoyed it immensely.

Roy Emerson had the unusual chance to know Stokowski in his most intimate and relaxed mood when he brought down test pressings of Tchaikovsky's *Aurora's Wedding* and Sibelius's First Symphony for the Maestro's approval at his villa in Vence, where Stokowski spent some three leisurely months a year.

"In that lovely and relaxed home, built along the lines of Nether Wallop," Roy said, "Stokowski was another person.

At the studio, everything was business, a brief greeting, then right to work. At the end of a session, we were all bushed, and left as soon as possible. Any talking was confined to records. But here, Stokowski took time to exchange ideas about music and personal things, to express feelings and to reminisce, to enjoy fresh food, French wine, and being a host —and there was none more gracious. Without the strain of strangers, he was very open and forthcoming."

After a leisurely lunch, they got to the test pressings. Stokowski sat on the sofa, in front of which stood a music stand with the score, red and blue pencils, and an eraser on it. "The music started, and Stokowski began to conduct with tiny motions," said Roy.

"He listened for the primary elements of the music— tempi, dynamics, rhythm, the melodic line, the sense of momentum, and balance. But above all, intensity, from the quietest pianissimo to the most thundering fortissimo, music had to catch you by the throat. How he communicated it to an orchestra so as to endow a piece they thought thy knew so well with unique color and excitement, no one knew, not even he. What a worker, and what a perfectionist he was."

Those who were in the midst of Stokowski's life during the last years marveled at his mental alertness. When Paul Myers told him, "You've been my hero for a very special reason," Stokowski asked, "What's that?"

"Because you're the only man I know who shook hands with Mickey Mouse."

"No, no, no," Stokowski objected, raising his forefinger. "He shook hands with *me*."

Most characteristic was Stokowski's obvious control of his own finances up to the last. Paul Myers recalled one of their last recording sessions when Edward Johnson came by to deliver something he had purchased on Stokowski's behalf. Stokowski reached into an inside pocket, produced a checkbook, had Natasha fill out a blank, signed it, handed it to

Johnson, and then returned the book to his pocket, patting it securely.

The only implication of age that he did not mind was the 1977 golden anniversary Grammy Award for his 1927 recording of the Bach-Stokowski Toccata and Fugue in D-minor. Equally in his style was the utterly unique CBS contract he signed in 1976 that would keep him conducting until his one hundredth year.

Nancy Shear, music librarian of the Curtis Institute, to whom Stokowski was "the greatest influence in my life," came to visit him in Nether Wallop in the late summer of 1977. "I couldn't believe that this was an old man of ninety-five who hadn't seen me in almost a year. When I walked in, without a second's hesitation he exclaimed, 'Nancy!' and throughout my stay was as sharp as ever. He was very excited about his next recording project, Rachmaninoff's Second Symphony, which was scheduled for rehearsal and recording on September 13. He had been studying it constantly a long time; it was actually a new work for him. He had a one-track mind. We would be talking and he would suddenly say, 'Please excuse me. I want to be with Rachmaninoff.'"

His wish was unexpectedly granted at Nether Wallop in the early morning of the day originally planned for the recording. Jack Baumgarten had phoned Paul Myers the day before to say that Maestro was feeling unusually fatigued and it would be necessary to postpone the session. No one was worried. This had happened several times before and Stokowski had rescheduled, full of new enthusiasm.

To Stokowski, death was as hospitable as life had been. On the night of September 12, 1977, he went to sleep and never awakened. The doctors said he died of heart failure. Stokowski did not die of anything. He just went to sleep. He was always functioning, always moving from one pulsating thought or action to the next. Eventually, he needed rest. No musician deserved it more.

A small private service was held in a chapel at St. Marylebone Cemetery, East Finchley, North London. The organist played some unhyphenated Bach. The members of the family attending the service were Stokowski's five children and his brother and sister-in-law, Mr. and Mrs. Stock. Present among his close friends and associates were Natasha Bender, Edward Johnson, Roy Emerson, Jack Baumgarten, Marty Wargo, and Oliver Daniel, music director of Broadcast Music Incorporated and a member of the American Symphony board.

As it was not a religious ceremony, there was no clergyman at the funeral. Edward Heath, by then out of office, officiated, reading from Stokowski's own book and paying tribute to his friend as "not just a great conductor, but the greatest of them all, and a great man."

Stokowski was buried in the churchyard of St. Marylebone, opposite the remains of his mother, father, and sister, Lydia. Eight months later I·visited his grave to find a six-foot plot of rain-soaked dirt and a stick marked D 10 147. Installation of the gravestone and the headstone had been inexplicably delayed. There lay Stokowski, alone in his last home of silence.

Now, at long last, the grave is covered. Now there is a tombstone with the inscription:

Leopold Stokowski
born April 18, 1882
died September 13, 1977
Music is the Voice of the All.

The quotation is from Stokowski's book. It has been held to be a mistake, a misprint, and that what was intended was "Music is the voice of us all." Whoever concludes this knows neither Stokowski's book nor Stokowski's transcendentalism.

Stokowski left a practical will, typical of one whose philosophy asserts the domination of the spiritual over the empirical. Each of the five children received a handsome and equal sum. Natasha, who did most for him and will miss him most, was left three times the sum left to each child. His business manager was left half the proceeds of Stokowski's record royalties for five years. Whether Stokowski left more or not, I have not troubled to determine. I would say, actually, that Stokowski was a very extravagant man. It is an accurate description of a conductor who gave his services gratis to the All-American Orchestra for two years and to the New York City Center for two years, who underwrote the Hollywood Bowl for extra rehearsals, and who gave the American Symphony some $60,000 or so annually while he himself remained unpaid throughout ten years of service.

He was nevertheless very well paid in other respects and honored by such prestigious rewards as the Bok Award, Ditson Award, membership in the National Institute of Arts and Sciences, honorary doctorates from universities, and honorary fellowships at the Royal College of Music and Queens College, Oxford. He was also the proud possessor of a ribbon as an officer of the Légion d'Honneur, a sword as a knight of the Polonia Restituta, a uniform of the Crown of Rumania— and a Houston deputy sheriff's badge.

One only wonders how and why Stokowski's unique musical achievements never received royal recognition from the British throne. Though I never heard of him mentioning this to a soul, it could well have been his crowning disappointment. This too we shall never know.

Amidst the outpourings of worldwide tributes that followed Stokowski's death, one could imagine him surveying the scene wearing one of his most enigmatic smiles. Surely, he would have been diverted to hear himself lionized by those whom his way with music had inspired to "roaring cataracts of nonsense." Surely, he would have been pleased to hear the music, some of it composed by him, some of it transcribed by him, and most of it long and lovingly associated with him.

From Philadelphia to Peking and London to Los Angeles,

from New York to New Delhi and Montreal to Moscow, every established orchestra officially opened its season with some formal dedication to Leopold Stokowski, ranging from an opening work to an entire program. On September 23, Eugene Ormandy came upon the stage of the Philadelphia Academy, silenced his audience's applause and without ascending the podium said, "In loving memory of Leopold Stokowski, who made an overwhelming impact on the world with this great Philadelphia Orchestra, we will play Bach's *Come, Sweet Death,* a work he loved more than anything else." A transcription emerged with a Wagnerian sonority and color that every music-lover immediately identifies as the Stokowski sound. In New York's Carnegie Hall on October 9, the American Symphony Orchestra dedicated the season's first program to its founder, Leopold Stokowski. The orchestra's director, Kazuyoshi Akiyama, also started with *Come, Sweet Death.* At its conclusion the audience rose and stood silently.

The newspapers and periodicals lavished maximum space on Stokowski obituaries and pictures. There were few radio stations that did not honor Stokowski's memory in some way. Those that specialized in talk programs paid oral tributes. The mammoth, twelve-hour musical marathon presented over Los Angeles station KPFK, extemporaneously guided by producer William Malloch, featured a revealing interview with Malloch taped in 1950 when Stokowski performed Mahler's Eighth Symphony with the New York Philharmonic wherein Stokowski disclosed very movingly his affinity for Mahler, for the composer's *Sehnsucht,* irony, and loneliness, and for his fantastic ability to change suddenly from misery to joy. One listened to Stokowski's Mahler with more understanding after that, not just because of what he said but because his emotional intensity matched that of his conducting of Mahler.

On the Sunday following Stokowski's death, St. Bartholomew's in New York, the church that first brought Stokowski the organist and choirmaster to this country, gave a memorial service that included the singing of two of Stokowski's original works, *Benedicite* and *Pianissimo Amen.* Two months later, the Brahms *German Requiem* was performed at the church in Stokowski's honor. The next month, a joint memorial service honoring Stokowski and Toscanini was announced by the combined choirs of St. Patrick's Cathedral in New York and the Cathedral of SS. Peter and Paul in Philadelphia. The program featured Handel's *Nisi Dominus,* Faure's *Requiem,* and Elgar's *Sospiri,* with an ensemble of Metropolitan Opera Orchestra members, conducted by John Grady, St. Patrick's music director.

The Philadelphia Orchestra's Women's Committee and Auxiliary formed the Leopold Stokowski Conducting Fellowship, "aimed to encourage the youthful talent that was so primary a concern of Stokowski throughout his long and productive career."

In Copenhagen, the Opperby Stokowski Collection was established, comprising a formidable assemblage of recordings, tapes, interviews, lectures, letters, programs, program notes, pictures, scores of original Stokowski compositions and transcriptions (with orchestral parts), and miscellany. "Preben and Mimi Opperby," said Philippa Thomson of the Royal College of Music, "head a sort of Stokowski Fan Club of Denmark. Their collection is completely unique. Mr. and Mrs. Opperby have willed it to the RCM, which in appreciation conferred upon them honorable memberships."

Back home, the Curtis Institute's first semester opened with a Stokowski memorial. The Maestro's closest associate, Sylvan Levin, said, "For me, Stokowski has not died and never will die."

On the evening of June 19, 1978, the Philadelphia Orchestra conducted by Eugene Ormandy presented a Leopold Stokowski tribute at the Robin Hood Dell. The program was

Stokowski's debut program of October 11 and 12, 1912: Beethoven's *Leonore* Overture no. 3, Brahms's First Symphony, Ippolitov-Ivanov's *Caucasian Sketches,* and Wagner's Overture to *Tannhäuser.* The speaker of the occasion was Stokowski's friend, Francis Robinson, a leading representative in many capacities of the Metropolitan Opera for over a third of its distinguished history. His eloquent eulogy concluded:

Leopold Stokowski was the greatest propagandist for music of his time, perhaps of all time. With this concert we honor this great musician, your great former leader and fellow townsman. No words of mine are adequate, so I beg to close with this quotation from Pericles: "For this whole earth is but the cemetery of famous men, and their names shall live on, not graven merely in the stones above them but far off, woven into the fabric of other men's lives."

Epilogue

No ONE COULD HOPE TO SAY within a single book all there is to be said about a man who possessed the most fortunate of human attributes, genius and personality, and who, for the superhuman span of three-quarters of a century, commanded such a towering position. This closing chapter at least enables me to offer a compressed account of some matters that stirred endless contention.

From his teens, Stokowski was compulsively concerned with the difference between abstract sounds as they spring up in the composer's imagination and those same sounds translated into the mute and imprecise symbols of musical notation, which he contemptuously called "fly specks." Almost militantly, he would also frequently assert the necessity of the interpreter to fathom the "emotional truth" of a composition as it arises within his hard-won individuality.

A great conductorial tradition lay behind Stokowski's arbitrary ways with the notation and interpretation of musical scores, those "lifeless diagrams" that await realization by the performer. Nikisch called it "the Wagner school," explaining that the composer simply gave the downbeat and after a little while stopped all pretense of keeping the orchestra together by beating time. Instead, he conducted with his whole being, creating a mesmerizing rapport with his expressive eyes and plastic gestures. From time to time, he would stop the orchestra to correct a misprint, to add or subtract a note, a phrase, or even an entire section, or to notate the need for a reorchestration of something that did not "sound," a surprisingly common occurrence.

But no composer ever found so much to change as Mahler the conductor, and not only when he performed his own works. Mahler's free-spirited interpretations and unshackled reorchestrations of Beethoven always created some sort of cause célèbre, particularly in the Fifth and Ninth Symphonies.

In our day, we are well aware that the integrity of music is not upheld but harmed by the interpreter who does not illumine and intensify its meanings through imaginative individuality. The personality of the performer being a fact, the rest is a matter of culture, proportion, and taste; and regarding taste, the old adage warns us against dispute. Stokowski himself said, "It is not only my privilege but my obligation to do what I must with the music I perform. I do not dispute your privileges to dislike it or to reject it."

In this conviction, Stokowski gained the courage to change anything ad libitum "always in the interests of clarifying and intensifying the music," he said, "of making it as vital and thrilling an experience as possible." These are admirable objectives. But when Stokowski's unbuttoned imagination was insufficiently supported either by stylistic understanding or by an adequate grasp of a composer's intentions, he could be misled into distortion and lapses of taste that outraged sensitive musicians and critics.

Several unfortunate examples linger—his 1934 performance of Bach's Mass in B-minor at Princeton University Chapel with the Westminster Choir School and the Philadelphia Orchestra and the 1953 recording of Tchaikovsky's Fifth Symphony with "his" Symphony Orchestra, which his most uncensorious critics found virtually inexplicable. Such extreme aberrations, however, were exceptions. Usually— which in Stokowski's case embraces thousands of examples—

a Stokowski performance, no matter what else transpired, was rarely less than a profoundly vital event.

Probably no aspect of Stokowski's career aroused more criticism and controversy than the virtuosic orchestrations signed "Bach-Stokowski." The question has been not alone how well he did them but also whether he did them at all. The topic is one over which the musical world has taken sides for half a century. Some of the wrangling is over technical and stylistic matters of minor interest and concern to all but professional musicians. But the rest of this obscure issue demands as much clarification as one can obtain.

Every effort to produce a manuscript of these works has been fruitless. When I asked people who were known to have copied orchestral parts for Stokowski if I could see the kind of score they had worked from or the sort of directions he had notated, none that were promised ever arrived. I have in my possession but one such document, a Xerox copy of a faded first page of Bach's D-minor Toccata in the Peters Edition of the organ version with copious marks in Stokowski's unmistakable hand. Strewn throughout the page are groups of notes (not on staffs) indicating rhythms, written in a tiny, exquisite, and fastidious musical script amazingly like Chopin's. In the Allegro, Stokowski indicated the division of the organ figure for alternating hands exactly as it should be played by strings. He alters the $4/4$ time to $4/8$. And so on. It is indisputably a clear indication of his wishes.

Those who maintain that these transcriptions are unquestionably Stokowski's offer as evidence his extraordinary knowledge of the full coloristic and dynamic potentials of the orchestra; his lifelong familiarity with, and love for the entire organ literature of Bach; and his devotion to the cause of popularizing works of genius. They have also contended that the orchestral sound of these transcriptions could only be achieved by an organist seeking an ideal instrument, which Stokowski undeniably created with his orchestra.

Those who maintain that Stokowski alone did not realize

Bibliography

Antek, Samuel, *This Was Toscanini*. New York: Vanguard Press, 1963.

Johnson, Edward. *Stokowski: Essays in Analysis of His Art*. London: Triad Press, 1973.

Kolodin, Irving. *The Musical Life*. London: Gollancz, 1959.

Kupferberg, Herbert. *Those Fabulous Philadelphians*. New York: Scribner's, 1969.

Leinsdorf, Erich. *Cadenza*. Boston: Houghton Mifflin, 1976.

Mencken, H. L. *Mencken on Music*. New York: Knopf, 1961.

Nettel, Reginald. *The Orchestra in England*. London: Alden Press, 1946.

O'Connell, Charles. *The Other Side of the Record*. Westport, Conn.: Greenwood Press, 1970.

Pleasants, Henry. *Serious Music—and All That Jazz*. New York: Simon and Schuster, 1969.

Reis, Claire. *Composers, Conductors, and Critics*. New York: Oxford U. Press, 1955.

Robinson, Paul. *Stokowski*. New York: Vanguard Press, 1977.

Rodzinski, Halina. *Our Two Lives*. New York: Scribner's, 1976.

Roussel, Hubert. *The Houston Symphony Orchestra, 1913–1971*. Austin: U. of Texas Press, 1972.

Russell, Charles Edward. *The American Orchestra and Theodore Thomas*. New York: Doubleday, 1927.

Sachs, Harvey. *Toscanini*. Philadelphia and New York: Lippincott, 1978.

Samaroff, Olga. *An American Musician's Story.* New York: Norton, 1939.

Schickel, Richard. *The World of Carnegie Hall.* New York: Messner, 1960.

Schonberg, Harold. *The Great Conductors.* New York: Simon and Schuster, 1967.

Stoddard, Hope. *Symphony Conductors of the USA.* New York: T. Y. Crowell, 1957.

Stokowski, Leopold. *Music for Us All.* New York: Simon and Schuster, 1943.

Thomas, Louis R. A History of the Cincinnati Orchestra to 1921. Dissertation submitted to Division of Graduate Studies, U. of Cincinnati, 1972.

Thomson, Virgil. *The Musical Scene.* Westport, Conn.: Greenwood Press, 1970.

———. *The Art of Judging Music.* Westport, Conn.: Greenwood Press, 1969.

———. *Music Right and Left.* Westport, Conn.: Greenwood Press, 1968.

Wister, Frances. *Twenty-five Years of the Philadelphia Orchestra.* Philadelphia: Stern, 1925.

Selective Discography of Available Stokowski Recordings

Assembled by Robert Bragalini (Associate Music Director, WQXR)

Abbreviations of orchestras used herein:

ASO	American Symphony
BPO	Berlin Philharmonic
CPO	Czech Philharmonic
CSO	Chicago Symphony
FNRO	French National Radio
HRPO	Hilversum Radio Philharmonic
HSO	Houston Symphony
LPO	London Philharmonic
LSO	London Symphony
LAPO	Los Angeles Philharmonic
NATPO	National Philharmonic
NBCSO	N.B.C. Symphony
NPO	New Philharmonia
NEW SO	New Symphony Orchestra of London
NYPHIL	New York Philharmonic
PO	Philadelphia Orchestra
RCASO	R.C.A. Symphony
RPO	Royal Philharmonic
SO	"His" Symphony Orchestra

SOA	Symphony of the Air
SRO	Suisse Romande Orchestra
SSO	Stadium Symphony Orchestra of New York (essentially the same as the New York Philharmonic)

ABBREVIATIONS OF RECORD COMPANIES USED HEREIN:

BACH	Bach Guild
BUENA	Buena Vista
COL	Columbia
CRI	Composer's Recordings
DES	Desmar
EV	Everest
LOND	London
ODY	Odyssey
PHIL	Philips
QUIN	Quintessence
RCA	RCA
SER	Seraphim
VAN	Vanguard
VAR/SARA	Varese/Sarabande
WALTER SOC	Bruno Walter Society

Isaac ALBENIZ
  Iberia: Fête Dieu à Seville (orch. Stokowski)
    NATPO   COL 34543

Fikret AMIROV
  Azerbaijan Mugam
    HSO   EV 3032

Johann Sebastian BACH
  Brandenburg Concerto # 5
    PO   ODY 33228

Easter Cantata: Chorale, Jesus Christus Gottes Sohn
(orch. Stokowski)
    CPO   LOND 21096

Jesu, Joy of Man's Desiring
    Luboff Choir, New SO QUIN 7019
    SO   BACH 70696;
                              VAN 363; VAN 701/2;
                              VAN 707/8

Cantata # 156: Sinfonia
    LSO   RCA 0880

Birthday Cantata: Sheep May Safely Graze
    Luboff Choir, New SO QUIN 7019
    SO   BACH 70696; VAN 701/2;
                              VAN 707/8

Sleepers Awake
    LSO   RCA 0880

Chorale, Ein feste Burg ist unser Gott
    SO   SER 60235
    LSO   RCA 0880

Chorale Prelude, Ich ruf zu dir, Herr Jesu Christ
    PO   ODY 33228

Chorale Prelude, Num komm der Heiden Heiland
    PO   ODY 33228

Chorale Prelude, Wir glauben all' an einen Gott
    PO   ODY 33228
    CPO   LOND 21096

Komm, süsser Tod
    SO   SER 60235
    LSO   RCA 0880

Mein Jesu, was für Seelenweh
    CPO   LOND 21096

Fugue in G minor (Little)
    SO   SER 60235
    LSO   RCA 0880

Christmas Oratorio: Shepherd's Music
    SO   SER 60235
    SO   BACH 70696

Passacaglia and Fugue in C-minor
    SO   SER 60235
    CPO   LOND 21096

Violin Partita # 1 in B-minor: Sarabande
    SO   SER 60235

Violin Partita # 2 in D-minor: Chaconne
    LSO   RCA 0880

Suite # 3 in D: Air
    LSO   RCA 0880

Toccata and Fugue in D-minor
    PO   BUENA 101
    SO   SER 60235
    CPO   LOND 21096

Prelude and Fugue # 8 in E-flat: Prelude
    CPO   LOND 21096

Bela BARTOK
  Concerto for Orchestra
    HSO   EV 3069

Ludwig van BEETHOVEN
  Piano Concerto # 5
    Gould, pf., ASO   COL 6888; ODY Y4 34640

Coriolan Overture
    LSO   RCA 0600

Egmont Overture
    NPO   LOND 21139

Symphony # 3
    LSO   RCA 0600

Symphony # 5
    LPO   LOND 21042

Symphony # 6 (abridged)
    PO   BUENA 101

Symphony # 7
    NPO   LOND 21139

Symphony # 9
    Harper, Watts, Young, McIntyre, LSO
                                     LOND 21043

Hector BERLIOZ
Damnation of Faust: Dance of the Sylphs
    LSO   LOND 21112

Symphonie Fantastique
    NPO   LOND 21031

Georges BIZET
L'Arlésienne Suites 1 and 2
    NATPO   COL 34503

Carmen: Suites 1 and 2
    NATPO   COL 34503

Symphony in C
    NATPO   COL 34567

Ernest BLOCH
America, An Epic Rhapsody
    SOA   VAN 346

Alexander BORODIN
Prince Igor: Polovtsian Dances
RPO   LOND 21041; 21111

Johannes BRAHMS
Academic Festival Overture
NPO   RCA 0719

Serenade # 1
SOA   VAR/SARA 81050

Symphony # 1
LSO   LOND 21131

Symphony # 3
HSO   EV 3030

Symphony # 4
NPO   RCA 0719

William BYRD
Pavan for the Earl of Salisbury (orch. Stokowski)
LSO   LOND 21130

Joseph CANTELOUBE
Songs of the Auvergne
Moffo, ASO   RCA 2795

Frederic CHOPIN
Mazurka # 13 in A-minor (orch. Stokowski)
LSO   LOND 21130

Mazurka # 17 in B-flat minor (orch. Stokowski)
NATPO   COL 34543

Prelude # 24 in D-minor (orch. Stokowski)
    NATPO   COL 34543

Jeremiah CLARKE
  Trumpet Voluntary
    LSO   LOND 21130

Arcangelo CORELLI
  Concerto Grosso in G-minor, op. 6, # 8
    SO   BACH 70696; VAN 363

Henry COWELL
  Persian Set
    SO   CRI 114

Claude DEBUSSY
  Children's Corner Suite: Excerpts
    SSO   EV 3327

  Clair de lune (orch. Stokowski)
    NATPO   COL 34543

  Estampes: Soirée dans Grenade (orch. Stokowski)
    NATPO   COL 34543

  Images pour Orchestre: Ibéria
    FNRO   SER 60102

  La Mer
    LSO   LOND 21059; 21109

  Nocturnes
    LSO   SER 60104

  Prelude to the Afternoon of a Faun
    LSO   LOND 21109

Preludes, Book 1: La Cathédrale engloutie
(orch. Stokowski)
    NPO   LOND 21006

Paul DUKAS
  Sorcerer's Apprentice
    PO   BUENA 101

Henri DUPARC
  Extase
    LSO   LOND 21130

Antonin DVOŘÁK
  Serenade in E for Strings
    RPO   DES 1011

  Slavonic Dance # 10 in E-minor, op. 72, # 2
    CPO   LOND 21117; 21130

  Symphony # 9
    { PO   }
    { NPO }   RCA CRL 2-0334

Sir Edward ELGAR
  Enigma Variations
    CPO   LOND 21136

  Enigma Variations: Nimrod
    CPO   LOND 21112; 21130

Georges ENESCO
  Roumanian Rhapsody # 1
    RCASO   RCA 2471

Manuel de FALLA
  El Amor Brujo
    Verrett, PO   ODY 32368

Cesar FRANCK
  Symphony in D-minor
        HRPO   LOND 21061

Reinhold GLIÈRE
  Symphony # 3
        HSO   SER 60089

Roger GOEB
  Symphony # 3
        SO   CRI 120

George Frederic HANDEL
  Messiah: Selections
        Armstrong, Procter, Bowen, Cameron, LSO
                                LOND 21014

  Royal Fireworks Music
        RCASO   RCA 2704

  Water Music: Suite
        RCASO   RCA 2704

  Xerxes: Largo
        Luboff Choir, New SO QUIN 7019

Lou HARRISON
  Suite for Violin, Piano and Small Orchestra
        M. Ajemian, pf.; A. Ajemian, vln.; SO
                                CRI 114

Gustav HOLST
  Planets
        LAPO   SER 60175

Engelbert HUMPERDINCK
  Hansel and Gretel: Evening Prayer
        Luboff Choir, New SO QUIN 7019

Jacques IBERT
  Escales
    FNRO   SER 60102

Charles IVES
  Orchestral Set # 2
    LSO   LOND 21060

  Robert Browning Overture
    ASO   COL 7015

  Symphony # 4
    ASO   COL 6775; D3 S-783

Werner JOSTEN
  Concerto Sacro
    ASO   CRI 200

  Jungle
    ASO   CRI 267
  Canzona Seria
    ASO   CRI 267

Aram KHATCHATURIAN
  Symphony # 3
    CSO   RCA 3067

Edouard LALO
  Symphonie Espagnole
    Thibaud, vln., NYPHIL
                        WALTER SOC 373

Franz LISZT
  Hungarian Rhapsody # 2
    RCASO   RCA 2471

Charles LOEFFLER
  Pagan Poem
    SO   SER 60080

Gustav MAHLER
  Symphony # 2
    M. Price, Fassbaender, LSO
                              RCA ARL 2-0852

Felix MENDELSSOHN
  Symphony # 4
    NATPO   COL 34567

Gian-Carlo MENOTTI
  Sebastian: Suite
    NBCSO   RCA 2715

Olivier MESSIAEN
  L'Ascension
    LSO   LOND 21060

Wolfgang Amadeus MOZART
  Serenade # 10 in B-flat for Winds (K. 361)
    ASO   VAN 707/8

Modest MUSSORGSKY
  Boris Godunov: Symphonic Synthesis (orch. Stokowski)
    SRO   LOND 21032; 21110

  Night on Bald Mountain (orch. Stokowski)
    PO   BUENA 101
    LSO   LOND 21026; 21110

  Pictures at an Exhibition (orch. Stokowski)
    LSO   LOND 21006; 21110

Ottokar NOVACEK
  Perpetuum Mobile
    NATPO   COL 34543

Carl ORFF
  Carmina Burana
    Babikian, Hager, Gardner, HSO
                  SER 60236

Amilcare PONCHIELLI
  La Gioconda: Dance of the Hours
    PO   BUENA 101

Francis POULENC
  Concert Champêtre
    Landowska, harp., NYPHIL
                  DES 106/7

Sergei PROKOFIEV
  Cinderella, Suite
    SSO   EV 3108; 3016

  Peter and the Wolf (also includes the orchestral suite)
    Keeshan
    SSO   EV 3043

  Romeo and Juliet: Suite
    NBCSO   RCA 2715

  Ugly Duckling
    Resnik, SSO   EV 3108

Sergei RACHMANINOFF
  Piano Concerto # 2
    Rachmaninoff, PO   RCA ARM 3-0296

  Prelude in C-sharp minor (orch. Stokowski)
    CPO   LOND 21130

Rhapsody on a Theme of Paganini
    Rachmaninoff, PO   RCA ARM 3-0296

Symphony # 3
    NATPO   DES 1007

Vocalise
    Moffo, ASO   RCA 2795
    NATPO   DES 1007

Maurice RAVEL
  Daphnis and Chloé: Suite # 2
    LSO   LOND 21059; 21112

  L'Eventail de Jeanne: Fanfare
    HRPO   LOND 21061

  Miroirs: Alborada del gracioso
    FNRO   SER 60102

  Rapsodie Espagnole
    LSO   SER 60104

Nicolai RIMSKY-KORSAKOV
  Capriccio Espagnole
    NPO   LOND 21117

  Flight of the Bumblebee
    NATPO   COL 34543

  Ivan the Terrible: Prelude to Act III
    NATPO   COL 34543

  Russian Easter Overture
    CSO   RCA 3067

Scheherazade
     LSO   LOND 21005
     RPO   RCA 1182

Arnold SCHOENBERG
     Gurrelieder,
         Bampton, Vreeland, Althouse, PO
                           RCA AVM 2-2017

     Verklärte Nacht
         SO   SER 60080

Franz SCHUBERT
     Ave Maria
         PO   BUENA 101

     Moment Musicale # 3 (orch. Stokowski)
         LSO   LOND 21130

     Symphony # 8
         LPO   LOND 21042

Alexander SCRIABIN
     Etude in C-sharp minor, op. 2, # 1 (orch. Stokowski)
         ASO   VAN 10095

     Poem of Ecstasy
         HSO   EV 3032
         CPO   LOND 21117

Dimitri SHOSTAKOVICH
     Prelude # 14 in E-flat (orch. Stokowski)
         NATPO   COL 34543

     Symphony # 5
         SSO   EV 3010

Romeo and Juliet
    SRO   LOND 21032; 21108

Serenade for Strings
    LSO   PHIL 6500,921

Sleeping Beauty: Excerpts
    NPO   LOND 21008
    NATPO   COL 34560

Song Without Words, op. 40, # 6 (orch. Stokowski)
    LSO   LOND 21130

Swan Lake: Excerpts
    NPO   LOND 21008

Symphony # 4
    ASO   VAN 10095

Symphony # 5
    NPO   LOND 21017

Symphony # 6
    LSO   RCA 0426

Virgil THOMSON
Plow that Broke the Plains
    SOA   VAN 2095; 707/8

The River
    SOA   VAN 2095

Ralph VAUGHAN WILLIAMS
Fantasia on a Theme by Thomas Tallis
    RPO   DES 1011

Wasps: Incidental Music
    SSO   EV 3327

Hector VILLA-LOBOS
Bachianas Brasileiras # 1: Modinha
    SSO   EV 3016

Bachianas Brasileiras # 5
    Moffo, ASO   RCA 2795

Uirapurú
    SSO   EV 3016

Antonio VIVALDI
Concerto Grosso in D-minor, op. 2, # 11
    SO   BACH 70696; VAN 707/8;
                          VAN 363

Four Seasons
    Bean, vln., NPO   LOND 21015

Richard WAGNER
Götterdämmerung: Immolation Scene
    LSO   RCA 1317

Götterdämmerung: Siegfried's Rhine Journey and
    Funeral Music
    LSO   LOND 21016
    LSO   RCA 1317

Die Meistersinger: Excerpts
    RPO   RCA 0498

Parsifal: Excerpts
    HSO   EV 3031